The Congruent Life

The Congruent Life

Following the Inward Path to Fulfilling Work and Inspired Leadership

C. Michael Thompson

Foreword by Robert A. Johnson

Jossey-Bass Publishers • San Francisco

Jossey-Bass books and products are available through most bookstores. To contact Jossey-Bass directly, call (888) 378-2537, fax to (800) 605-2665, or visit our website at www.josseybass.com.

Substantial discounts on bulk quantities of Jossey-Bass books are available to corporations, professional associations, and other organizations. For details and discount information, contact the special sales department at Jossey-Bass.

The epigraph for the Introduction is reprinted by permission of the Estate of Dorothy L. Sayers and the Watkins/Loomis Agency.

The epigraph for Chapter One from *Good Work* by E. F. Schumacher is copyright © 1979 by Verena Schumacher and is reprinted by permission of HarperCollins Publishers, Inc.

Epigraph within Chapter Ten excerpted from *Merton's Palace of Nowhere* by James Finley is copyright © 1978 by Ave Maria Press, P.O. Box 428, Notre Dame, IN 46556, and is used with permission of the publisher.

Epigraph within Chapter Ten excerpted from *The Empowered Manager* by Peter Block is copyright © 1987 by Jossey-Bass Inc., Publishers, and is used with permission of the publisher.

 Manufactured in the United States of America on Lyons Falls Turin Book. This paper is acid-free and 100 percent totally chlorine-free.

Library of Congress Cataloging-in-Publication Data

Thompson, C. Michael, date.
  The congruent life : following the inward path to fulfilling work and inspired leadership / C. Michael Thompson; foreword by Robert A. Johnson.
    p.   cm.—(The Jossey-Bass business & management series)
Includes bibliographical references and index.
  ISBN 0-7879-5008-4
  I. Title.   II. Series.   1. Work—Psychological aspects.   2. Work—Religious aspects.   5. Quality of work life.
  BF481.T48   1999

                                                  99-006852

FIRST EDITION
HB Printing 10 9 8 7 6 5 4 3 2 1

Contents

Foreword

A number of years ago I gave a lecture in a southern city on the legend of Parsifal and the Fisher King, which had formed the basis for my book *He.* The next morning, through one of those twists of good fortune which we create by being open to them, I found myself across a breakfast table from a young man who had been present at my lecture the night before. Earnest and serious minded, he was full of questions about his career, his journey, and the choices arrayed in front of him. A genuine seeker, to be sure; but I had to wonder if, like Parsifal, his challenge lay not so much in answering the questions he had posed as in asking the right one. I had little idea that I would one day be writing the foreword to his first book. Even less, I suspect, did he.

Michael Thompson has come to ask the right question. It is not "how to," "what to," "when to," or "where to." Those questions can be important in their place, though they are all too often symptoms of our cookbook, quick-fix culture. The ultimate question is *for whom:* What is the central principle for which we live our lives and give our energies? Whom (or, if you prefer, what) does our life serve?

To answer this ultimate, a priori question requires that we go deeply inside ourselves, to the very core of who we are. It requires that we listen for, and then learn to hear, the voice of our deepest wisdom. And it requires courage and resolve to begin and sustain that journey—courage because it takes stepping far outside our zone of comfort, resolve because the cultures in which most of us live do not always encourage us on our way.

There is a place inside each of us that could aptly be called *Egypt.* We know we are enslaved there, as were the Hebrew people, but we are unable now to leave. Like the twelve sons of Jacob, we went there originally to assure ourselves of a good living and of the means to fill our basic wants and desires. But soon we forget why we journeyed there. The means to a more comfortable life have now become our only end, and we are willing to endure our masters and our plight to keep the money coming and our false sense of security intact. And what if someone should offer a new vision— a land flowing with milk and honey, some painful distance away but real nonetheless? Remember the people of Israel. Many did not want to go and stayed behind. Those who did leave tried to turn around the first time they got the chance, and moaned or mutinied practically every step of the way. The devil that you know, as the saying goes, is always better than the devil that you don't. If you were to be shown a plausible route out of your own Egypt, out of the land of narrow materialism, would you, too, cling to the devil you know?

This book begins by asking the right question: What is the ultimate meaning and purpose of the work we do? Whom does it serve? And it shows those willing to make the journey how they might flee the Egypt within themselves for a land flowing with meaning, purpose, and value. The journey out of this Egypt is a journey inward, to the place where we encounter the source of that flow.

No good exodus worth its name can be completed without some time in the desert. That seems one of life's laws, and one must be prepared for it. But Thompson's premise is that the fruit of that inner journey is so desirable—indeed essential—that it serves as a beckoning reward for the leaders of our human organizations who undertake it. Moreover, I have the sense that, with more and more men and women today embarking on this journey, you may find your sojourn shared by a multitude even greater than those who so long ago forsook Egypt, endured Sinai, and crossed over into their Promised Land.

Encinitas, California   ROBERT A. JOHNSON

Preface

This book began a dozen years ago—or maybe it was a lifetime. As vice president and counsel to a Fortune 500 company, my legal and business backgrounds were providing me with all the indicia of a "successful career." I little suspected that my definition of *success,* even of *career,* was about to be exploded.

You could call it a midlife crisis and I'll not be offended. In fact, I've come to agree with M. Scott Peck that the goal may be to see just how many such crises we can pack into one lifetime. But the result was that my life became less like following a predictable, sequential path and more like following a string—one laid out specifically for me, complete with funny twists, sharp turns, unexpected reversals, and times when I lost sight of it altogether. And I came to know the personal God who had laid that string out before me and bidden me to follow.

I also learned to call the confusion and disorientation so common to such crises by its true name: *spiritual pain.* It was the pain of being separated from my authentic self, of having to live someone else's life in order to "go along and get along" that well-trod, sequential career path. It wasn't just that the organizational structure had supplanted the educational and family structures in telling me who and what to be; I had become its very willing adherent. In a thousand subtle (and not so subtle) ways, my ego and its needs fled from the demands of the larger Self, drowning them out with a cacophony of successes, raises, anxieties, meetings, parties, projects, and intrigues. I was, myself, untrue to myself.

We live in an age of spiritual pain. And thank goodness! We are awakening at last to that profound sense of separation, with fewer and fewer ways to bridge over the abyss. We are allowing ourselves both to experience and to question the distance we feel from our

deepest values and beliefs, from our hopes and dreams for ourselves and our lives, from our families and spouses—and from God.
We endure this separation in the name of our careers, our businesses, and who we are expected to be at work. But for many, the
ride no longer justifies the fare.

This book is for those people for whom that separation is no
longer bearable; for those who, if they have but one life, can
no longer bear to spend it living someone else's. It is for those for
whom the traditional coping mechanism—walling off one's business from one's personal life—no longer works. It is for those
whose vision of themselves and their organizations eclipses their
current reality; for whom "that's just the way business is" no longer
rings true.

My "string," of course, would be laid in different places than
yours. It has led me to an intensive study of depth psychology and
adult counseling, through the Shalem Institute's program in traditional spiritual direction, and on the most wonderful and terrible (often at the same time) journey of personal spiritual growth.
It has wound out of business to the halls of academia, called me
back to business as a consultant, and led me on to executive development and coaching work with businesspeople seeking to follow their own strings. And, as it turns out, bidden me to write this
book. It is my fervent hope that you will find in the pages ahead
many places where our strings intersect—and greater courage to
follow your own.

The story told in my family is that my great-grandfather started our
Easter tradition many years ago. He would get up long before dawn
and, while all still slept, run a string from the house out to the garden. At its end he would place a beautiful Easter lily for the delight
of the first child who arose to find it. Just as I did many years earlier, my children now excitedly awake on Easter morning looking
for the string that's been laid for them, complete with unexpected
twists and turns. The only difference is that, like all children these
days, they prefer baskets of candy and toys to lilies.

The symbolism of this tradition, like that of many others, can
be understood on more than one level. To follow the string in your
own life means to be led, in some fundamental ways, by the urgings

of something other than your own conscious ego. It means being accepting of abrupt changes and reversals and still staying the course; for there is mortal danger in leaving the string, assuming that *you* know where it is going, and never finding it again. And it may mean losing your life—your version of what your life should be—in order to truly find it. Just remember that at the end of that string blooms the lily, the symbol of life reborn and renewed, full and free.

Sunset Beach, North Carolina   C. MICHAEL THOMPSON
December 1999

To my father,
who in gentleness and strength
taught me about the
best in business

And my mother,
who showed me the door to
the inner life

This work was conceived in them

Acknowledgments

Because this book has been so much a part of my life these past few years, practically anyone who has touched my life during that time (for good or ill) has had a part in it. But special gratitude goes to a few extraordinary people.

First, to my wife, Jane, and my daughters, Ann Elizabeth and Catherine: to Jane for her endless proofreading, patience, and encouragement; to Ann Elizabeth for her creative spark and late-night chats when I most needed them; to Catherine for her never-give-up desire behind a heart-melting smile.

To those who reviewed portions of the manuscript and shared their wisdom: Jack Behrman, Robert Burnside, Tilden Edwards, Gloria Karpinski, Jerry May, Tom Taylor, and Peter Vaill.

To trusted friends who through their conversations helped me flesh out the concepts of this book: Bonnie Favorite, David Fouche, Sam Gladding, Clay Hipp, and Russ Moxley.

To Jim Autry, who has mentored me through the birthing of this life-work.

To Robert A. Johnson, for his generosity in writing the Foreword, for his serendipitous four-leaf clovers, and for appearing in my life at just the critical moment, much as Dr. Jung did for him.

To my colleagues John Todd Llewellyn and Randy Rogan for their collaboration on the projects that led up to this endeavor, and to Meg Dowell, our research assistant.

To typist extraordinaire and spiritual friend Jim Clinard.

To my favorite sister, Bethany T. Kelly, for giving me my first chance to try out these concepts on real people.

To my editor, Byron "The Velvet Hammer" Schneider, for his faith in this book and his patience with this particular rookie.

And, especially, to the dozens of men and women whose journeys of life and work I have been privileged to share, and whose stories form the backbone of this book.

Finally, while we all have many teachers in life, three have always stood out for me; and, like most students, I am long overdue in my acknowledgment of their place in my life story. My inexpressible gratitude to Veena Wilburn, who instilled in me the delight of learning; to Ardyss Woods, who taught me the joy of the written word; and to Anne Berry, who gave me my earliest lessons about life and leadership.

Our age has its own particular mission or vocation—the creation of a civilization founded upon the spiritual nature of work. [These] are the only original thoughts of our time, the only ones we haven't borrowed from the Greeks. It is because we have been unequal to this mighty business, which was being conceived in us, that we have thrown ourselves into the abyss . . .
SIMONE WEIL, *The Need for Roots*

Introduction

Life in the Lost Provinces

*It may well seem to you—as it does to some of my
acquaintances—that I have a sort of obsession about
this business of the right attitude to work. But I do insist
upon it, because it seems to me that what becomes of
civilization after this war is going to depend enormously
on our being able to effect this revolution in our ideas
about work. Unless we do change our whole way of
thought about work, I do not think we shall ever escape
from the appalling squirrel-cage of economic confusion in
which we have been madly turning for the last three
centuries or so.*
DOROTHY SAYERS

Our world has changed profoundly in the fifty-plus years since Sayers, the famous mystery writer turned religious critic, wrote the
words above. No aspect of our culture—social, political, economic,
or religious—has escaped the tumultuous effects of the chaotic and
unrelenting change that the second half of this century has brought.

Yet one might wonder if she would see any real difference in
our attitudes toward work and business. The squirrel-cage turns
much faster now, of course. But our cultural view of work is still
largely instrumental ("I owe, I owe, it's off to work I go"); many of
us still conceive of business as somehow walled off from the rest of
life ("It's just business"); and the popular model of business management has evolved only from Dagwood to Dilbert. Is there really
something immutable in our society, after all?

1

This book is about how these conceptions are, slowly but perceptibly, changing. It is about *why* they are changing. Most important, it is about why they *must* change. By the time we finish our explorations, I hope you will be convinced of four things:

1. The very human desire for meaning and purpose in life is increasingly being met for many in the work they do. This is no longer true just for those entering the ministry or "socially conscious" vocations but also for those in business, government, and other occupations as well. They are seeking it, but the way their work must be approached in the new century will *require* it.

2. That need for meaning and purpose is for an increasing number being met through a "spirituality" of work, though it is seldom called that. For spirituality in our day is not adherence to creed or dogma but a life-orientation that finds meaning and purpose through devotion to a higher reality in *all* the aspects of one's life, including productive work.

3. There is a new and more unified way to look at organizational leadership. Good and effective leadership in business, nonprofits, churches, and other organizations is not so much a set of skills and competencies as it is the fruit of that devoted life-orientation. It is a developmental process of growth and maturation fed by the leader's inner spirit more than by his or her outer strivings.

4. Such "in-spired" leadership won't just be a nice thing for our companies and institutions to have in the century to come— it will be absolutely essential to meet the challenges the future holds in store.

At the end point of our inquiry together, this much will be clear: *not only does personal spiritual growth foster qualities and traits that both adult developmental theory and depth psychology have identified with the highest stages of human development, but these are just the qualities and traits most needed for life and leadership in the workplace of the twenty-first century.*
For those who can suspend their assumptions about life and work for long enough to make this exploration, there is an excel-

lent chance of convincing you that I'm right. For those who can't, at least remember what George Santayana said about being married to the spirit of the current age: you are destined to be widowed in the next.

The Congruent Life

"No need is so compelling," wrote the late Willis Harman, "as the need we all feel for our lives to make sense, to have meaning."[1] However dimly conscious it might be amid the chaos and complexity of our daily lives, there is a need in almost all of us for a sense of connectedness and purpose in the events of our outer lives, and a deeply rooted desire for our inner lives to have a harmonious connection to a higher source of meaning and value. Whatever we individually choose to call that source (for me it is God), the reality of the search for it remains the same.

But—and this is critical for understanding this book—such a search is not one-way. Remember the well-worn parable of the prodigal son?[2] Recall that all the wayward boy had to do was make up his mind and *begin* the journey home. While he was "still a great distance off," goes the story, his father ran to meet him with great joy and celebration, and brought him the rest of the way home. There is a great truth here: to seek the ultimate source of meaning and value in the important aspects of your life is to open yourself to being *found* by it. You are, in one of those paradoxes so common to Truth, both the seeker and the sought.

That this double search should find its way into business and the lives of working people is not surprising and is in fact long overdue. For something that consumes so much of our lives and energy to have *only* the material purposes we ascribe to it is a recipe for illness. Put the other way around, work that *lacks* meaning and purpose does not deserve our life-energy and will likely receive only the smallest amount we can get away with giving.

Consider this analogy: I love to cook and spend a fair amount of my spare time at it. Now, one of the reasons I cook is so that I will be able to eat, which is rather necessary to continue living. But that in no way explains the time, effort, and attention that goes into one of my dishes—I could just as well accomplish the goal of staying alive with a can of beans and a vitamin pill. So it is with our work, to a greater extent than we seem able to admit. If we really believed that our work was nothing but an unpleasant necessity, then, following E. F. Schumacher, there would be "no use talking about good work, unless we mean *less* work. Why put any goodness into our work beyond the absolute minimum?"[3]

That's not how most of us act: we take pride in what we do; we seek to improve; we try to leave a mark; we value those who work with us and want them to value us; we enjoy ourselves or else we find another job or career path where we can. This behavior belies a purely instrumental view of work. Moreover, it is not a far walk from there to the kind of search I am talking about, for it is clear that many of the ways we measure meaning and value in our lives are intimately linked to who we are at work and the caliber of the work we do.

Perhaps it is still true that most businesspeople are either "devoted only to non-transcendent materialistic purposes such as career advancement; or they have a transcendent purpose that doesn't mesh with the purpose of the company they work for."[4] In other words, although we bring many of our values with us to our workplaces, we can concede that at the close of the twentieth century most of us don't pretend that our working lives are adequate reflections of our deepest need for meaning and purpose. But the great advances in our culture are not decided in advance by plebescite. They happen because they answer a fundamental need and attract to them one by one the adherents who create a new reality.

And the need has never been greater. While the institutions of society that fulfilled the role of providing our sense of connection and purpose are in decline, the so-called New Economy is requiring so much more of the time and energy of working people that the workplace is assuming that role by default. We all know that businesspeople are working harder, longer, and with more stressors than they were ten years ago. But a natural consequence of that, for good or ill, is the ascendancy of our work, careers, teams, and coworkers over our civic groups, churches, and even families. We find a sense of connection, meaning, and purpose in the former, or often not at all.

It may seem at a glance that the New Economy is not very conducive to this search for meaning. A recent survey found that three out of four of us get "totally stressed out" at work at least once a week (25 percent said *daily!*), and almost half worry "frequently" about losing their jobs.[5] Yet the tumultuous environment in which we do our jobs may be the best reason to look for meaning—even transcendent meaning—in what we do. As observed by *Fortune* magazine: "Executives generally aren't an introspective lot, but in the dawn of the New Economy—with no job security or clear career path, with more responsibility and less certainty than ever—stressed-out managers increasingly are turning inside for answers."[6]

This book is about what "turning inside" might mean—how that happens, what we encounter, what the fruits of that might be, and the implications for work and organizational leadership. It is not a "religious" book, except in the sense that it does seek to "bind together" (that's one original meaning of the word *religion*) some things long separated by Western culture. You will find that I borrow heavily from my own Judeo-Christian heritage, precisely because it is my home ground, but I trust you will not find this approach exclusionary of other, equally valuable religious orientations. In fact, my intent is to speak to anyone who believes in a power greater than our humanity, however you understand that power.

I am also taking Carl Rogers at his word when he said that what is most personal to us is also most general. This book grows out of my own experience, research, work—and struggle—over the last three decades as a practicing attorney, business professor, and leadership consultant. It also comes from my work over the last dozen years as a spiritual friend or counselor to others. During that time I never worked with a single searcher who did not wrestle mightily with the issue of how to integrate her deepest values and her professional life. Their struggle, and my own, form the basis of this book.

The "Lost Provinces"

So here's a question: If the vast majority of people in this country consider themselves "religious" or otherwise express belief in a higher power,[7] and explicating the connection between human activity and the transcendent is one of the purposes of religion, why do we hear precious little from the traditional church about the one activity that consumes most of our waking time?

One rather unpleasant answer came during a panel discussion in which I participated several months ago. At the table with me was an older and venerated professor of religion, formerly dean of one of the foremost theological schools in the country and an outstanding biblical scholar. As the discussion turned to living one's values in the workplace, the distinguished professor made a remark that has haunted me since: "The work most people do, you see, cannot be said to have any spiritual significance. They must find that kind of fulfillment in other parts of their lives—in their spare time." Although perhaps he did not intend it, he had just excluded everyone in the room, save *himself,* from the possibility of living their deepest longings through their work. That is not only elitist, it is wrong—maybe even heretical—because it presumes that God can be present only in some types of human endeavors (such as being a theology professor) and not in others. It is wrong because (as we will see in Chapter Two), it is not the substance of the work itself that makes it more or less "spiritual" but our approach to it. This is not to say that there aren't some jobs where finding spiritual significance is harder than others—which is another reason for this book—but as individuals *we* get to determine the extent to which our productive work both reflects and cultivates our inner life—that is, unless we buy into the heresy.

The two main sources of literature in this area—business and religion—talk past one another and miss the ear of most working people in the process. "Those who discuss the economics of work," write Harman and Hormann, "seldom deal adequately with issues of meaning, and those who are concerned with the ways people seek to discover the meaning of life seldom appear competent to deal with the economics of work."[8] As to the latter, it is instructive that the term *theology of work* did not even appear in print until the early 1950s.[9] There are many reasons for this dearth, including the bias of the Greeks (our intellectual forebears) against common work, the paucity of explicit guidance in the Judeo-Christian Bible on the subject, and our emphasis on the social issues surrounding work at the expense of the religious meaning of the work itself. But whatever the cause, the conspicuous lack of theological reflection on the meaning and purpose of human work has relegated it to the hinterlands—the "lost provinces"—of organized religion.[10]

Despite notable individual contributions, the literature arising from the business realm suffers from the opposite problem: a lack of theological grounding. Although this lack is understandable considering the background of the authors, the resulting works are often purely idiosyncratic—a stringing together of personal stories and platitudes that strikes a chord with the reader more or less by chance. Moreover, most of the books about spirituality and management are popular works, not theoretical or empirical, and one surefire way to ensure sales is to offer formulae for greater efficiency and profitability. Those things are important in business, of course, but the danger to which some works have succumbed is in pandering to those seeking yet another way to sharpen a competitive edge rather than speaking to the need men and women have to connect their work to their highest values. They ask the wrong question.

But the greatest shortcoming of the business-spirituality literature is this: by excluding nothing it includes everything. In seeking to offend no one (a laudable goal, mind you), the language is often so sanitized that it is robbed of its meaning. To read some of it is to come away with the impression that a warm bath is in and of itself a spiritual experience, or that the "team spirit" that just caused a defensive tackle to crush an opposing running back is tantamount to an experience of the holy.

None of this is terribly helpful to men and women who are struggling to find the deeper purposes in what they do for a living, regardless of their religious persuasion. Nor is it helpful to organizations seeking to understand the growing phenomenon of workplace spirituality and what it means for their future. What is needed is a new understanding of spirituality and work that shows the natural connection between the two and connects *both* to the deep human longing for meaning and purpose. And that understanding needs to be made accessible to those working men and women for whom the longing is most real.

About This Book

It is true, as Thomas Kuhn observed, that any new paradigm always first appears as a rough draft. This book is but one attempt to apply a bit of sandpaper to a corner of that paradigm—the corner occupied by work, business, and organizational life.

We begin in Chapters One and Two by examining the box we have built for ourselves in our thinking about work. That's what a paradigm is, of course: a set of boxes we as a culture have to put things in so that the world makes sense to us. But what most people tend to forget is that those boxes are our own creations and get broken down and re-formed every so often. The box we had for "work" in the industrial age is breaking down before our eyes, as an ever increasing number of people seek to find meaning in their working lives in ways that their parents could only seek in the "rest" of their lives.

This meaning is found most deeply and authentically in a "spirituality" of work. I put quotation marks around that word only because it has so many and varied meanings, some of which challenge our notions of what is appropriate in a business context. But we will see in Chapter Three that there is nothing about the word *spirituality*, once understood, that is at enmity with the demands of a life thoroughly immersed in the world of commerce. You may find, in fact, that you have been living—or aspiring to—a life more spiritual than you have heretofore realized. Yet it is a concept often misunderstood, and in Chapter Four we will seek to separate wheat from chaff—to distinguish the kind of authentic spirituality on which all great religious traditions agree from that which merely appropriates the name.

For those of you who like your arguments served with a healthy side order of utilitarian logic, Chapter Five examines why we would *want* to explore the spiritual side of work and business. From the rising tide of worker expectations to the need for new forms of incentive and motivation, we will see how the New Economy is spawning this deeper view of business and its purposes. Moreover, we will recognize in these changes a need for a quality of organizational leadership that only a deepened inner life can foster.

Chapters Six through Eight are at the heart of this book's message: that such a deepened inner life leads directly to those characteristics, qualities, and traits that are the very marks of good and effective leadership. Perhaps they always have been, but we are only now coming to realize that organizational leadership at its best is not the sum of certain skills or competencies, or charisma, or facile style, but rather the sum of who the person *is*. This exploration will take us into an emerging theory of how humans continue to develop in adulthood—emotionally, psychologically, and spiritually— and how that developmental process can determine a person's potential for effective leadership. This process of growth, for which an inner life is so essential, does have certain "fruits" in the outer productive lives of those who stay that path.

Chapter Nine is a forecast ahead, though not without clear signs in the present. We will look at what business will be like in the twenty-first century, how its values and priorities will differ from those of this transitional time. And we will see why it is safe to say that the fruits of a spiritual life will be indispensable—not just desirable—in the new millennium.

Chapter Ten is simply an attempt, constrained by the limits of a single book, to lay out the essentials of an inner life for those disposed to seek it. I don't claim comprehensiveness, only that the chapter describes the guideposts that were important in my own struggle and in the journeys of those working people whose spiritual lives I have been privileged to share. I do claim with some confidence that Chapter Ten is consistent with the truth contained in the world's great religious traditions and that it fosters the development of the "fruits of the spirit." My hope is that you will find it a starting place for the sacred task of living and working in concert with Ultimate Reality—of living the Congruent Life.

Spirit and the New Organizational Leadership

"If there is no transformation inside each of us," writes Peter Block, "all the structural change in the world will have no impact on our institutions."[11] If our goal is to so reshape our organizations that they will survive and flourish in the new century, our most immediate task is to shape ourselves. We do this not by surface changes in behavior or skills, no matter how valuable such add-ons may be; true transformation takes place in the deepest parts of us, over time and with great courage and effort. But here's the good news: if we seek that inner transformation through aligning ourselves with Ultimate Reality, we find ourselves on a path well worn by the many over the centuries who have sought the same—a path this book tries to describe. Moreover, you may find yourself *sought after* along the way. It is this double search that makes "spiritual" the resulting growth and transformation.

For decades now, writers have tried to define leadership. Libraries are full of our attempts to decode this complex human phenomenon. But we usually do it by trying to *reduce* leadership to some formula or recipe or set of principles. It's as if we think that, consonant with the scientific method, we can find a sort of genetic key that will unlock the whole mystery. Perhaps the problem is that we have been searching by microscope for something that can be grasped only in panorama. Perhaps leadership in business and elsewhere is, as Warren Bennis has put it, the natural expression of a fully integrated human being, and can thus be seen only through the wide-angle lens of the leader's total growth and development. And part of what that human being must integrate is the animating and creative spirit within that is intimately connected to a larger source of meaning beyond.

The truth of this idea is beginning to dawn. A strong inner life plays a key and indispensable role in personal growth and development. And such personal growth, with the emotional, attitudinal, and behavioral changes it produces, is not simply a helpful adjunct to organizational leadership these days—it is its essence. The logic is simply this: of the literally hundreds of skills, competencies, traits, characteristics, and qualities used in the literature to define leadership, those that are most essential in the fluid and chaotic reality of the world today are in fact the outer fruits of that devoted inner life.

Part One

Work and the Search for Meaning in Our Age

Chapter One

The Great Divorce

> *The Cartesian Revolution has removed the vertical*
> *dimension from our "map of knowledge"; only the*
> *horizontal dimensions are left. To proceed in this flatland,*
> *science provides excellent guidance: it can do everything*
> *but lead us out of the dark wood of a meaningless,*
> *purposeless, "accidental" existence.*
> E. F. SCHUMACHER

In one of the final scenes of Coppola's epic film *The Godfather,* the once-loyal Tessio finds himself in a delicate situation. His part in the plot to assassinate Michael Corleone has been uncovered, and he must now answer to Tom Hagan, the don's right-hand man. Several large associates of the Corleone family stand ready to whisk their former colleague to a place of final rest. A sheepish Tessio offers an explanation: "Tell Mike it was only business. I always liked him."

"He understands that," Tom Hagan responds. The needed reassurance now given and received, Tessio calmly submits to his fate.

Now, let's see if we've got this right. A man tries to murder (do in, rub out, kill) his longtime friend and associate. His excuse is that it was "only business"; as if this would somehow make Michael less dead or in any event less upset about being so. Moreover, now that the business deal has gone sour, the conspirator willingly accepts his own murder as the natural consequence of poor strategic planning. And everyone—intended victim, perpetrator, and the entire audience—"understands."

As with much literary hyperbole, there is truth here. We accept in the context of our working lives all sorts of behavior that we would find unacceptable elsewhere. We may complain about it, of course. In fact, complaining about our bosses and colleagues is a sort of national pastime. But despite twenty years of increasing emphasis on "business ethics" and the conscious efforts of many to bring their personal values to the workplace, there still exists a deep divide between the expectations we have for ourselves and others "in business" and those we have in the other important aspects of our lives. How would we judge a man who determines how much of his time and support his daughter will receive based on how she grades out at her piano recital? Or a woman who encourages her son to steal the playbook of the opposing peewee league football team? We would be appalled by the overemphasis on technique and the importance of winning at the expense of our other cherished values. Yet every day in business we place such primacy on quantifiable results that we can make downsizing decisions based on little or no other input, and competitive advantage is so important that corporate theft has become an accepted norm. Then we create sanitizing terms like *reengineering* and *corporate espionage* to shield us from the fact that such behaviors are in fact very far away from our ideal view of ourselves.

All of this comes with a cost. Confronted with the reality that we live in two different worlds that operate on different value systems, we can stand outside of business and throw rocks, or we can tenuously rationalize our own behavior inside business, or we can abandon altogether the effort to make sense of the split we feel.

Yet the split remains, both without and *within* us. Depth psychology teaches us that any serious discord we experience in the world around us is often "introjected" into us personally—we take on that conflict within ourselves and feel its effects directly. The symptoms vary but are readily apparent in most of us. We may feel a vague sense of malaise or of something missing in our lives. We may be among the astounding 31 percent of the U.S. population who report experiencing depression or other mental health problems.[1] Or, consistent with our human tendency to deal with opposites by identifying with one or the other extreme, we may either immerse ourselves wholly in the "world of business" with its perceived norms and rewards, poking fun at those who just don't understand the demands of the marketplace, or run willy-nilly to a moral high ground (e.g., universities, seminaries) from which to lob righteous judgments at "big business."

Imagine for a moment that there existed a town where, for some unexplained reason, most of its citizens have fallen ill. Some mysterious malady so robs them of their sense of meaning and purpose that a sizable number are clinically depressed, while others suffer from a kind of mania that makes them so obsessively pursue their daily tasks that a disproportionate number die each year from heart attack, stroke, or other stress-related diseases. Even those less dramatically affected suffer from an observable loss of initiative and productivity. And what if such a disease threatened to spread across the entire nation? Wouldn't we call for an investigation? Alert the media? Send in the Centers for Disease Control?

No, there is just enough Tessio in each of us that we accept as "only business" the disease and its effect on our lives. Perhaps, as James Autry puts it, we think business either too important to be shackled by our everyday values or not important enough to deserve them. Perhaps business is just deemed "different." Whatever the rationale, we have so thoroughly internalized the split between work and the rest of life that we quite naturally understand Tessio's point.

How did we come to this view of ourselves and our world? How could such a split within and without come into being? Make no mistake, it has not always been so. There are many times and places in human history where the division of life into categories "work" and "other" was unthinkable and the application of different values to each considered simply wrong. To understand how this split occurred is to grasp two things: (1) it was not inevitable—that is, it was not merely "progress"—and (2) it does not, therefore, have to continue.

The Evolution of Our Concept of Work

We understand why the study of history is important in formal education. We see the connection between events and how they influenced our own time and culture. We read about the lives of great people and see how their actions and ideas shaped our own. But the evolution of concepts—even concepts as important as our ideas about work—is not as easily traced through time. As a result, even those fairly well versed in textbook history may presume that our current ideas have been with us forever. It's rather like assuming that humans have always thought the world is round because you've never heard the story of Christopher Columbus.

To follow the development of our modern attitudes toward work and industry requires that we go back at least as far as the agrarian societies of medieval Europe. Here the defining dichotomy was not between work and nonwork but between the sacred and the secular. It is part of our humanness, of course, that we must always have such dichotomies to truly understand anything of importance—dark is only recognizable as dark because there is light; good is only good when juxtaposed with bad; and so on. And as Eliade points out in his classic work *The Sacred and the Profane*, there has been a fundamental human tendency across many cultures and centuries to separate sacred time, sacred places, and sacred activities from their secular counterparts as a way of making sense of the world.[2] For the medieval mind, the dividing line was clear: the monk lived solely within that favored world, whereas the man with a lesser calling could but venture into sacred time and space by invitation, to partake of the mass or a sacrament.

Yet the two men shared this in common: for both, life was work and work was life. Any division between the values and demands of the two was simply not a part of his psyche. For the monastic this was made explicitly clear in the writings of the early church fathers.[3] From St. Benedict's famous statement *Ora et labora* ("To work and to pray") and as far back as the second-century writings of Clement of Alexandria, the religious were given specific instruction and encouragement to weave physical labor into the structure of every day, balancing such activity with spiritual reading and prayer. In the enduring words of one monk, a worker in the monastery's kitchen: "The time of business does not with me differ from the time of prayer; and in the noise and clatter of my Kitchen . . . I possess God in as great tranquility as if I were upon my knees at the blessed sacrament."[4]

Although accounts of (and certainly by) a typical medieval peasant are rare, we know that in some important respects it paralleled agrarian life as it existed in the West well into this century, at least until the advent of modern transportation, communication, and conveniences. Anyone raised on or near a rural family farm will know what I mean. The rhythm of daily life was as seamless as the seasons. Work began early in the day and early in each life, and flowed without schedules, appointments, or (gulp) weekends through all the other aspects of family and community life. High points were just as likely to include the birth of a new calf as some village merriment. The hardness of the work was matched by the hardness of living itself. To ask people living in that time and place to parcel out for you the difference between their work and "other" lives, and to explain to you the differing values of each, would at best get you an odd look. That distinction would have no real meaning for them.

But something very important began to happen with the onset of the Protestant Reformation—portentous for our ideas about work and ultimately about that way of organizing work that we call business. The rebellious monk Martin Luther refused to see the world along the traditional sacred-secular dichotomy. For him, it was not only the monks ("as idle as they are numerous") who possessed a sacred vocation; *every* type of work could serve God equally. Salvation lay in the faith of the individual and in the fulfillment of the duties his station in life (his "stand") required of him. Common work, provided that it was done to serve God, was now given as great a value as the sacred activities of the monastery.

And what of the rise of the new mercantile capitalists in Europe, with their rampant greed and rapid accumulation of wealth? For Luther, of rural agrarian origins, the answer was simply for the individual merchant to repent of the sins of greed and avarice. Embrace those aspects of worldly vocation that serve God—reject those that don't.

Left in a vacuum, Luther's theology of vocation raised work to an unprecedented level of importance in the life of the individual. It imbued work with meaning and purpose, while attempting to restrain its temptations. In a sense, Luther preserved the medieval relationship between life and work but *sanctified* it as a marriage.

But it was John Calvin's extension of Luther's thoughts that contained within it the seeds of what we will call the Great Divorce. Calvin was from the bustling financial center of Geneva. He could decry as well as Luther the excesses of the new capitalism, but for him, unlike his contemporary, the institutions of business, trade, and banking were so central to his world that he had to encompass them in his theology. This he did through the doctrine of "the elect." Man's sinful nature could be redeemed only through God's grace, which was given to the individual directly without the intercession of the priest. But it was not given to *everyone*. Because justification could not be earned, it was given freely as a gift of God to those who were chosen by Him. And how could you know that you were among the elect? Calvin himself provides no easy answer; but as argued by Max Weber in his highly influential treatise *The Protestant Ethic and the Spirit of Capitalism,* the Reformed preachers who took Calvin's message to the people taught that God's favor could be seen in one's degree of vocational success. Because the measure of that success in business is material gain, it was not much of a leap to equate wealth with the type of vocational "good works" that showed your inclusion among the chosen. Of course, material gain did not *produce* salvation, but it was strong *evidence* that you were on the right track. In any event, to be *un*successful in one's trade or business sent a sufficiently frightening message to the anxious medieval mind that it provided the needed fuel to drive the phenomenon of the Protestant ethic.

We had now moved from the idea of faithfulness in work as part of the path of salvation, to one of observable, measurable success in work as the mark of salvation. But what of the accompanying dangers of increased wealth? Isn't it supposed to be easier for a camel to go through the eye of a needle than for a rich man to enter the Kingdom of God? About this Calvin and the Reformation theologians were in concert: your duty to work with industry and persistence is matched by your duty to be frugal, restrained, austere, and steadfastly honest. John Wesley's famous command to "Gain all you can; save all you can; give all you can" is but one example. As an early capitalist, you were thus encouraged to use the whip on the racehorse of material gain while simultaneously reining it in.

Nowhere did this doctrine more firmly take hold than in the fertile soil of the United States. As pluralistic as our society now is, we tend to forget that the nation was formed at a time when nearly 90 percent of the population was descended from Puritan or other related Calvinist backgrounds.[5] Strongly embedded in the American psyche were the Calvinist notions of work as a calling and the assiduous devotion to work as salvific, to which the Puritan added an even greater sense of seriousness, austerity, and perseverance, born not only of their view of a righteous life but also of the hard demands of colonial existence. The resulting "work ethic" was largely responsible for the creation of the kind of self-motivated workforce indispensable to a successful capitalist economy—of which the United States became the most shining example.

Puritan thought was equally insistent on the dangers of excess, however. Such influential theologians as William Ames and William Perkins counseled moderation in the enjoyment of worldly gain and the use of profits for the common good. A doctrine of stewardship began to emerge in an attempt to bridge the theological gap between the encouragement of worldly success and the proscription against greed and avarice. While devotion to one's calling could of necessity be profitable in business, the use of those profits for Godly purposes was the necessary corollary. Without both, individual gain was immoral. The uneasy tension between the whip and the rein was thus tenuously maintained in the Puritan mind.

But not for long. In the eighteenth century the social and intellectual movement we call the Enlightenment began firmly to take root in practically all aspects of American thought. While the influence of the Calvinist clergy on daily life waned, the secularizing influences of Enlightenment thought began to redefine the Protestant ethic. By the close of the century it scarcely would have been recognizable to the Puritan of the early 1700s. The change was alarmingly simple: "making profit became a value in its own right,"[6] rather than the means to a religiously inspired end. The seminal thinkers of the day, such as John Locke and Adam Smith, helped over time to move the mind-set from vocation, call, and the common good to individual rights, personal will, and material success. The heady freedom from all forms of collective tyranny, which was the great gift of the Enlightenment, truly "liberated" the common man from the restraints that organized religion had placed on his economic life. The rein was loosed altogether.

The Protestant ethic lived on, of course, but in the version we now recognize. Hard work, thrift, industriousness, perseverance, and discipline were key traits; but rather than serving some distant notion of salvation, they became the virtues one must cultivate in order to achieve material success. To look at the writings of Benjamin Franklin is to see the Americanized version of the ethic in its purest secular form. The purpose of work and industry was now disconnected from any religious or spiritual significance, and even from any particular notion of the common good. Its purpose was the individual advancement and material success of the person living a life of respectability, adhering to Franklin's proverbs and platitudes.

A wedge was being driven in Western thought between human work and ultimate meaning. Slowly, but quite inexorably, we were coming to see work not as a part of the fabric of our life with its larger (and for most people, religious) significance, but more as a means to fulfill narrowly personal ends. All that remained was for the Industrial Revolution of the nineteenth century to institutionalize these beliefs into the physical structure of our economic life.

Work and the Industrial Age

Whatever may rightly be said about the hardships of life prior to the Industrial Revolution, work as experienced by the farmer, merchant, or craftsman of the eighteenth century had certain common characteristics. Most of it was done in close proximity to the home, contributing to a sense of continuity with the rest of life's activities. There was generally a good deal of control over the time at which the work was performed, further weaving it into the day. There was a high degree of control over the product from start to finish and thus a sense of ownership and responsibility, which was heightened by the fact that the worker could usually point to the place where his or her work product was being used in the community.

We are witnesses to the ways the Industrial Revolution changed all that. We work some distance—often great distances—from our homes, in environments that are meant to emphasize the differences between the two. Most of us have no control at all over our "business hours." We often work on only a small portion of a product or project and, except for the latest "consumer profile" data, we have no clue as to how our products are used. It's the situation epitomized by Frank and Ernest, two colorful working-class cartoon characters, when one says to the other, "I'm retiring tomorrow—and I'm going to walk down to the end of this line and find out what we've been making for the last thirty years!"

The end result has traditionally gone by the name *alienation*—the physical separation of the worker from the other aspects of his or her life and the emotional and psychological estrangement from both the process and product of the work. For our time, though, perhaps a better term would be the *de-meaning* of work, for ultimately the greatest consequence of the eighteenth and nineteenth centuries was to deprive us of practically any chance of finding deep meaning in our daily business. To do so we would have had to overcome both our inherited cultural attitudes about the ends served by work and the prevailing ways in which work was organized. For most, that was too steep a hill to even bother to climb.

As we come to the end of the twentieth century, we can see how these cultural attitudes have crystallized. As predicted with frightening accuracy by Daniel Bell in 1956,[7] our culture has so accepted the assumption that work can have no intrinsic value that it is no longer a subject of discussion. It is the "standard of living" that is the goal, says Bell, "aided and abetted by advertising and the installment plan, the two most fearsome social inventions of man since the discovery of gunpowder," and work is nothing more than the tedious but necessary vehicle for getting there.

For most of the time the Great Divorce was taking place, any discussion of work and its place in our lives likely came from economists, sociologists, and philosophers—not from theologians. Probably the most humane and articulate voice for meaning and purpose in work was actually Karl Marx, but our fear of the Bolsheviks and years of Cold War doomed most of his more thoughtful works to the periphery. Our economic manifesto, on the other hand, was Adam Smith's *An Inquiry into the Nature and Causes of the Wealth of Nations*. Smith seemed clearly to understand the alienating nature of work as it was being reconceived in the eighteenth century, but unlike Marx, he simply thought it worth the price. Indeed, Smith observed, one forfeits "a portion of his ease, his liberty, and his happiness" when he works,[8] but there seemed to Smith no way to avoid this in the new industrial economy. Of necessity, it seemed, work lost its human dignity in exchange for its usefulness.

Against the backdrop of this thoroughly secular discussion, organized religion was largely silent. As pointed out by Williams and Houck, by the end of the nineteenth century "Protestantism was almost totally identified with the status quo, and was the source of little prophetic insight for business and political life."[9] Moreover, despite its relative significance in American life today, the Catholic church had very little influence on the formative years of the world's greatest economic power. The organized church "allowed work and religion to become separate departments, and is astonished to find that, as a result, the secular work of the world is turned to purely selfish and destructive ends, and that the greater part of the world's intelligent workers have become irreligious, or at least, uninterested in religion."[10]

So, here we are. The medieval marriage of work and life has been thrown out along with the ignorance, superstition, and collectivism of that age. Instead of Luther's vision of all vocations as sacred callings through which one served God and the common weal, our inherited view is that our work is merely the necessary vehicle for obtaining purely personal ends—paying the debt service, getting that new car, or sending the kids to college so they can start the cycle all over again. "The habit of thinking about work as something one does to make money is so ingrained in us," says Dorothy Sayers, "that we can scarcely imagine what a revolutionary change it would be to think about it instead in terms of the work done."[11] The Great Divorce now final, we must find ways of measuring our success in work that have little to do with the deepest values of the "rest" of our lives—measurements like positional advancement, a good "rep" in the company, status in the larger community, success in the "game of life." As Max Weber put it in his conclusion to *The Protestant Ethic and the Spirit of Capitalism*:

> The rosy blush of . . . the Enlightenment seems to be irretrievably fading, and the idea of duty in one's calling prowls about in our lives like the ghost of dead religious beliefs. Where the fulfillment of the calling cannot be directly related to the highest spiritual and cultural values, or when, on the other hand, it need not be felt simply as economic compulsion, the individual generally abandons the attempt to justify it at all. In the field of its highest development, in the United States, the pursuit of wealth, stripped of its religious

and ethical meaning, tends to become associated with purely mundane passions, which often actually give it the character of sport.[12]

It isn't God; but our sporting passion for wealth demands of us such tribute that in earlier ages it would have been necessary for us to build an idol to such a powerful force and give it a name. How about the goddess Success, or the god Respectability?

What Do We Think Work Is?

There is a great difference between the ability to observe and explain something and the ability to capture its essence. Many people could report the news, but only someone like Charles Kuralt could uncover the essential human meaning of the events and stories that crossed his path. There are many who are trained to observe nature and report their findings, but it took someone like Thoreau to open our understanding of the world at a much deeper level. Not that the ability to observe and explicate isn't important, of course; it's the basis of the scientific method and the source of much of our modern knowledge. But there is quite a great difference between stating what *is* and recognizing the potential inherent in a thing or unlocking its deeper meanings.

After the Great Divorce, most of what has been written about human work has been of the observing-explicating kind. Consonant with the scientific method, we have looked at what motivates the economically minded worker of our day, using primarily the lenses provided by sociology, psychology, and economics. It has been left to a few scattered philosophers and theologians to look beneath the studies, surveys, and findings for the truth behind the facts.

The contributions of the behavioral sciences to our understanding of work motivations have been rich with insights. In many of these writings, such as Michael Maccoby's influential book *Why Work: Motivating the New Workforce*,[13] we are given credible explanations for the various reasons (what he calls value drives) why people perform as they do on the job. None of these constructs are necessarily *wrong* despite their wide range of viewpoints—they simply reflect the richness inherent in such a fundamental human activity as work. The problem is that they can be only partial explanations because they see work motivation in the context of their own disciplinary perspective. They aren't incorrect, just incomplete.

Thus an economist tends to see work in terms of a commodity that is exchanged for direct or indirect compensation (salary and perquisites, respectively). True, but even the most jaded among us would have to admit to having broader purposes in mind when they work. A psychological analysis of work may focus on man's ego-needs as met by a sense of inclusion, achievement, approval, or power. I find such studies compelling, but still must admit that they give me a view of human nature that is incomplete. And for many decades the discussion of work came largely from the sociological and political arena, from Marx and Engels to the birth of the OD movement; yet it seems clear that the multifaceted reality of work cannot be adequately discussed in the context of human institutions and our relationship to them. Each picture we get from these differing disciplines can contain a large measure of truth and still not contain the whole story. Of necessity, this fundamental and complex part of our nature evades the tidy categories of our sciences.

Observing and explaining what *is*, is insufficient here for another reason. What is being observed is a cultural construct, something that *is* but has not always *been* and thus may not always *be*. It is a construct based on current reality, to be sure, but is limited by its inability to envision a different reality. The movie *Nell* made this point nicely, while exploring the difference between observing what *is* and searching for deeper meaning. Jodi Foster played the title role, portraying a young girl raised in the Appalachian mountains in total isolation from the modern world. While the scientific community wanted to study her from afar with eavesdropping devices and telephoto lenses (producing, of course, the requisite scholarly article at the end), one man sought truly to understand Nell at a more basic level. He learned her unique language with painstaking difficulty and slowly gained her trust, eventually penetrating through her outer reality to glimpse the beauty of who she was as a person. Having gone beyond observing and reporting, he was able to see in his relationship with Nell how her current reality was shaped by the events of her life, and he came to grasp (though reluctantly) how much fuller her life could be without the limitations of her current environment.

Such a shift is necessary in us too if we are to move from understanding what *is* to the larger context of meaning and potential. As valuable as it is in its place, our observing-explaining cannot alone penetrate to the essence of the thing observed. Nor can we see the inherent potential of the thing if we insist on defining it only in terms of its current context. Observing and explaining work-related behavior doesn't confront, or even attempt to, the deeper enigma of work and its place in our lives. Observing-explaining doesn't address, nor should it try to, the need we all have for our lives to have meaning and purpose, and therefore the need for our work to be meaningful as well. Partial truths are helpful to us only when we acknowledge their incompleteness.

One very interesting study that comes out of the observing-explaining literature, now replicated several times, gives a hint as to the existence of this deeper meaning and purpose. The participants were asked to assume that they had the freedom to retire immediately or to go into any type of work they wanted. In the latest version of the survey, less than 2 percent said they would want to retire! Although the majority would prefer some other job to the one they now had, the overwhelming conclusion is that work in general is sufficiently important to us that we want it to be a part of our lives.[14] Our gripe seems to be with our jobs, not with work itself. Clearly, for most people work is more than just a means to an end (debunking at least the economist's narrow view of human nature), and it contributes to the meeting of much more complex human needs.

What Sayeth the Church?

The task of uncovering deeper, transcendent meaning in our common experiences has long been the province of the theologian and religious philosopher. But for a variety of reasons, I feel we've been let down—and left to our own devices—by this traditional source of sense-making. Certainly the Great Divorce has so driven its wedge between work and transcendent meaning that most people haven't felt the need, or perhaps the permission, to think deeply about such issues. But apropos the religion professor's comment reported in the Introduction, the organized church has so bought into the Great Divorce that it has given little attention to the meaning of work from either the pulpit or the typewriter. Add to this the decline in the influence of religion generally in American life, and you get an idea of why so little theological reflection on work has made it to the consciousness of working men and women.

This paucity of theological reflection has, by the way, left any discussion of work and ultimate values to the burgeoning business of "business ethics." Here I have a particular bone to pick, as I have taught that subject for many years to undergraduate business majors. Even at universities with religious backgrounds, there is great unease among administrators and most faculty with the notion that there is a connection between ethical behavior and personal religion. Even if they can see the possibility of a connection, they are much more comfortable if it is ignored. The message sent to students (who fortunately seem adept at surviving our fallacies) is twofold: first, that our values exist as abstract products of our reasoning and our ethical theories (deontology, utilitarianism, and so on), apart from our beliefs about Ultimate Reality—a proposition that Allen Bloom rightly calls "the stupidest and most pernicious illusion";[15] second, that the word *business* modifies and limits the word *ethics,* so that there is perceived to be some separate category of ethical behavior that applies to our commercial dealings—an institutionalization of the Great Divorce at the level of our universities. Unfortunately, our religious sense-makers have been equally unsuccessful in influencing the leadership of our educational institutions.

One important reason for the failure of theology to connect with most working people is its insistence on trying to fit its thinking about work within the confines of the tenets of traditional church dogma. Thus much of the reflection is on such topics as the place of work in the eschatological coming of the "new heaven and new earth" of God's Kingdom, or on work as participation in the creative nature of God, or on work as the curse resulting from mankind's original sin as chronicled in the book of Genesis. These speculations may have benefit for those deeply steeped in the doctrines of the organized church. What they *don't* do is provide any guidance to a man or woman who has discovered (or is trying to discover) a *personal relationship to God and is struggling with how work fits into that relationship.* For those people, much of the theological reflection on work must seem like so many angels dancing on the head of a pin.

But perhaps an even bigger reason for the failure of theology may be found on the other side of the same coin: the church's attempt to fit modern work into traditional dogma is matched only by its attempt to model itself after the institutions of the prevailing commercial culture. It increasingly borrows its structure, its procedures, and even its bottom-line measures of success from business, losing all the while its ability to stand outside the dominant culture as a prophetic and inspiring voice. Working people who enter its doors seeking a more congruent life often simply find themselves in the same spin of activity, conflict, and intrigue that marks their experience of the workaday world—chairing committees, raising money, and attending endless meetings just as they do at work. They're fed the same food they eat of necessity every day on their jobs, with not so much as a side dish of the meaning, hope, and purpose for which they came.

There are indeed voices that are speaking about business and work using the language of traditional faith—words like *vocation, service, stewardship,* and *calling.* These concepts are accessible to businesspeople and relevant to the struggle of aligning outer life with inner faith. But those voices, more often than not, come from people like Peter Block, James Autry, and the late Robert K. Greenleaf—people in and of business who have lived the struggle, rather than from the sense-makers of organized religion. With a few fortunate exceptions, our theologians, religious philosophers, and ministers have contributed little to the mending of the Great Divorce.

This dearth but mirrors the larger crisis in the organized church. Swirling around it is the increasing desire for a personal and immediate experience of the transcendent, in which dogma is replaced by deep knowledge, and faith is cultivated from within rather than prescribed from without. The church, long the container and medium of individual experience, is losing its hold on its position as intercessor. A new Reformation of sorts is taking place, one through which millions of people are giving life to their deeply religious yearnings by trying to find their "own way" to God. The desire is to experience transcendent reality for oneself, sometimes through a bewildering array of nontraditional approaches—from Eastern ascetic practices to transpersonal psychology to all manner of New Age potions—but distinctly not through the church or synagogue. The consistent failure of organized religion is not that it fails to embrace such approaches but that it too often insists on taking the new wine of individual experience, as explosive as it is intoxicating, and putting it into the old wineskins of centuries-old dogma.

The church has done no better with the burgeoning desire of men and women to connect their spiritual yearnings to their jobs. To the extent the phenomenon has even been addressed by organized religion, it has all too often been given a context that does not speak directly to the passions and struggles of working people committed to this new and truly groundbreaking task. The result is an institution that may have many valuable social functions but surprisingly little of relevance to say about something as central to modern life as the deeper meaning and purpose of work and business. For that, it just may be necessary to look more carefully inside *ourselves*.

Questions and Exercises for Further Reflection

1. Can you identify the last time you made a decision relating to your work that felt really uncomfortable to you? What were the values that you ultimately relied upon in making that decision? One way to tell is to ask yourself *why* you made that particular choice, and then continue to ask yourself "Why is that important?" until you reach the rock-bottom reasons why the decision came out as it did. Once you discover the bedrock values and assumptions on which you based the decision, you might ask yourself the following questions:

Where else in my life do these values hold such sway?

Where did I learn that these were the ground rules for the ways in which work and business should operate?

Would these values be equally controlling if they were applied to an analogous situation involving my family, friends, or community? On what bases do I justify the distinction between work and personal life?

2. Think back on the religious influences in your own up-bringing during your childhood and adolescence. Make a list of things you were taught by those influences or that you heard from them that concerned the meaning, purpose, or significance of work. How long is the list? Are the teachings consistent, or do some actually contradict others (for example, work as a curse and work as stewardship)? How have these things influenced your own views of work and business? How have they influenced how you feel about the job you are in right now?

3. When was the last time you heard a sermon, homily, or other religious address that touched on the meaning and purpose of work and business—not admonitions about how it should be conducted but rather on its religious or spiritual significance? (Have you *ever* heard one?) Did it challenge or reinforce your assumptions?

Chapter Two

The Meaning of Work and the Work of Meaning

Meaninglessness inhibits the fullness of life and can, therefore, be equated with illness; meaningfulness makes a great many things endurable, perhaps everything.
C. G. JUNG

If I were to ask you, "What is the meaning of life?" I would be unlikely to get a very coherent or original answer from most of you, if I got one at all. Heck, I don't know the answer either. But if I asked you, "What is the meaning of *your* life?" I would get a rich variety of responses that spanned the broad reach of human experience and ranged from the inspiring to the mundane, the sublime to the ridiculous. So it is with the "meaning of work." It does us little good to fiddle with work's *objective* definitions—what it means to economists or theologians or the writers of Funk & Wagnalls' dictionary. But it is extremely important for you to consider what *your* work means to *you*—its individual and *subjective* meaning. This chapter will lead us on a very personal exploration of the place work occupies—or perhaps should occupy—in your life. Only then will you be in a position to see what effect the Great Divorce has had in your own life and be ready to look at the ways of healing that split that are offered in Part Two of this book.

Let's say you are engrossed in a sunset or gazing at a painting, and I ask you what either of those things meant to you. You wouldn't send me to a dictionary to look up the words *sunset* or *painting,* would you? You wouldn't send me to some scientific text on why sunsets are colorful or to some art history book that discusses the painting. No, you would likely tell me how it affected you; the value it had for you; why it was worth the expenditure of your time and energy. Most objects and events do not *inherently* have any meaning—we *bestow* meaning on them in accordance with the importance we give to them out of our own thoughts and emotions. And so it is with this thing we call work. No kind of work is *inherently* meaningful. We give meaning and value and importance *to* it—or don't, as the case may be. And the conclusion that logically follows, whether we wish to resist it or not, is this: *no kind of work is inherently more meaningful than any other; all work is capable of addressing our core needs for meaning and purpose.*

Now, before trotting out the usual objections to this statement, consider first your own experiences. On the one hand, every one of you can likely name one or more ministers, social workers, or other "helping" professionals you have known who have burned out along the way, finding in the end that their idealistic vocation became "just a job." On the other hand, most of you would be able to point to someone like Gus, the custodian of my small rural high school, whose humor and affection combined with selflessness and hard work to teach me a valuable lesson about work and human dignity. This isn't to say that there aren't jobs with greater *potential* than others for personal meaningfulness. Some do have, if you will, larger hooks than others on which to hang our deepest values. But the point is that *we* do the hanging and can do so on any of the infinite variety of jobs, trades, occupations, and life engagements that make up our human experience of work. To argue otherwise is to make the mistake of locating meaning outside the person as something objective—of looking in the dictionary for something best found inside ourselves.

The meanings we give to our work are richly varied, and most of us have several of them operating within us at any given time. But there is a way to categorize them that can give us insight into whether *our* work, as it is done by *us,* is capable of being an outlet for our deepest values or is merely an unpleasant means to a necessary end.

Concentric Circles of Meaning

A good starting point is John Haughey's distinction between immanent and transcendent meanings of work.[1] By *immanent* we refer to those motivations that are part of the immediate experience, personal concerns, and ordinary "reality" of our world. As such, immanent meanings are also grounded in the thoroughly secular aspects of our lives. They range from monetary rewards to a sense of achievement, gaining of status, family security, "attaboys," a sense of competence, and so on. This shouldn't suggest that our immanent meanings of work are somehow bad or wrongheaded. We are, all of us, motivated by some unique mixture of them every day in our jobs. One day, the satisfaction of money and purchasing power may be paramount; the very next day, the currency may consist of our feeling a part of a community at work. As Freud said, how we work (along with how we love) says a great deal about our mental and emotional health, and such immanent meanings have a tremendous influence on how we are socialized into our families and communities. Even more fundamentally, work "helps establish the regularity of life, its basic rhythms and cycles . . . [and] organizes, routinizes, and structures our lives. It allows a safe outlet for our competitive strivings and often helps to keep us sane."[2]

But for practically all of us, there is a need for our lives in general to have meaning that goes beyond the immanent—beyond the narrow horizon of our immediate, personal concerns, perhaps even beyond the bounds of our limited version of reality. To talk of these types of meaning beyond the immanent, we choose the word *transcendent,* for lack of a better one.

When we use the word *transcendent,* we commonly are speaking of the holy—the things of God. But that is only one of its definitions. Think instead in terms of concentric circles, such as those you would make by throwing a rock into a placid lake. As the rippling circle spreads outward, it becomes larger, more expansive in its breadth, its horizon ever widening. Yet it contains all of the smaller circles within it. It "transcends," but also includes, the numerous smaller horizons emanating from the stone's impact. Such are the transcendent meanings of work. Any time we find our horizons broadening to include interests beyond our own, principles beyond self-interest, and powers beyond those of the visible world, then we are beginning to experience the possibility of a transcendent meaning for our work.

The immanent meanings do not vanish, of course, nor do they even necessarily become less important. It is their *primacy* that is displaced. A well-paying job that utilizes our talents; an enjoyable working community; the positive feelings of self-worth that come from advancement, competence, and the like—all these remain important parts of who we are at work and why we give it so much energy. But they can be supplanted from their ruling place (consider yourself warned), and to some extent modified, by the transcendent.

For some idea of the form the concentric circles might take (and perhaps their logical progression?), consider the following adaptation of the well-worn story of the stone masons and the cathedral. In our version there are seven commercial bankers hard at work in their offices, each grappling with a separate aspect of a complicated financing arrangement that will result in construction of a new and much-needed regional hospital. Each of our commercial lenders responds to the question, "What are you doing?" in a different way:

First Banker: I'm trying to keep my boss off my butt. If I don't finish this project by the end of the day tomorrow, I'm toast.

Second Banker: I'm pulling down forty-two five a year.

Third Banker: I'm trying to make my family financially secure. They are all-important to me.

Fourth Banker: I'm working on a genuinely creative financing arrangement for this hospital deal. My team and I can put together a construction package that's five basis points lower than anyone else in the industry.

Fifth Banker: I'm providing a service to my company and community. That's my obligation.

Sixth Banker: I'm helping to build a hospital; something that will positively affect the health and well-being of the whole community for many years to come.

Seventh Banker: I'm serving God and mankind the best way I know how. Oh, yeah, and I agree with what most of the others said, too.

Do you notice the ways in which the circles widen? They go from (1) fear of punishment, to (2) personal gain, to (3) approval of family or peer group, to (4) an emphasis on knowledge, skill, or craftsmanship, for which the level of performance and the approval of those similarly skilled is paramount, to (5) duty to the community and larger society, to (6) universal principles, to (7) God. We might argue about which circles go inside which, but this at least is true: there is a progression from immediate, ordinary, personal concerns to the interests of others to overarching values and finally to Ultimate Reality. Each wider circle includes yet transcends the narrowness of the concerns of the preceding bank lenders.

Which one of the bankers' responses comes the closest to capturing how you would answer the question "What are you doing?" in your daily work? Put a different way, what's the widest concentric circle of meaning you can honestly claim for your own work? Beginning in the 1950s and 1960s with the work of Jean Piaget and Lawrence Kohlberg, researchers began to articulate a theory of how people grow and develop—not only in childhood but in a process that lasts throughout their lifetime. We will discuss adult developmental theory, as it is called, in detail in Chapter Six. Suffice it now to say that the concentric circles we have described are, in roughest outline, the stages of human moral development as they apply to our views of work. Thus when we talk about the widest concentric circles, we are talking not only about the transcendent meanings of work but also about urges toward the higher reaches of human development.

And who among us aspires to such higher reaches? Do you? Considering the constant pull of work's immanent meanings and a culture that relegates transcendence to a small corner of the working world, what sort of person would dare to swim against the cultural stream? It would have to be someone for whom the need for meaning and purpose in life was real and alive, and who felt that need as strongly in her work as she did in life's other aspects. What kind of person is that?

In the early years of his psychoanalytic practice, Carl Jung began to notice that he had two very different types of patients. Most would bring to him their symptoms and difficulties and, once sufficiently patched up that they could continue normal functioning, they would go on their way. Yet a few would remain long after their presenting symptoms were cured, urged along by some inner need to go more deeply into their own mysteries. They seemed impelled to further growth as persons, despite the fact that their psychoanalytic work was often quite painful (and more than a little costly). To Jung this phenomenon was a manifestation of a human drive toward wholeness, a fundamental and deep-seated desire to grow beyond the bounds of the ego and its needs toward some larger sense of connection to the inner self, the community of mankind, and God. He called this process *individuation* and devoted much of his prolific body of work to it. Although the stirrings of individuation were visible in practically everyone, Jung felt that at least in his own day (he died in 1961), those who consciously and committedly embarked on this journey remained the rare exception.

Is it any different today? The answer is a guarded yes. As the great symbol systems of Western culture and religion continue to lose their potency and meaning for us, the drive toward wholeness—an ever powerful human force—continues to find expression in the lives of many people. And there is some evidence that their numbers are growing. Whether they feel a vague malaise of something missing in their lives or experience the bright realization that they are on their own individual paths of growth and development, millions of people have found that they cannot accept the dearth of meaning and purpose offered by contemporary society and are increasingly drawn toward a very personal path to wholeness. For them—and perhaps you are among them—individuation becomes a way of life.

The implications of this sea change are enormous for business, but for the present let's look at the ways it is manifesting itself in the lives of individual managers and executives. From the mass of immanent meanings that have been the staple of our business lives for so long, there are emerging transcendent meanings that reflect the growth and development of the individuals who have grasped them. These people themselves may not even recognize the importance of this shift, but they have slowly widened their circles from the concerns of self and group to the interests of God and the common good. They have heard the call of transcendent meaning, even as they have attended to work's necessary immanent meanings.

That call is being answered today by an increasing number of working people. You may be trying to find your own answer, right now. But I want to suggest that if you will look around you to the managers and executives whom you most admire, to the men and women who find their work most fulfilling, to the organizational leaders who are truly most effective with their people, and, perhaps, to deep inside yourself, you will find that call answered in one or more of three ways.

Work as Self-Development

E. F. Schumacher, in his wonderful little book *Good Work,* suggests that human work has three purposes. It does, of course, provide necessary and useful goods and services. But beyond that, work "enable[s] every one of us to use and thereby perfect our gifts like good stewards [and] 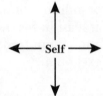 to do so in service to, and in cooperation with, others, so as to liberate ourselves from our inborn egocentricity."[3] Written more than twenty years ago, this statement expresses what is now one of the most commonly held transcendent meanings of work. We use our working lives as the anvils on which we hammer out our inconsistencies, hone our skills, and temper our weaknesses. Along with the competencies required by our trades and professions, we learn the fine (and often more difficult) arts of dealing and working with others. Long before 360-degree feedback was in vogue, the workplace was already the arena in which we could learn more about ourselves, if open to doing so, than we could from any other activity. Whether we are struggling to get ahead of the learning curve, or dealing with our petty-tyrant boss, or confronting the terminal illness of a friend and coworker, work can provide the raw material for our own self-construction.

When we approach it consciously and committedly, this process of development can be part of what Abraham Maslow calls self-actualization. Although Maslow's hierarchy of needs may seem overly simplistic today, it is still true that the desire to become authentically oneself, to express creatively one's unique gifts and talents, is one of the deepest motivations of highly developed people and one of the requirements of effective business leadership. As James MacGregor

Burns observed, the true innovation and creativity necessary for leadership might only come from a "self-actualization through work"—the expression of mankind's higher needs through the context of human activity.[4]

But doesn't this business of self-development seem terribly self-absorbed? How can it lend transcendent meaning to our work if there is so much emphasis on self? Think of the Schumacher quotation just cited: to be a steward of our gifts implies that we hold and use them *for* someone or something outside ourselves. Moreover, we use them not in the service of our own egos but to liberate ourselves from our natural tendency to egocentricity. In other words, we can *transcend* the narrow concerns of the ego through our committed attention to actualizing our true self. That is why the arrows in the figure that begins this section all point outward. Maslow expresses the seeming paradox this way: "S-A [self-actualizing] work transcends the self without trying to, and achieves the kind of loss of self-awareness and self-consciousness that the easterners . . . keep trying to attain. S-A work is simultaneously a seeking and fulfilling of the self *and* also an achieving of the selflessness which is the ultimate expression of the *real* self. It resolves the dichotomy between selfish and unselfish."[5]

The emergence of the empowerment movement, increased self-directedness of workers, and more enlightened management styles have all contributed to making self-development an accessible goal for more working people. Not long ago I was sitting in the office of a new coaching client, a manufacturing plant supervisor who learned his management skills in the early 1970s. As we watched the blue shirts come and go with the change of shifts, I asked him what most motivated his employees. "Money is still in the top five," he replied, "as I guess is fear of me firing them. But the thing that's new—maybe over the last ten years—is that practically every one of them gets really juiced over their promotability and their skill development. They're all pretty good at what they do—they just want to get better." When I asked what he did to tap these various motivations, he had plenty of answers relating to fear and money, and none with respect to self-development—a good indication of both when he learned his management style and why I was called in by his superiors to coach him! But for our purposes the point is that, in practically all corners of business, the opportunity to view work as an instrument of self-actualization is present as never before. And for an increasing number of people, work thereby acquires a transcendent meaning.

Work as Service

For far too long, we associated service to God exclusively with the occupation of the clergy, or at best with certain helping professions. We were robbed by the Great Divorce of any cultural sanction for the view that our lives in business could somehow directly serve our creator. Fortunately, this began to change in the 1970s with the publication of Robert K. Greenleaf's *Servant Leadership*. A longtime executive of AT&T  and a devout Quaker, Greenleaf spoke with both wisdom and experience of the centrality of service in the life of business, and, even after his death, his influence has continued to expand with the work of his influential foundation and the reprinting of his writings. Current authors such as Peter Block, James Autry, and Max De Pree are clearly influenced by Greenleaf's work and continue to keep the central premises of servant leadership in mainstream thought. Service, too, is an emerging source of transcendent meaning for millions of people.

For Christians particularly, the theme of work as service is a natural extension of their theology. Although Jesus said very little about occupational work as such, his teachings are replete with references to the ultimate value of service to God and others in all aspects of life: "He who is greatest among you shall be your servant" (Matthew 23:11); "The Son of Man did not come to be served, but to serve" (Matthew 20:28). With such statements Jesus turned on its ear the prevailing norm of the day, where rank and status were carefully prescribed, and one's place in the social hierarchy determined everything from the greeting you would receive in public, to the place you would sit at gatherings, to the services to which you were entitled. As a natural extension of the Christian faith, many businesspeople are choosing to subjugate their status as managers and executives to the service of God and of those who work "for" them. They are taking Jesus' admonition to "love the Lord your God with all your heart, with all your soul, and with all your mind . . . and your neighbor as yourself" (Matthew 22:37, 39) and giving it life in the workplace.

You might ask why the figure that begins this section only shows an arrow to God and not to the many other sources of transcendent meaning that our work could serve. Other people might well choose words like *humanity, justice, society, higher good,* or *ultimate values,* and they will get no argument from me. I simply choose to be explicit about service to God because I believe that, at bottom, our notions about moral values and our duties to others are founded in our beliefs about the ultimate source and meaning of our existence—and for me that is God. Moreover, all the world's great religions are clear that a necessary corollary of fealty to God is service to mankind and obedience to the high moral values that are God's laws. The latter is simply an extension of the former. So while much of what has been written about servant leadership stays safely within the realm of service to people or ideals, it is clear that behind the "inclusiveness" of the discussion are strong assumptions about the existence and expectations of an Ultimate Reality.

Business is becoming for many the primary arena in which to realize the transcendent meaning of service. Not only has the workplace annexed most of the time and energy we have for such meaningful pursuits, but for managers and executives it presents an unparalleled opportunity to assume the role of servant to those who look to them for leadership. Business has truly filled the void left by the decline of our religious and social institutions by providing the forum in which the desires for service and contribution, so valuable to society as a whole, can be met.[6] Greenleaf, ever prophetic, saw this coming two decades ago: "[I]n the next few years, more will be learned in business than in any other field about how to bring servant leadership into being as a major social force."[7]

Work as Vocation

Some months back I was observing a leadership development course filled with businesspeople from around the country. One of the participants, a very intelligent and likable woman named Anne, was relating to the group how she had left her secure position with a Fortune 200 company after nineteen years, in hopes of finding work that provided a greater sense of satisfaction. With kids now educated and a recent divorce final, she felt it vitally important to find a place that more fully engaged her talents and her affections. The group was full of very practical advice with respect to her "career path": avoid this particular industry for its poor growth potential, posture your résumé in this particular way, act quickly to avoid the appearance of vague career goals. As she listened she seemed clearly to be losing patience. Finally she blurted out, "Look, I don't *have* a career any more—I have a *vocation*."

There is indeed a difference. As Robert Bellah puts it, our career is our means of achieving social standing and our source of self-esteem, but our vocation is what "connects work's purpose with the proximate and ultimate end of a person's life" and links us to a larger community.[8] It is, literally, our "calling" in life, coming from the Latin root *vocare,* "to call." And of course, for those who feel its reality, that call is from God.

The idea of getting one's vocation from God has deep roots in Western religious tradition. As recounted in Chapter One, Luther vehemently opposed the notion that only priests and monks were called by God, insisting not only that all Christians had religious vocations in life but that *every kind of work* could be blessed as a calling. Whatever theological differences may later have developed among the Protestant reformers, they were in accord as to the *universality* and *individuality* of vocation. That is, every person has a calling in life if he or she will but hear it, and that call is unique to him or her alone.

What Anne was saying was that she had heard that call, or was trying to. She, like the many others who have discovered this transcendent meaning of work, had forsaken the sequential, linear career path fashioned by the needs of her ego and the expectations of society. She had embarked on the difficult but ultimately rewarding task of seeking her true vocation from God.

How in the world does one do that? How do we "listen" for such a call, or know that we've "heard" it? Discernment of God's movements in our lives is never easy, of course, particularly in those areas of our lives that the Great Divorce has taught us to classify as secular. Matthew Fox even calls vocation one of the six great mysteries of life.[9] But there is a kind of calculus we can use, which has been best summarized by Frederick Buechner:

> There are all different kinds of voices calling you to all different kinds of work, and the problem is to find out which is the voice of

God rather than that of society, say, or the superego, or self-interest. By and large a good rule for finding out is this: the kind of work God usually calls you to is the kind of work (a) that you need most to do and (b) that the world most needs to have done. If you really get a kick out of your work, you've presumably met requirement (a), but if your work is writing TV deodorant commercials, the chances are you've missed requirement (b). On the other hand, if your work is being a doctor in a leper colony, you have probably met (b), but if most of the time you're bored and depressed by your work, the chances are that you've not only bypassed (a), but probably aren't helping your patients much either. . . . The place God calls you to is the place where your deep gladness and the world's deep hunger meet.[10]

God does not call us to work for which there is no genuine need or for which we are not suited. But within those parameters there is a wealth and variety of work that can answer the call of vocation—that is, if we are but open to the unexpected paths down which God may lead us. But the moment we become too closely wedded to the immanent meanings of work—to a certain status or income or means of satisfying our ego-needs—our "hearing" begins to fail us.

Those who understand the call of vocation know that the work need not be some grand thing in the eyes of the world, precisely because it serves the interests of God, not status. In fact, I believe that both of the examples Buechner uses are unnecessary exaggerations that, if we aren't careful, could lead us into the trap of thinking that only a narrow band of careers can qualify as vocations. One conceivably *can* serve the needs of the world through writing deodorant commercials. Not only is it a useful product (I assume Dr. Buechner would agree), but the *way* in which such work is done can have everything to do with God's interests in the world. Similarly, one need not retreat to a leper colony to serve the world's most pressing needs. Our businesses, our families, and our neighborhoods are just as full of the deep hunger of which he speaks.

Nor are we necessarily called once and for all to a single vocation. The world's needs and our own gifts continue to evolve over time. If we are truly to keep our "ears" open, it may be necessary to make changes—even radical ones—along the way. M. Scott Peck points out that midlife is a particularly propitious time for this, not because the old jokes about midlife crises are correct but because "[i]t is a time when God calls us to revitalization, and frequently that revitalization requires a radical shift in activity or focus."[11] Such seemed to be the case with Anne.

I have found this to be true in my own life. Now well into my third career, it is clear to me that everything I did before was both perfect for that time in my life and preparatory for the future. The practice of law gave me an in-depth understanding of the world of business, and my time as an academic exposed me to most of the theoretical constructs of this book—which I am now in turn applying to business. For those who view work as a calling there are no wrong turns, no derailments—just chances to grow.

Viewing work as vocation in many ways subsumes the other emerging transcendent meanings we have discussed. To answer God's call is to commit oneself to growth and self-development as a faithful steward of the gifts one has received. This is perhaps the clearest meaning of Jesus' parable of the talents, in which the servant who merely hid his master's coin for safekeeping was most severely punished (Matthew 25:14–30). And, of course, to try to answer the world's deep hunger is to put oneself in the service of others. God never seems to ask for our love and service without asking us to give the same to our neighbors as well (Deuteronomy 6:5; Leviticus 19:18; Matthew 22:37–39).

Wrong Turns and Potholes

The road to meaning and purpose in our lives is strewn with wrong turns and littered with potholes, as anyone who has tried to find his or her way along this path will surely tell you. Western society puts a not-so-subtle pressure on all of us to seek meaning in externals—the company, the economy, the country, science, the "good life"—rather than our own wider circles of meaning. It is also difficult to focus on the transcendent—and correspondingly easy to grasp at the immanent—when we are as stressed and stretched as we often feel at work. It is no secret that, for almost all of us, work requires more in less time with fewer resources and incentives than it did a single decade ago. So in a country like the United States that has more multiple jobholders than any other on earth,[12] and where fully 73 percent of the workforce regularly works weekends,[13] it takes a conscious act of will to look beyond the culturally defined meanings of work and vocation. Many don't bother, as perhaps evidenced by the fact that only 39 percent of Americans in one survey rated work "more important" than leisure—far less than most other countries.[14]

Inviting "wrong turns" in our workplaces abound. The obsessive connection to our jobs that we call workaholism is an increasingly common one—made more alluring by the fact that our employers may encourage it! Workaholism starts with the understanding, now thoroughly instilled in Western culture, that our work is the primary means by which we define ourselves and others.[15] Men and women in search of a sense of meaning for their lives can thus easily fall prey to the belief that their visible success at work and the approval of their peers can provide externally what is felt to be lacking internally. The overinvestment in work comes to serve the same function as overindulgence for the food addict or overimbibing for the alcoholic. The ego's need is temporarily met, but often with the kind of diminishing returns that make the workaholic have to invest more and more time to achieve the same psychological sense of well-being—claiming all the while that his or her behavior will change just as soon as this project is finished or that deadline met. The sense of meaning found, such as it is, consists only of the thoroughly immanent and personal. Even if we can convince ourselves (usually with a healthy dose of rationalization) that we are toiling for the good of our families or the benefit of our companies, we have only slightly enlarged our circle and continue to disregard the wider circles outside our narrow horizons.

Certainly, hard work is sometimes called for—often in the service of transcendent meaning. Gandhi is but one example of a person who worked selflessly and ceaselessly in the service of those wider circles. But we must always take care to be certain that we are called to such work and that it is truly a transcendent purpose we are serving rather than the needs of a lesser god.

We can avoid a wrong turn in our work—even very hard work—by focusing on its transcendent meanings, while attending to work's perfectly appropriate immanent purposes as well. It is not always or easily done, but to the extent that we can align ourselves with those widest circles of concern within us, we put ourselves in a position to live lives that are not only successful but also meaningful and connected to our deepest values. Work so done is meaningful because it flows from and is connected to our innermost core, rather than

simply serving some external object or cause. Our work may be objectively valuable—providing income, security, and the like—but
derives its primary meaning from the subjective.

As if the road to transcendent meaning weren't rough enough
given our inherited cultural terrain, we have added some giant potholes in recent years. Technological advances, especially those related to business communication, were supposed to reduce work's
burdensome aspects while freeing time for creativity, increased production, and leisure. For most of us, our experience is to the contrary, of course. Yes, productivity has been enhanced, but most
people feel more tethered to their jobs than connected to their
creativity by the ceaseless intrusions of voice mail, e-mail, pagers,
faxes, and cellular phones. As one frustrated executive recently
said, "Voice mail has replaced prayers for me. It's the first thing I
do when I get up and the last thing I do before I go to sleep."

Many others have been subjected to an alarming loss of privacy
as a result of widespread use of various techniques for monitoring
employee activities and communications. This can create potholes
in some professions you might not expect—the practice of law, for
example. When I became a lawyer twenty-some years ago, our bills
to clients were largely based on our individual, subjective view of
how much our efforts had been worth, how much time the job had
taken, and what the client could afford to pay. You eyeballed all of
that and came up with a figure, generally without anyone questioning your judgment. But in 1975 the world as I knew it changed.
Our small firm bought a machine that could, in the words of our
managing partner, "help with our billing" by providing a printout
of the time we had spent on a particular client-task. It was a nice
tool, I had to admit, in helping me make a judgment of an appropriate fee. But one day, in a moment that was doubtless repeated
in law firms all over the country, that same managing partner fig-
ured out that you could press a button and get a printout of what
every lawyer was billing on a yearly, monthly, or daily basis, down
to the tenth of an hour. You can guess the rest. Before you could
say "Law is a business," there were minimum billable hour requirements, oversight of attorney billings by a central committee,
and (oh, yes) an increase in the hourly rate charged so that the
firm could buy a new and better billing machine. In the midst of
all this, a young lawyer found it increasingly difficult to sustain his
search for transcendent meanings in the work he was doing.

But the most enticing detour, the veritable siren's song of our culture, is of our own making. Many years ago I sat on a front porch step with a bright and talented young man fresh out of graduate school. The world was his oyster, as they say, as he talked of the many exciting paths along which his training and abilities could lead him. The possibilities seemed truly limitless. But then he shared an insight that has haunted me—and perhaps him— ever since. "There is a trap I could fall into," he said. "There are a lot of exciting things out there; but the higher the income and lifestyle I become accustomed to, the fewer the number of possibilities that will be open to me if I want to sustain it. In a way, I could become trapped in a gilded cage." Now, some two decades later, I am aware that he did. He has changed jobs and even professions more than once, but always to feed the yawning mouths and voracious appetites of larger houses, fancier clubs, nicer cars, and more private private schools. I do not know if he is happy, but I do know he is trapped.

But then there are stories of people like Carl, a cardiac surgeon with a fine reputation. By age forty-five he had reached the highest levels of his profession, with some three thousand open-heart surgeries under his belt. What's more, if we applied Frederick Buechner's calculus to Carl's medical career, we would have to say that he was doing work that he was exquisitely capable of doing and that the world indeed needed to have done. But at that point in his successful life, Carl began to hear another call. After an intense and sometimes painful period of faithful searching, he came firmly to believe that his vocation for the next phase of his life lay in preparing himself for the ministry and doing medical mission work in impoverished countries. He is now the associate pastor of a small church in South Carolina, frequently on leave to the mission fields. I think he is reasonably happy, although he hits a pothole every now and then just like the rest of us. But I know he is free, and he has used that freedom to give his life and work a transcendent meaning and purpose that far too few of us ever know.

The Vocation of Business Leadership

Steve sat behind his cluttered desk, listening intently as I finished rolling out the feedback from his direct reports. The written comments from his subordinates would have been the envy of anyone who supervises others in business. A sampling: "Makes people feel worthy and valued." "Excellent business sense combined with exceptional people skills. A great motivator and coach." "He is the BEST supervisor I've ever had. I feel he will support my decisions and help me in any way he can." And finally: "Don't ever retire!"

He leaned back, clasped his hands behind his head, and allowed himself a wry smile. "Well, they know I probably will retire in another year or two, but we'll try to get somebody in here who cares about 'em as much as I do."

I probed a bit: "What does caring mean to you?"

"Growth—that's really what it's all about. I've learned something every day—or at least every other day—ever since I've been here, and I want all of our people to do that too. If you can't grow and develop, learn new skills and more about yourself, and get better at dealing with people, then you probably need to be someplace else. Or dead!"

"And how do you make their growth and development happen?"

"Mostly by getting out of the way. Ideally, my job is to get them the resources they need, make suggestions when they ask for them, be sure they get the recognition they deserve, and then become damn-near irrelevant. If I do my job well, there really ought to come a time when they don't need me at all."

"Why is that kind of management style important to you?"

"Well, first of all, I just think in the long run you get more out of your people that way. But beyond that, it's just something I believe in. It's how people deserve to be treated, at least after they've shown that they're basically capable and trustworthy—and these folks did that long ago. I mean, we don't talk much about religion around here. That may be illegal or something. But this is just part of what I believe."

So goes one blunt, cut-to-the-chase version of the vocation of business leadership. It is growth and self-development; but it is also committed service to the growth and development of those around you, particularly those in the organization who look to you for leadership and guidance. And although they might not be as guardedly explicit about it as Steve, many leaders have gone a step beyond to consider "for whom" (or what) such service is being rendered. The first time I met James Autry, he put it this way in a speech:"Management is a calling, a life engagement, that combines technical skill with vision, compassion, honesty, trust, and courage in order to create a place where people can do good work, grow personally, spiritually, psychologically, and emotionally—as well as financially—and reap the professional results of a job well done."

The vocation of business leadership is not the same call as that answered by Carl the surgeon. It requires different talents and fulfills a different need. But its purposes are just as transcendent and its meaning just as encompassing. And perhaps, just perhaps, the need for it in our own time and culture is even greater.

———————

A few years ago a study published in the *Journal for the Scientific Study of Religion* found that 15 percent of the sizable sample explicitly viewed their work as a "calling"—a vocation.[16] The findings suggested that merely being a church member or exposed to religious influences was not enough. Denominational affiliation, pastoral influences, and sermons were all deemed to have "no effect." But the study did find that "when religion is *internalized,* it causes some people who are already inclined to think of work as important to take the additional step of viewing it as a calling, not just a career"[17] (my emphasis). Moreover, the characteristics of the people most inclined to make that leap were those of precisely the people you would expect to find in executive and managerial positions in business—and, not surprisingly, reading this book. They were well-educated men and women who enjoyed relatively high levels of job security, worked with people instead of objects, and were well paid. In short, the study stands for the proposition that a sizable portion of our population, having many of the characteristics of the typical business manager, are ready to move beyond the career culture to the transcendent meanings of work and vocation. The key to such a move seems to lie not so much in the extrinsic trappings of the organized church but in "internalized," personal religion. What may be meant by such a personal, inner religious urge is the subject to which we now turn.

Questions and Exercises for Further Reflection

1. Workaholism is a little like putting on weight. You start with a few extra pounds (hours per week) and convince yourself the gain is only temporary. Then you find yourself making all sorts of

subtle adjustments in order to accommodate the extra weight. You become accustomed to the new, heavier you, which now becomes what is "normal" for you—that is, until it causes some debilitating health problem. Does this pattern sound familiar in the context of your current job? Have you put on far too many "pounds" the past several years? What is your "ideal weight" when it comes to spending your productive time and energy at work, and how have you been successful at ignoring or rationalizing the warning signs of overwork? What would it take for you to "go on a diet"? What are the immanent meanings that are served by your overwork? (Don't kid yourself, you wouldn't do it if there weren't any.) Is there not a more healthy way to productively serve those meanings?

2. Think of your own work—and, more important, the way in which you do it—in the context of Frederick Buechner's calculus of vocation. How effectively does your work engage your strengths, talents, and interests? Does your work and workplace bear the unique stamp of your own God-given abilities and gifts? What could you do day to day to be able to answer that question more unequivocally? As to the second portion of Buechner's calculus, does the work you do and the way in which you do it serve God's interests in the world? If the holiest man or woman you can think of in history were to approach you and inquire what you did for a living and how you did it, would you be embarrassed to say? Proud?

3. Recall the story in this chapter of the young professional who feared that he might find himself trapped in a gilded cage. Does his fear resonate at all with you? If you discovered a vocational call to a different career path from the one you are currently on, would you feel trapped into staying where you are? What are the immanent meanings of work for you that have become so important that they could actually prevent you from seeking out transcendent meaning?

Part Two

Spirituality
An Answer Ancient and Ever New

Chapter Three

Spirituality—And Other Misunderstood Words

Let days speak,
and many years teach wisdom.
But it is the spirit in a man,
the breath of the Almighty,
that makes him understand.
JOB 32:7–8 (RSV)

The process of uncovering meaning in our lives is both personal and internal. It is unique and subjective to each individual meaning-maker and relies more on the workings of the inner world than on the logic and influences of the external order. Meaningfulness is in the eye—or more accurately the heart—of the beholder.

But to dig a layer deeper, how do we in this very individual, internal process determine what is meaningful to us? Where does meaning "come from"? How do we come to attach deep significance to something? The simplest answer is that meaning derives from the things we most highly value: we sense the presence of meaning in an event, thought, or action to the extent that it sounds a chord consonant with the most essential and immutable values within us. And, for the greater number of us, such values ultimately stem from our beliefs in a supreme being, the nature of life, and our place in the universe, whether or not we are explicit about that. For a great many of us, something acquires meaning—is greatly valued—*insofar as it serves, obeys, or is otherwise consonant*

51

with the will of a superordinate power or purpose, however that may be understood and by whatever name it may be called. Bestowing meaning is the ultimate act of valuing; and for those whose ultimate value is a supreme being, such is the source of greatest meaning.

It is in this context that we will first use that much-misunderstood word *spirituality.* For as we will use the term, human spirituality is the way in which people connect the activities of their daily lives with their wellsprings of deepest meaning. It is the place where spirit and flesh consciously meet and interact. Without spirituality, transcendent meaning in work or elsewhere is just an intellectual concept, never capable of being real-ized.

Why then, is the word so misunderstood? Why, to quote Parker Palmer, is the word considered one of the "vaguest" in our language? To give but one recent example of the baggage this word carries with it, I attended a conference some months ago at the renowned Center for Creative Leadership on the subject of "spirit and leadership." Despite the obvious linguistic connection between *spirit* and *spirituality,* a sizable number of the participants said they would not have attended if the conference title had employed the second word rather than the first! What gives?

The Language Problem

To be so rich in many ways, the English language is impoverished in others. As any romantic knows, the Greeks have three words that translate as *love* in English, which help them differentiate between the varieties of loving emotions. We Anglos have to rely largely on context to determine whether a person expressing love for another is talking about Platonic affection, familial devotion, torrid passion, or something else entirely. Other languages make the point more vividly. Eskimos have literally dozens of words for snow that convey how hard it is coming down, how compact it is, how deep, the size of the flakes, and so on. In Arabic there are sixty words for types of camels and no word for camel in the abstract. The camel's gender, age, species, and the like are all differentiated by its name. And why? Because the camel is as vitally important to the Arab as snow is to the Eskimo—central to their lives, culture, and civilization. It says much about the place of spirit in our rationalistic and materialistic culture that most of us would be unable to think of a

single synonym for *spirituality*. In fact the only ones listed in my the-
saurus are a couple of unused relics of the language, *ethereality* and
rarefaction, whatever they mean. We simply do not have the tools in
our language to talk about such concepts satisfactorily.

Moreover, we have found uses for the word in our modern discourse that are questionable at best. Let me (perhaps unfairly)
choose one example. Two of the most prominent voices in the
business literature on spirituality in the workplace have said the
following about building successful teams in modern corporations:
"[T]eam building at its heart is a spiritual undertaking. It is the creation of a community of believers, united by shared faith and shared
culture."[1]

Well, excuse me, but believers in *what*? Faith in *what*? In a corporate goal or team project? In a particular product or service? Of
course we want people to be committed to their companies and
coworkers and excited about their work products. But to assert that
this constitutes a spiritual experience stretches the term to the
point where it becomes essentially meaningless. We might just as
well say that the process of building a street gang or organizing a
militia group is a spiritual undertaking. After all, aren't they equally
"a community of believers united by shared faith and shared culture"? A more descriptive term for this dynamic is *participation mystique*—the innate human desire to connect with persons and ideas
outside oneself and to identify with their purposes.[2] But for reasons we will get to shortly, this dynamic does not necessarily have
anything to do with human spirituality.

The prevailing state of confusion says a great deal about the
split we feel in our religious life these days. We either confine spirituality to the rigid cast of centuries-old religious dogma or see it
as part of the "whatever" world of nebulous New Age rhetoric. Our
definitions thus tend either to be too narrow or too broad, "too archaic and pious sounding [or] too trendy and slick."[3] We cannot
seem to find the middle ground where we can speak intelligibly to
the religious yearnings of ordinary people and their felt desire to
find connections between daily life and ultimate meaning.

To do so, I believe, is not so much a challenge of language and
its uses as it is a matter of understanding and imagination. The language is there. Despite its limitations it has been adequate for centuries in allowing seekers to describe their quest for a meaningful

connection to Ultimate Reality. It's just that, like a landscape we've passed so often that we really don't see it, or a verse we still remember long after the emotions that prompted us to memorize it have faded, the words have lost their freshness and immediacy to us. They have lost their *power* to act as vessels of expression for our deepest concerns. Like so many of the symbols of the organized church, they have lost their ability to act as transmitters of meaning.

We need to understand afresh how the language of our Western spiritual traditions can give expression to the timeless human desire for meaning and purpose in life. In the words of Harrison Owen, one of the pioneers in the modern exploration of spirit in organizational life: "It is my conviction that when speaking of things of the spirit, we will do well to remember, explore and utilize the powerful words of Western traditions. To the extent that this is off-putting, I apologize, but I would also ask you to look beneath the surface and consider whether those familiar old words are truly lost or do they, in fact, contain some of their age old power."[4]

Can our language be revivified? I believe it can, if we are capable of two things. The first is a new *understanding* of an old reality. We need to look at what spirituality has meant in our Western traditions (which, by the way, is strongly consistent with other traditions as well) and see just how accessible that concept remains to our busy, thoroughly modern lives. The second is the *imagination* required to see how our own life journey reflects—or could reflect—the struggles and triumphs of the many who came before us. The arena may be different—business, corporate life, and the hectic world of commerce—but the path is much the same. To recapture for yourself the truths of the wisdom traditions is to escape the morass of the current dialogue about spirituality and perhaps to light your own authentic spiritual path.

Spirituality as a Life-Orientation

Spirituality is a descriptive term. Like other descriptive terms, such as *love, beauty,* or *ugliness,* it cannily avoids nice, neat definitions. The dictionary attempts are often tautologies like "the quality of being spiritual," which only send us scurrying to another equally vague definition. Yet it will profit us to look closely at what the word attempts to describe (and what it doesn't, as we shall in Chapter Four) for a measure of clarity about its meaning. Spirituality is concerned with the *relationship between the human spirit and the Universal Spirit—between the human being and God*. Now that is not to say that spirit, human or divine, cannot be manifested, observed, or experienced in an infinite variety of other ways. Spirit truly, as Jesus said, blows where it will. But a "-uality" of spirit, at least as I will insist on using the term, has to do with the relationship and interaction between the fully human and the truly divine. That is its theological definition, but I submit that unlike many other theological constructs it is also the word's most practical and useful meaning for our daily lives.

What we are describing is a special type of subject-object relationship. In one sense we are the subject, and God (or whatever you choose to call Ultimate Reality) is the object. And let's be clear about this: such a relationship is not the same as the ones we might have with a team, an army, a country, or another person, though all of those may in certain circumstances have the ability to attract our commitment, loyalty, or love. To use the common parlance, they may legitimately connect some quantum of our "spirit" (enthusiasm, zest, life energy) to theirs by engaging our emotions and beliefs. But to say that our relationships with such people, entities, and ideas constitute a spirituality leads us back into the definitional morass.

In another sense, of course, we are the object of an unfathomable subject who acts in the world and seems somehow to seek a relationship with us. Thus Peter Vaill rightly observes that spirit is generally experienced by us either as a "search" or a "stirring within"[5]—the first because of our innate desire to move toward it and the second because of its incomprehensible desire to move toward us.

There is theological truth here. Spirituality is the orientation of one's life toward God—not away from others and not even away from the legitimate needs of the self, but *toward God*. One of the classics of Western religious thought puts it in these words: "The spiritual life involves both dealing with ourselves, and attending to God. Or, to put it the other way round and in more general terms, first turning to Reality, and then getting our tangled, half-real psychic lives—so tightly coiled about ourselves and our own interests—

into harmony with the great movement of Reality."[6] It is the relationship of which Jesus spoke when he said to his disciples, "Abide in me as I abide in you. Just as the branch cannot bear fruit by itself unless it abides in the vine, neither can you unless you abide in me. I am the vine, you are the branches. Those who abide in me and I in them bear much fruit" (John 15:4–5 [NRSV]).

Spirituality is the "double search" of which I spoke in the Introduction; a reciprocal relationship with the source of ultimate meaning, through which we are enabled to discover meaning and purpose for ourselves. But to live such a life, to live in such a relationship, requires of us four critically important things. Or, put another way, true spirituality has four essential prerequisites.

First, we must be *open* to the influence of a higher power. The attitude of openness paves the way, breaches the door, prepares us for an encounter with that which truly transcends our personal concerns and petty fears. "Spirituality is a decision to search beyond what one can do *to* or *on* or *within* oneself. Spirituality perceives the inadequacy to lie fundamentally not in the material props but in the self that would do the propping. Thus, to be spiritual is to turn away from material props and to open oneself to a transcendent source of meaning."[7] Both modern research and the wisdom of the ages tell us that such openings come most often from the experience of despair or natural beauty, or as the result of prayer or meditation.[8] Whatever the antecedent for the opening, it is the first and necessary prerequisite for the spiritual life—one that all too many of us are too busy or too self-absorbed to achieve.

Second, spirituality requires that we *acknowledge* that power as the ultimate source of meaning and value. The more direct and unveiled our contact with Ultimate Reality, the more inescapable that acknowledgment becomes. "Woe is me, for I am undone" was Isaiah's cry when he first encountered his Lord (Isaiah 6:5 [NKJV]). Our own encounters may prove less wrenching if only because they are not so face-to-face. There is credence to C. S. Lewis's observation that only the pure in heart will see God because only the pure in heart would *want* to. But any experience of being touched by Ultimate Reality sets off a sort of Copernican revolution within us. Unless we are successful in denying the event or repressing its activity inside us, we can no longer claim for our ego the centrality we once thought it had. Our smallness is exposed in the immensity of the light we have seen. Whether it happens quickly or slowly, whether it is an event or a process, our encounter with the Almighty dis-illusions us about our place in our own inner universe. We are no longer the sun around which other people, events, and even God revolve. We are displaced into an orbit around that which was central all along. Like Copernicus, we just now discover it. What Jung so often said is true: the experience of God is always a defeat for the ego.

Third, we must *align* ourselves with that power and its aims. This is a far broader notion than just being committed to living one's life in accordance with certain principles (though it will include that). It is more in the nature of a *covenant,* a solemn and deep-seated promise to pursue the relationship with God with such constancy and commitment that God's aims become as second nature to us, and our aims consonant with God's. To put the same idea in an Eastern cast:

> To those identified with Tao,
> Tao will gladly extend welcome.
> To those identified with virtue,
> Virtue will gladly extend welcome.
> To those identified with failure,
> Failure will gladly extend welcome.[9]

To align one's life with the aims of Ultimate Reality—the Tao—involves a sense of striving and the inevitable experience of defeat or setback, because it is impossible to achieve with the totality on which our control-freak natures generally insist. A person with a life devoted in this way will often describe it in terms of a quest or a journey, where the end destination is not nearly so important as staying the path, and success is measured only in the ability to move past frustration.

Commitment to virtuous principles in one's life, in and of itself, is a one-way street. Principles have no life, no "spirit" on which a "-uality" may rest. But to attempt consciously to align oneself with God and God's aims is to establish a relationship, a mutuality, that is the beginning of genuine spirituality. It is to step off into the flow of the river rather than remaining forever on its shore. It is to create the possibility of being acted upon—changed—by that relationship. As William James observed: "When we commune with [God], work is actually done upon our finite personality, for we are turned into new men, and consequences in the way of conduct follow in the natural world upon our regenerative change."[10] The reason is simply this: "Our spiritual life is his affair; because, whatever we may think to the contrary, it is really produced by his steady attraction, and our humble and self-forgetful response to it. It consists in being drawn, at his pace and in his way, to the place where he wants us to be; not the place we fancied for ourselves."[11]

But history teaches us all too well the dangers involved. For every Mother Teresa of Calcutta, there seems to be a David Koresh of Waco. We humans seem possessed of an endless capacity for self-deception and rationalization, and some of our greatest human atrocities have been committed by those who claimed to be aligned with God's aims. That is why the fourth antecedent, the *cultivation* of God's presence, is so important. Although specific practices may differ by religion and culture, all the world's spiritual traditions insist that we are able to maintain our alignment with God's aims only through the steady and consistent use of proven disciplines. We will talk more extensively of these disciplines in Chapter Ten and discover that they are not nearly as fearsome or foreign to us as one might think. Suffice it now to say that our greatest hope of avoiding the most destructive of our human failings lies in the discernment, humility, and self-awareness that come from the proven cultivating practices. Without them, the way is easily lost.

Spirituality, then, is a relationship made possible by our opening to the influence of a higher power, our acknowledgment of that power's rightful place, our conscious alignment with its aims, and our assiduous cultivating of its presence. This is not to say, however, that the relationship is a purely private matter or that it leads to a kind of pietism that focuses only on self. Most traditions are rightly suspicious of any purported relationship with God that lessens our love for others. To the contrary, as Jay Conger observes, spirituality "lifts us beyond ourselves and our narrow self-interests. When not misused, it is the most humane of forces. It helps us to see our deeper connections to one another and to the world beyond ourselves."[12]

Although the two terms are not identical, *spirituality* has much in common with what has come to be called *intrinsic* (as opposed to *extrinsic*) *religion*. Gordon Allport first developed this terminology in the 1950s to describe two alternative dimensions of religiousness. Those with an extrinsic orientation "may find religion useful in a variety of ways, e.g. to provide security and solace, sociability and distraction, status and self-justification. The embraced creed is lightly held or else selectively shaped to fit more primary needs."[13] Persons with intrinsic religion, however, "find their master motivation in religion. Other needs, strong as they may be, are regarded as of less ultimate significance, and they are, insofar as possible, brought into harmony with the religious beliefs and prescriptions. Having embraced a creed, the individual endeavors to internalize it and follow it fully."[14] In short, the extrinsically motivated *use* their religion, while the intrinsically motivated *live* it. By its very nature, a genuine spirituality presumes an intrinsic religiousness, but with a difference. The spiritual life is more concerned with relationship than with creed. Its primary concern is with the Ultimate Reality in whose service the creed was formed, and it is capable of going beyond the letter of the creed when the discerned demands of Ultimate Reality require it. The creed, like any principle or discipline, is followed to the extent that it serves and prospers the relationship, but the relationship is capable of a richness and depth that cannot be confined by any creed.

"In almost all religions," write Kanungo and Mendonca, "spirituality is associated with a belief in relating oneself with a higher-order influence."[15] It is the establishment and maintenance of that relationship that is at the heart of practically all the world's great spiritual traditions. The maturing of that connection, the deepening of its intimacy, is what we commonly refer to as spiritual growth. Such concepts are neither new nor confined to Western traditions. Says William James in his classic study of religious thought, *The Varieties of Religious Experience:* "This overcoming of all the usual barriers between the individual and the Absolute . . . is the everlasting and triumphant mystical tradition, hardly altered by differences of clime or creed. In Hinduism, in Neoplatonism, in Sufism, in Christian mysticism, in Whitmanism, we find the same recurring note, . . . an eternal unanimity which ought to make a critic stop and think, and which brings it about that the mystical classics have, as has been said, neither birthday nor native land. Perpetually telling of the unity of man with God, their speech antedates languages, and they do not grow old."[16]

To James, "[t]he warring gods and formulas of the various religions do indeed cancel each other, but there is a certain uniform deliverance in which religions all appear to meet." That uniformity consists in the realization that "there is something wrong about us as we naturally stand" and "that we are saved from the wrongness by making proper connection with the higher powers." That connection, in practically all of the case examples James examined, was "describable in these very simple general terms. They allow for the divided self and the struggle; they involve the change of personal centre and the surrender of the lower self; they express the appearance of exteriority of the helping power and yet fully account for our sense of union with it; and they fully justify our feelings of security and joy. There is probably no autobiographical document, among all those which I have quoted, to which the description will not well apply."[17]

Opening, acknowledging, aligning, and cultivating—about the need for each there is no serious dispute among the world's great traditions. It is only in questions of god or gods, grace or karma, reincarnation or immortality, and the other endless speculations that we carry on our inveterate disputes. But to James this much was clear: "We and God have business with each other; and in opening ourselves to his influence our deepest destiny is fulfilled. The universe, at those parts of it which our personal being constitutes, takes a turn genuinely for the worse or for the better in proportion as each one of us fulfills or evades God's demands."[18]

The Psychological Perspective

The process of opening, acknowledging, aligning, and cultivating is practically identical to Jung's concept of individuation. For Jung, to individuate was to become most truly oneself, to become a living expression of the uniqueness with which we are each endowed. It is a lifelong process in which we seek to develop the wholeness of our personality. Jung believed that the urge to individuate was a central instinct of human nature and the psychological basis for our religious and spiritual yearnings.[19]

For the process of individuation to take place, the conscious part of our personality (the ego) must come into relationship with a larger reality that Jung called the Self—a paradoxical concept that Jung used to denote both the totality of our personality and a larger reality that altogether transcends personality. Because Jung sought to speak as a scientist and not a theologian, he stopped short of naming this reality God. It is clear, however, that he considered the Self to be the observable, phenomenological equivalent of God. He put it this way: "Intellectually the self is no more than a psychological concept, a construct that serves to express an unknowable essence which we cannot grasp as such, since by definition it transcends our powers of comprehension. It might equally well be called the 'God within us.'"[20]

The aim of individuation is both to divest the ego of its false sense of self-sufficiency and to establish a vital relationship between the ego and the Self. But for that to happen, there must first be an *opening* by the ego to the effects of this larger reality. Fritz Kunkel, a student of Jung whose works developed the connection between Christianity and Jungian psychology, termed this moment of opening the *ego crisis*.[21] The crisis may come through a sense of inner turmoil or a confluence of outer events (or, more commonly, both); but whatever the causation, our carefully constructed egos "hit the wall." We find that our own resources and reserves are simply insufficient to meet the inner and outer challenges that have been laid in our path. We look instinctively for "something more"—to a minister, to therapy, to a book or seminar, to drink—anything that will give us from the outside the strength we seem to lack from within.

Predictably, Jung viewed such crises as blessings, even if dangerous ones. In his unique (and often dense) style, he describes both the opportunity and peril represented by the crisis:

> When a summit of life is reached, when the bud unfolds and from the lesser the greater emerges, then, as Nietzsche says, "One becomes Two," and the greater figure, which one always was but which remained invisible, appears to the lesser personality with the force of a revelation. He who is truly and hopelessly little will always drag

the revelation of the greater down to the level of his littleness, and will never understand that the day of judgment for his littleness has dawned. But the man who is inwardly great will know that the long expected friend of his soul, the immortal one, has now really come . . . to make his life flow into that greater life—a moment of deadliest peril![22]

When successfully navigated, the experience of the crisis leads the egocentric will to *acknowledge* its limitations and to seek a true relationship with the Self—the "immortal one." To borrow an image from Jungian analyst Edward Edinger, that relationship can be visualized in terms of an axis, a literal connection between the Self and the ego. To the extent that such a connection is strong and vital, the process of individuation can take place and the ego can maintain its psychological health. But when the axis is defective or nonexistent and the process of individuation thwarted, an infinite variety of psychological and spiritual maladies can result. In short, the ego-Self axis is the *alignment* necessary for spiritual and psychological growth.

And what of the *cultivation* of that relationship? Jungians believe that the communication between the ego and the Self is quite literal. It may come in the form of dreams or other incursions from the unconscious, which should be consciously studied and understood in order to cooperate with the great movements of the Self. Moreover, the traditional disciplines of prayer and meditative practices are recognized by Jungians as important ways in which the lines of communication can be kept open.

For Jungians such as Fritz Kunkel, there is no significant difference between the psychological notion of individuation and the theological doctrines of spiritual growth in the world's great religions. The Self is seen as the creative energy of God, both alive within us and manifested in the world—both immanent and transcendent. To align ourselves with it is to both live from our center and live in accord with God's will; to deny it in favor of our own egos is sin and illness.

Jung was also clear about the purposes of individuation for the larger society. "As the individual is not just a single, separate being, but by his very existence presupposes a collective relationship, it follows that the process of individuation must lead to more intense and broader collective relationships and not to isolation."[23] Or as John Sanford has put it: "From [individuation] comes the capacity to love, the ability to sacrifice oneself for others, and the ability to lead others for their benefit and not for our own egocentric gratification."[24]

It has been said with some accuracy that depth psychology has usurped the place of religion in the twentieth century as the backdrop for explaining human nature. It certainly provides a language that is safer and more "scientific" for an age that values only the objective and the observable. But the template for human growth and development was not discovered, much less created, by Jung. It was simply observed and described in a way that only a brilliantly insightful mind such as his could do, and given to succeeding generations wrapped in the modern language of psychology. By his own admission, Jung sought only to "take these thought-forms that have become historically fixed, try to melt them down again and pour them into molds of immediate experience."[25] But what was observed and described by him would be easily recognizable to spiritual masters of past centuries, as it should be to modern theologians. It is only the psychological manifestation of the relationship that *is* spirituality.

The Confusion of Causes and Effects

What, then, of the ways in which we use the term *spirituality* these days? To read the recent literature, particularly that concerned with spirituality and business, is to hear it described as a cognitive concept ("a realization that at the core of human existence there is a set of cardinal virtues and capital vices"[26]) or an emotional effect ("a subconscious feeling that energizes individual action"[27]) or a set of behaviors ("the effect of this experience on his behavior when he actively attempts to harmonize his life with the Beyond"[28]). Is it any of these? All? None?

Remember what we said earlier: spirituality concerns the relationship between the human spirit and the divine spirit, between the human being and God. It can be *manifested, observed, or experienced* by us in an almost infinite variety of ways (certainly including concepts, effects, and behaviors), but spirituality itself is *that which partakes of the relationship between the human and the divine*. What we observe and experience are only the effects of that relationship, not the cause. To become confused about that is really rather dangerous, because it can allow us to mislabel a wide array of thoughts, feelings, and actions that merely mimic genuine spirituality.

Consider this analogy: Sitting inside your house, you hear the sound of the wind chimes outside. You say, "That is the wind," and perhaps you are right. But you do not mean that the sound itself is the wind, any more than you mean that the steel pipes that are clanging together to produce the sound are in fact the wind. Moreover, it is possible that the sound was actually produced by the damned neighbor's cat batting the chimes around or, for that matter, by a bull rhinoceros that is currently charging through your yard.

Or think about lying in bed on a weekend morning, in that foggy place between waking and sleep. You hear feet padding about in the kitchen and the sound of cabinets opening, and you say, "That's my daughter." What you mean is that the sound and the behavior are consistent with what your daughter would do. Neither are "her"—and in fact there is at least some chance that what you hear is a hungry, noisy intruder.

This simple point seems lost on us these days. When we say that "team building is a spiritual experience," what we mean (or should) is that it *can* be—that by partaking of and contributing to the relationships among the vital spirits of the individuals involved and between those spirits and the source of ultimate meaning, the building of any team (or group or community) can take on a spiritual character. From that can flow all sorts of behaviors, emotions, and thoughts that we can rightly label *spiritual* because they are the observable manifestations—the effects—of a spiritual cause. Another team, motivated by hatred, testosterone, and a first-rate butt-kicking speech, can pound an opposing football team 56-0. That has about as much to do with spirituality as the charging rhino has to do with the wind.

The point is that we must be clear about causation before we can throw around words like *spiritual* and *spirituality*. A group of people, in business or elsewhere, whose shared opening, acknowledging, aligning, and cultivating assists in producing a common goal and corporate vision has succeeded in truly creating a spirituality in the organizational life of the group's members. The same team cohesiveness can be produced by greed, fear, or just good old-fashioned love of success, but those effects come from quite different places in our human natures. We may, by the same token, rightly describe someone we know as a spiritual person or say that she has about her a certain spirituality. I feel fortunate to know a number of such people and find that, in one way or another, they each exhibit qualities and traits that are the outer manifestations of the inner relationship we are here describing. But I have also met a good many people in my practice who, through personal style and charisma, can mimic many of the same pleasing qualities despite the fact that they are card-carrying narcissists, egocentrists of the first order. I submit that despite the impressive persona many of them have built for themselves, there is nothing spiritual about them. They are, in fact, very dangerous people. Look at the "causes" of such people, groups, events, and experiences. You are less likely to be fooled by the effects.

A Spirituality of Work and Organizational Life

For an increasing number of people, work has become a natural expression of the relationship that is spirituality. They want their working lives to serve, or at least to be consistent with, the higher power that has touched them. They want the productive energy spent at work, no less than any other aspect of life, to serve as a response to the experience of opening to a higher-order influence and acknowledging its claim. They want this despite the struggles and obstacles that daily life in the workplace can, and usually does, present.

In fact, it's often those struggles that get people to *open* to God in the first place. Most of the people I see in executive coaching have hit something of a midlife wall, with work at the center of their difficulties. It is perhaps a familiar picture to many of you: attitudes and responses that worked well earlier in life lose their effectiveness; attributes once considered to be strengths now show their shadow side; things that held great significance in the past seem to fade in importance, and there is a grappling for some renewed sense of meaning. The complexities of life's "second half" call on us to access parts of our personalities that heretofore played minor roles for us. So the highly rational businesswoman may need to better acknowledge her own feelings, and be aware of the feelings of others, if she is to manage her subordinates effectively. The businessman whose well-developed sensing function (in Myers-Briggs terminology) helps him analyze complex data may now need to develop his intuitive functions if he is to move from being a good technical manager to the strategic leader he is otherwise qualified to become.

The tremendous stress that comes from such struggles can lead, on the one hand, to a midlife crisis in its traditional and negative sense, complete with regressive behavior, derailed careers, and damaged relationships. On the other hand, it can also spark us to *acknowledge* the need for lasting changes in our life. The Chinese character for *crisis*, remember, is the combination of those for *danger* and *opportunity*. We may seize the opportunity by coming to seek new outlets for our creativity, becoming more self-aware, and looking for new sources of meaning and purpose in our daily activities. We may even consider a career change or look for ways to modify our current work situations—not so much to escape the struggle as to ensure that our work is consonant with our deeper values and fully uses our innate and unique talents. For many, this linchpin moment in life provides the impetus to seek a vital connection to a more profound source of wisdom, creativity, and power.

When we do try consciously to *align* ourselves with that source and *cultivate* that alignment, a true spirituality of work begins to brew. This can take a myriad of outward forms: some would say that they consider their work an offering to God, others see themselves as stewards of their gifts and talents, and still others would say that (at least on their better days) they feel like they are answering a call to do a certain kind of work or to do it in certain ways.

Although expressions of spirituality may take a variety of forms, conversations with people who are seeking to live their spiritual lives though work reveal a couple of common themes. First, work and the work environment are fertile soil for spiritual growth and maturity. There is no place in our lives that more exposes our weaknesses or stretches our limits, teaching us about who we truly are. We are thrown together with people who are often very different from ourselves, forcing us to appreciate both their value and our own. It may be the one area in our lives that teaches us the hard lessons of humility. It has indeed been observed that we are in need of our "petty tyrants" at work, for they force upon us the situations and emotions that are our growth edges. Spirituality is not quiet contemplation apart from the rest of humankind—it is the growth and development that seems only to come in our contact with others. It's as if our rougher edges have to be worn smooth by the slow process of rubbing against the edges of others, and work is the preeminent place for that process to occur. Such growth has the capacity to strengthen our alignment with God because it helps us remove the obstacles within ourselves to a fuller relationship—a clearer axis—between ourselves and the ultimate source of wisdom and creativity. It allows us to "hear" God's call more clearly in the mundane matters of our daily lives and to *act* accordingly.

Second, work can also be a spiritual discipline, a way of offering yourself, your actions, and your productivity to God's purposes—being, as Christians are fond of saying, God's hands and feet in the world. Traditional spiritual disciplines are meant to cultivate the special relationship between the human being and the divine and to form habitual behaviors that do not come naturally to us. Considering the time and productive energy we pour into work and the challenges we face there daily, what better proving ground could we have than the work we do and the *way* we do it?

Whether viewed as an opportunity for spiritual growth or as a spiritual discipline, work and life in the workplace take on the kind of transcendent meaning that we explored in Chapter Two. Our work fosters and furthers the relationship with the Ultimate Reality that is the basis of true human spirituality and thus is imbued with ultimate meaning.

When the discussion moves from individual to organizational spirituality, I must confess to some initial skepticism. I know that genuine spirituality can exist in the context of a modern organization—I've seen it. But I've also heard the term confused with all sorts of mundane concepts and clichés like *company spirit, team spirit, capitalist spirit,* and the *spirit of this place.* As we have observed, these may have much to do with the emotions of camaraderie and the phenomenon of participation mystique but nothing necessarily to do with genuine spirituality.

Like individuation, the relationship that forms the basis for human spirituality takes place within one human individual at a time. Legal fictions aside, human groups such as business corporations have no life apart from the individuals they comprise. This is not to say that spirituality can't be manifested in the life of an organization through the collective efforts of its members, with all the outer observable effects that relationship has in the lives of individuals. I have seen small business organizations, and pockets within larger ones, where I felt this was happening. After all, we do have a model for organizational spirituality—religious communities—if that notion doesn't frighten off too many of you. A number of years ago I spent several weeks in a Jesuit retreat center, living and working among the monks and other retreatants. I was deeply impressed with the way the brothers strove together to grow spiritually in the common matters of daily life, and with how they viewed all their activities, certainly including work, as a part of their spiritual discipline. I'm not suggesting that there is enough homogeneity in the modern business organization to ever mimic that entirely, nor am I saying that there are not a variety of very human problems in monasteries (as you will learn from practically any candid monk or nun). But I am saying that the life of an organization—*any* organization—can partake of spirituality and exhibit its effects to the extent that a significant number of individuals within it have embarked on their own spiritual path.

The best examples are still, unfortunately, in the nonprofit sector. I recently participated in a cultural audit for St. Joseph's Health Care Systems in Atlanta. Formed by the Catholic Sisters of Mercy more than one hundred years ago, St. Joseph's distinctive philosophy of service to mankind is more than just a mission statement; it lies at the root of practically all organizational decisions and activities, large and small. Interviewing a random sampling of people from all corners of the organization left me with the impression that many, if not most of them, viewed their work as some sort of response to their deepest inner values. Some were explicit about that. Some had specifically chosen to work at St. Joseph's because of the outlet it provided for their personal spirituality. Many came from faith traditions very different from Catholicism, yet they valued the underlying philosophy as it expressed itself in the care of patients.

To be in that environment for several days was to come away with a palpable sense of "something different" about organizational life there. Yes, there were people who were frustrated, disgruntled, or overworked—all the usual stuff. But people treated each other with a rare degree of respect and concern. Beneath the usual pleasantries there was almost a reverence in the interactions with patients, their families, and each other. And everywhere were the visible signs of shared purpose; not the usual company-framed mission statements that everyone is expected to exhibit, but little personal quotes and mottos sitting on desks or tacked to the walls of cubicles, each attesting to the meaning each person found in his or her work. There was, as in many other organizations whose doors you might enter, a "spirit of the place." But this one clearly bespoke the spiritual lives of a significant number of the people who worked there. If I ever get sick in that part of the world, that's where I want to go.

With my for-profit clients, I see occasional pockets of organizational spirituality. These generally exist where one or more individuals have embarked on their own spiritual journey, are consciously intentional about living out that journey in the workplace, and give to others the freedom to do the same. (Keep in mind that last phrase. We'll come back to it in the next chapter.)

Does it bother me that I see only glimpses of organizational spirituality in secular, for-profit corporations? Not at all. In fact, it would bother me if it were suddenly "popular." The worst thing that can happen to a valuable idea is for it to become a fad. Better for it to slowly, naturally, almost organically take root and grow in the lives of people and institutions that are ready for it.

Spirituality is, after all, a very natural life process. It is not some ethereal concept, accessible only to the saintly and pure of heart. It is a very earthly and universal process known to both psychology and religion—the two domains merely use different language to describe it. It is the fundamental human urge to outgrow the boundedness of our ego and its petty fears and desires, the timeless desire to find connection to our deepest sources of wisdom, power, and creativity—both within and without. To borrow an image from John Sanford, the spiritual journey is as natural as the journey from acorn to oak tree. It's just that, unlike the oak, we must grow into the full measure of our humanity with consciousness, effort, and will.

Questions and Exercises for Further Reflection

1. Think back about the "opening" experiences you have had in your life. They may have felt like hitting a wall, where despair or pain or the pressures of life seemed so great that you felt forced to search outside your own resources for the necessary strength. They may have been graced moments of unexpected beauty or serendipity that overwhelmed your senses. There are many different ways in which our egos can open to the Other. What did you "do" with those experiences? Has their memory faded, either by conscious effort to forget or through the dimming effect of passing years? Did they have the effect of truly opening you to a higher-order influence for a while, only to yield to your ego's reassumption of its accustomed control once things returned to "normal"? Or were they truly the beginning of your own Copernican revolution?

2. For your own Copernican revolution to take place, what would your ego have to give up? A sense of self-sufficiency? A sense of control? What does your ego most fear from acknowledging that it is not the center of your universe? Naming that fear, acknowledging it, and exploring it may be very important for you to do. That fear may be the very thing that stands between you and continued psychological and spiritual growth.

3. Quoted in this chapter is Jesus' very evocative image of the vine and the branches from John 15: 4–5. If you were to visualize yourself for a moment as the branch of a vine or the limb of a tree, to what are you attached? From what do you draw your nourishment and sustenance day to day? Is it from a person? A family? An organization? Possessions? A branch can't live for very long apart from the vine, nor can it bear a different species of fruit. What is the quality of the sustenance you get from your vine? Where are its roots? What kind of fruit does it produce?

4. Who is the "petty tyrant" in your workplace? You know, the boss who makes unreasonable demands, the coworker who drives you crazy with her power games, or the subordinate who is bad enough to ruin your day but not bad enough to fire. Practically everybody has one. While it will feel quite unnatural at first, resolve

that you will do two things to honor the petty tyrant in your life. First, spend some time every month reflecting on the things that he or she has taught you about yourself over the past four weeks. What have you learned about your patience, your tolerance, your ego-needs, your strengths and weaknesses? Once you have been able to see beyond your anger and frustration (come on, now, you can do it), what have the lessons been? Second, say a little prayer of gratitude for this person. It's all right if you also ask that he be transferred to your company's new plant in the Andes, but express gratitude for the ways in which he has forced you to grow and mature.

Chapter Four

Beware of Cheap Imitations (or, What Spirituality Is *Not*)

> *Man is incurably religious. . . . If one thinks of religion as the ultimate concern, most men have it. The American who does not worship an authentic God is almost certain to have a substitute deity: The American Way of Life, Free Enterprise, The Standard of Living, the arts—or sex—at least something.*
> CHAD WALSH

Spirituality is a natural, life-driven and life-giving force. So why would Tom Peters, ironically one of the first and most effective authors to argue for more human values in the workplace, say that "when the talk turns to the spiritual side of leadership, I mostly want to run"?[1] To be honest, if I defined spirituality the same way that Peters apparently does, I'd want to run too.

We've done a bold thing to try to give some clarity to the concept of spirituality—something many writers whose work I respect have thought it unwise to do. It is indeed true that when we define something we limit it, we give it boundaries; and for something as expansive and powerful as the idea of human spirituality, that has some admitted dangers. But words are workable vessels of meaning only insofar as they have definitional limits and boundaries—when the word can successfully convey that something *is* this but *not* that. A pig is not a stick, and with at least some measure of clarity our language needs to allow us to differentiate between the two. Even a concept as elusive and multifaceted as spirituality requires some degree of clarity, or else we need to be content to let it mean anything at all—in which case it means nothing at all. If I read Peters aright, his problem is that he is including in his understanding of spirituality a good many things that do not fit. He has confused a pig with a stick.

Spirituality Is Not Creedalism

In a syndicated column that first appeared in 1993, Tom Peters offered his usual praise for the empowerment movement and "spirited" work, but refers to things "spiritual" with wry derision: "It should be enough if I work like crazy, respect my peers, customers and suppliers, and perform with verve, imagination, efficiency and good humor. Please don't ask me to join the Gregorian Chant Club, too."[2]

He misses, first of all, that the work characteristics he is praising often come directly from the inner work and life orientation that are the very heart of human spirituality. (We will look at this phenomenon in detail in Chapters Six through Eight.) Moreover, his choice of words, though clever, betrays an antiquated view of spirituality that is very far from the relationship and process we have described.

Peters's discomfort seems to come from the notion that acceptance of spirituality would "blur the borders between church and corporation."[3] In a subsequent interview he was more explicit: "There's nothing I believe in more than the Bill or Rights. When you cross the line between the secular and the spiritual you're edging up on something that bugs me."[4] He is wrong on two counts: not only is he confusing organized religion with a spiritual life, but he shares a misconception with many others in U.S. society about what our Constitution and laws require.

Some of the people I know who have rich inner lives belong to organized faith communities. Many don't. But what they have in common has always been abundantly clear to me. They are interested in *giving:* they give of their time and energy to foster the relationship with God; they give to themselves the "cultivating" influences and practices that make their inner lives richer and strengthen their alignment to the source of still greater strength; and they give to *others* the freedom and opportunity to find their *own* way in their *own* time. They may offer their insight and experience when asked, but they seem remarkably uninterested in convincing or convicting you of anything. We all know the people of whom Peters could be justifiably wary: they are interested in *getting,* whether that takes the form of converting you, gaining support for their positions, or simply obtaining the spoils of their self-styled "salvation" to which you, being different, are not entitled. This has decidedly not been my experience of those people who are endeavoring to live truly spiritual lives.

Spirituality, as we have come to understand it, is intensely concerned with the individual and his or her relationship to God, work as it relates to that relationship, and the communities of work in which that relationship is cultivated. Spirituality does not concern itself (as some religions and "religious people" have been known to do) with converting others, proselytizing, or expecting adherence to a particular creed or doctrine. Organized religion is a path, and a vitally important one to many people, for most of us need the system of attitudes, beliefs, and practices that the institutional church provides. But spirituality is more a journey than a path, and there are in fact many different paths that one can legitimately take to set upon that journey. Or, to use another metaphor, religion is the container for the human experience of relating to Ultimate Reality, and for most a very necessary container. It is, in truth, very difficult to drink deeply with your own hands. But the container is not the relationship itself, and in fact there are manifold containers that through the centuries have held and preserved their precious contents. My own view is that Peters and others have little to fear from expressions of genuine spirituality in the workplace. Spirituality is poles apart from the kind of fundamentalism that would "seek to coerce the world at large into conformity with their story."[5] It is not even the same as religion in general, at least as we use that term to denote an authoritative system of belief. In other words, spirituality is not creedalism.

Were that not so, I indeed think we would have good reason to be concerned. For example, I share with James Autry a great deal of unease every time I hear a businessperson say, "I run my business in accordance with Christian principles." With alarming frequency, that statement seems to translate less into lofty goals and admirable actions than "prescribed standards of behavior . . . which are more often used for restricting or policing than for liberating and enabling."[6] A bit of empirical proof for such unease popped up in the results of a survey done several years ago on the characteristics and practices of "Christian-based" companies.[7] When a number of such companies were examined with an eye toward their treatment of primary stakeholders (employees, customers, communities, and suppliers), an interesting dynamic emerged. Less than half of the companies stressed product or service quality as an extension of their "Christian principles," and there was a similar paucity of emphasis on employee values and behaviors (for example, acting in accordance with the Golden Rule). However, 81 percent emphasized the importance of the company's profitability, and 92 percent of the respondents stressed engagement in on-site religious activities. My take on those figures is simply this: such companies want the external trappings of religiosity, and they want profitability—and they likely feel that the first contributes to the second. However, when it comes to more important but less visible manifestations, such as their concern for their employees and how they treat their stakeholders, there is significantly less organizational emphasis.

The picture painted of such "Christian-based" companies comports with my own experience. They are all too often concerned with the outer trappings of religiosity, but their underlying corporate behaviors lay emphasis on what they can *get* (there's that word again) from it: a pleasing corporate image in the community, a stronger self-image for the CEO (who is usually the driving force behind the religious emphasis), and a rationale for moving out individuals who are seen as not "fitting in." It's a phenomenon that Jack Hawley refers to as "believeurism": "people, in the grip of a materially oriented, 'worldly' world, unthinkingly treating belief power as another commodity that can be bought, something to be exploited for worldly gain."[8] There is unfortunately a great deal of truth here. Managers who are desperate to make their mark in very competitive environments will look to any perceived source of advantage. It may be well intentioned enough, but at its base believeurism is simply an attempt to exploit the power of religious conviction without the bedrock of the conviction itself. It is the plight of the executive who once said to James Autry after one of his speeches: "If it'll help my bottom line, hell, I'll be spiritual!"

Spirituality is not religion; much less is it creedalism. To quote Jung on the difference:

> A creed coincides with the established Church or, at any rate, forms a public institution whose members include not only true believers but vast numbers of people who can only be described as "indifferent" in matters of religion and who belong to it simply by force of habit. . . . To be the adherent of a creed, therefore, is not always a religious matter but more often a social one. . . . It is not ethical principles, however lofty, or creeds, however orthodox, that lay the foundations for the freedom and autonomy of the individual, but simply and solely the empirical awareness, the incontrovertible experience of an intensely personal, reciprocal relationship between man and an extramundane authority which acts as a counterpoise to the "world" and its "reason."[9]

The Legal Issue

As to his concerns about the Constitution, Peters shares with many Americans a fundamental misconception about the Bill of Rights. The First Amendment requires *government* to be neutral in matters of religion, but (as with the rest of the Bill of Rights) it says nothing at all about private individuals and their organizations. What people choose to do to express their religious values at work (unless they work for the government) does not and never has had anything to do with the constitutional separation of church and state. It is one of the most pernicious results of our inveterate controversies over school prayer (that is, *government*-sanctioned prayer) that we have come to think there is a legal requirement that we leave our religious values at the workplace door. However I may disagree with the religious right on other scores, its political rhetoric has at least been helpful in reminding us that the First Amendment also allows us *free expression* of our religious values.

Although the Bill of Rights is the wrong tree to bark up, there are some legitimate legal concerns in this arena. Consider, for example, a company like R. W. Beckett Corp. of Ohio, which makes oil burners. Like a good many other "Christian-based" companies, employees are encouraged by management to attend lunchtime Bible studies; they say prayers before company-sponsored dinners and are personally urged by the CEO to attend Billy Graham rallies in nearby Cleveland.[10] How would it feel in such an organization to be Jewish? Or Hindu? What if your advancement in the firm was tied to your participation in these events and your adherence to Mr. Beckett's personal religious creed?

Actually, the protection in this case has nothing to do with the Constitution but with the Civil Rights Act of 1964. That landmark federal legislation (as amended now several times) made it illegal to discriminate in any term or condition of employment on the basis of race, color, religion, gender, or national origin. Just as with its legal cousin sexual harassment (much in the news these days), it is illegal to create for an employee a "hostile or offensive work environment" that results from the employee's religious preferences or beliefs. Thus, companies that want to *get* something from their employees, such as adherence to certain practices or belief in a certain creed, run a substantial risk of violating the law. Often driven by the personal religious beliefs of the founder or CEO, such companies might actively discriminate against those with different (or no) beliefs or make working there so uncomfortable as to create a "hostile or offensive" workplace. A federal appeals court in San Francisco, for example, has ruled that companies are prohibited from requiring workers to attend devotional services;[11] a New York federal district court has held that proselytizing or attempting to convert employees (again, trying to *get* something) can result in the same illegality.[12]

Merely *allowing* religious expression in the workplace does not present the same legal peril, as long as employers keep a basic distinction in mind. Employees should not be allowed to try to *get* something from other employees any more than the company itself should. That is, proselytizing, attempting to convert others, or arguing about creedal precepts, if tolerated by the employer, has the potential of creating the same hostile environment as company-sponsored activity itself. As an employer, you are within your rights to stop such behavior, and it is legally prudent to do so.[13]

And what if, as an employer, you would be more comfortable with no religious expressions at all in the workplace? The budding case law in this area seems to indicate that you would be within your rights, as long as all expressions of religion were treated equally. In other words, you are welcome to make your workplace a "religion-free zone" as long as you enforce that rule across the board. Remember, the Constitution's Bill of Rights prohibits governmental limits on personal religious expression but says nothing at all about what private employers can do in their own place of business. The problem is that expressions of religion are often cleverly disguised as political issues, and vice versa. (The abortion question is a familiar example.) A safer and more reasonable policy, it seems to me, is simply to allow the expressions but forbid the proselytizing.

Fortunately, for those practicing traditional spiritual disciplines, none of the issues I just described are much of a problem. Companies that positively view such practices and their effects tend simply to allow them to happen—mostly by just providing time, space, and understanding. The individuals who engage in them do so in response to a personal desire to cultivate their relationship with God and to carry that relationship into the workplace, perhaps with others of like mind and heart, but they typically feel no need to convert others to a particular way of thinking.

In this regard I was heartened by a survey recently conducted by the High Tor Alliance, with support from the Fetzer Institute and the Nathan Cummings Foundation. The sample was composed of men and women who engaged in personal spiritual practices such as meditation, silence, conscious listening, prayer, and the study of sacred texts. Most of them felt free to engage in such activity in their organizations; in fact, only 1.3 percent said they were "not at all" free. At the same time, a majority of the respondents said that their organizations did not share a common spiritual or religious orientation. This is encouraging—it says that despite the diversity of religious points of view in most organizations, those who wish to engage in spiritual or contemplative practices generally feel that they can do so in the context of their organizational life. Because the focus of the spiritual life is on *giving* and not *getting*, these employees and their employers feel that they can make room in the work environment for the relationship that is spirituality. Perhaps what the apostle Paul said to the Galatians some centuries back, he could well say to Tom Peters: "The fruit of the spirit is love, joy, peace, patience, kindness, generosity, faithfulness, gentleness, and self-control. There is no law against such things" (Galatians 5:22–23 [NRSV]).

Spirituality Is Not a "Feeling"

Consider this: a mulberry bush has leaves, and a giant oak tree has leaves. Does that mean that the bush and the tree are the same? Hardly. We cry at the death of a close friend; we cry at the birth of a child. Does that mean that the death and the birth are the same thing? Of course not. The simple logical principle is that although A may include C, and B may include C, that does not mean that A and B are identical. One would think that the error of confusing similar effects (having leaves or feeling like crying) with very different causes would be a simple one for most of us to master, yet we seem determined to make this mistake all the time in our discussions of spirituality.

For example, I have attended a number of conferences and seminars on the common boundary between psychology and religion. Many of the programs are indeed thought-provoking and often engage some very deep emotions in the participants. But over the years I have heard practically every possible aspect of such gatherings described by one participant or another as a "spiritual experience"—from the food to the lectures to the sunsets to the socials. My favorite example was the man and woman, each married to another back home, who reported to the group in embarrassing detail the "spirituality" of their physical explorations the night before. There is absolutely no doubt that human spirituality can and does express itself in a limitless number of ways. (Martin Luther, for example, tells us that one of his greatest spiritual insights came while sitting on the toilet.) But many times what these conference participants were telling me had nothing to do with their relationship to God or their connection to the deepest parts of their beings. They were reporting emotions, physical sensations, or thoughts that made them feel a certain, pleasant way.

Although spirituality is uniquely individual and experiential, it is not insular. We can experience and observe its effects in a wide range of human emotions, thoughts, and behaviors; but just because a person gets an analogous feeling from a completely different source does not make that feeling a truly spiritual experience.

For my fellow conference participants, the feeling often came instead from a moment of insight, from connection to a long-repressed emotion, or perhaps from a feeling of community. For our star-crossed couple, it might just have been the sex. But in any event, these were insular causes that produced certain feelings that people blithely labeled as spiritual, when what they really meant was that these causes produced a particularly enjoyable personal effect. Much of what I call New Age narcissism relates to people engaging in the same ruse, bouncing from one "spiritual" experience, book, or self-styled guru to another, when what they're really after is the feeling of significance and superiority that their personal "enlightenment" provides. It's a great way to dress up one's egocentricity.

The literature in this area becomes trapped in much the same way. In an effort to appear religion-neutral, authors couch spirituality in purely personal terms without reference to any power or source of meaning outside the self. Thus spirituality becomes a "life-giving principle within a human being" or a sense of personal "significance,"[14] begging the questions, Given by whom? Significant for what reasons? Surely what is personally significant to a mass murderer like Jeffrey Dahmer—or, for that matter, to a particularly ruthless manager—does not automatically qualify it as spiritual.

I see the logical fallacy repeated in some of the most prominent streams of business literature. For example, there is much interest these days in the role of spirit in the work of "high-performing" individuals and organizations. Most of us know from experience what it is like to feel "inspired" in our work, and the tireless energy and enthusiasm such a feeling can give to our efforts. We also know how important "spirit" is to any group endeavor and how directly the quality of products and services is affected by the amount of it we can sense in the employees around us. We've been tempted, then, to label as spiritual any number of things that merely have the *effect* of increasing individual work commitment or organizational morale. Thus the number of recent books and articles on the spiritual aspects of team building, engaging the employee's "spirit" through organizational vision, and the like. It is true that among the fruits of a genuine spirituality are greater enthusiasm for one's work and a greater sense of organizational purpose (as we will discuss in Chapters Seven and Eight), but one needn't read too deeply in most of these recent works to discover that they are merely attempts to produce the same effect with some cheap substitute causes.

We need to keep this dynamic in mind when we look at concepts such as the flow state, popularized through the research of Csikszentmihalyi.[15] A flow experience is probably the fullest measure of what it is like to do "inspired" work (or play). As Csikszentmihalyi describes it: "[A]ction follows upon action according to an internal logic that seems to need no conscious intervention by the actor. He experiences it as a unified flowing from one moment to the next, in which he is in control of his actions, and in which there is little distinction between self and environment, between stimulus and response, or between past, present and future."[16]

Such states, Csikszentmihalyi notes, are often described as transcendental or religious, and one need only look at the writings of the great contemplative masters to see how well this describes many of the experiences that grow from their spiritual practices. But it could also describe the mind of a serial killer or a rapist in the throes of the crime, could it not? The point is that, as one writer has been good enough to point out, spirituality may provide the internal motivation and the setting for a flow experience to occur, but spirituality and flow are not at all the same thing.[17]

We know, after all, that there are many kinds of people who are capable of putting great energy into their work, some for reasons having quite nothing to do with their spiritual growth. The unrelentingly ambitious are capable of strong purposiveness in their work, as are opportunistic brownnosers. The deadly combination of poor self-esteem, denial, external referencing, and obsessiveness that form the basis for the disease of workaholism[18] can yield the same result. The difference is not so much in the character of the work done or in the energy put into it or in the place the work holds (or strangleholds) in someone's life—the difference lies in the *end* to which the work is directed. For all such obsessions, the end served is the self, its narrow needs and wants. It is not that people endeavoring to live a spiritual life are unconcerned with individual desires but that the dominant source of meaning in their work is the extent to which it serves ultimate purposes outside the self—their "original cause," if you will. As we will explore a bit further on, the fruits of an authentic spirituality can go far beyond the "hard work" and task competency that such obsessions may collaterally produce, but do so without the accompanying perversions of the human spirit.

My intent here is to introduce an element of caution into our discussions of "spiritual" experiences. I am convinced that the discussion of spirituality in our time has become so watered down, and our use of the language so loose, that we describe as spiritual a great many things that merely make us *feel* a certain way. I believe we come much closer to the truth when we look at the root causes of those feelings, and reserve the designation *spiritual* for those thoughts, emotions, and behaviors that grow out of our relationship with God and our own deepest center.

That said, we need to make the obvious point that God's manifestations in the world are not limited to those that happen within the context of human spirituality. There is a sense in which every bush is burning, and there are opportunities for "showings" (as Juliana of Norwich called them) throughout the physical world around us, in all of our interactions and relationships, and in every human experience. I do believe it true that those with rich inner lives are more open and attuned to such showings, but God's inbreaking upon the world can happen in countless ways and at any moment. The activity of God's spirit may indeed be felt within a group, an organization, or an individual. It may be experienced as a gentle stirring, a persistent urging, a relentless hammering, or in many other ways both pleasant and not-so. But those experiences, no matter how powerful, can bear no fruit within us unless they are understood, appropriated, and lived out within the context of the relationship that is human spirituality. Otherwise they are like a dream not remembered or a lesson long ago forgotten—they can't make the difference in our lives that God must surely intend. They are like the seeds of which Jesus spoke that were cast abroad by the sower only to be eaten by the birds, scorched by the heat, or choked by the thorns (Matthew 13:3–9, 18–23). They cannot live and grow. They are only ephemeral "feelings."

Spirituality Is Not the Merely Supernormal

Several years ago I accepted an invitation to participate in a "community-building" workshop at a scenic retreat center nestled along the Housatonic River in western Connecticut. There were sixty or so participants, mostly supporters of or potential contributors to the Foundation for Community Encouragement, but otherwise without any prior connection to each other. Now, before continuing the story, let me say that I have the utmost respect for the work of this foundation and a great affinity for the books of its founder, M. Scott Peck. But something happened during this four-day event that clarified my notions of human spirituality.

The foundation posits that there is a certain "technology" to community building and that even the most disparate of groups can enter into a sense of true community (as opposed to what it calls pseudocommunity) in a relatively short period of time. This particular group, carefully following the techniques laid down for us at the outset, seemed indeed to be moving through the various stages of community building in a fairly predictable way. This included, as we found out, a segment during which everyone pretty much got at each other's throats, saying the most incredibly hurtful things to people whom they had just met forty-eight hours earlier.

Then it happened. One of the participants, in an effort to play peacemaker during one of the most contentious sessions, attracted the ire of the entire group. It was as if the group needed a lightning rod, someone to attract the negative energy being manufactured in the room so that they could move on to the next "stage." Only a few people in the room seemed to notice what followed: that man was *scapegoated*. Like the Biblical animal that is loaded with the sins of the community and sent to the wilderness to die,[19] for the rest of that day and night the man was required to bear the hostility of the other individuals in the group and was excommunicated from his former place of inclusion. True to his symbolic function, he withdrew his participation from the group, carrying their sins with him.

The next day, the last of the four-day retreat, began with a remarkably different tone. People were suddenly cheerful and friendly. They eagerly shared what the previous day's experiences had meant to them, their conversation heavily peppered with the words *spirit, spiritual,* and *spirituality.* But, at the urging of one of the conference facilitators, many people also shared the "odd" and "weird" dreams they had the night before. Dr. Jung would have had a field day! One after another, they related the same basic symbolism: things being buried, things going underground, things highly polished on the outside with crud found inside them. Without being at all aware of it, this "community" (or pseudocommunity?) had just reenacted the timeless mythology of the scapegoat, complete with the symbolic extinction of the group's individual and corporate evil—effectively repressing it from conscious view.[20]

This was not a spiritual experience. It *was* highly unusual, well out of the ordinary, with a somewhat mythic character to it. But it had no seeming connection to opening, acknowledging, aligning, and cultivating God's presence in the participants' lives—unless, perhaps, you were the scapegoat! This is the problem I have with the "community" movement and with those who have seized on community as a workplace concept. There is nothing inherently spiritual about the feeling of belonging to a group. It is, at the risk of repeating myself, simply a feeling. Moreover, both history and the work of Reinhold Niebuhr have taught us that human groups and organizations are capable of particularly malicious behaviors that the individuals who compose the group might never undertake.[21] Those who advance the very laudable goals of creating a sense of community in organizations would do well to remember the advice of Dorothy Sayers: while it is certainly true that the two great commandments of the Judeo-Christian faith are to love God and your neighbor, "the second commandment depends upon the first, and without the first, it is a delusion and a snare."[22]

To give one's allegiance to something just because it is supernatural goes by the name *occultism*. The world is chock-full of such opportunities these days, from telephone psychics to healing crystals to past-life regressions to space travelers cleverly hidden in the tail of a comet. Some of that stuff may have value; but my insistence is that it has value only to the extent that it fosters and furthers the opening, acknowledging, aligning, and cultivating that is human spirituality. All else is at best entertainment and at worst an opportunity for genuine evil. I don't purport to know much about the ontology of evil, but I am quite satisfied that not everything inhabiting the unseen realm is concerned with or conducive to our spiritual growth and development. I believe, in fact, that M. Scott Peck's *People of the Lie* was right in its assertion that evil objectively and independently exists in the universe and that it works in the world through the self-absorption, willfulness, and—yes—scapegoating behavior of individuals and their human groups.[23]

The Myth of Self-Actualization

In Chapter Two we discussed Abraham Maslow's concept of self-actualization as one of the ways in which businesspeople are coming to find transcendent meaning in their work. But the term has come to be quite liberally applied in recent years to practically any successful entrepreneur who achieves sufficient notoriety through making a ton of money, publishing a book chronicling their successful entrepreneurial experiences, or both. The descriptions and self-descriptions of these successful businesspeople—from Tom Chappell (Tom's of Maine) to Anita Roddick (the Body Shop) to Bill Gates (Microsoft)—often have them at the pinnacle of Maslow's hierarchy of needs, examples to the rest of us of what enlightenment can do for our bottom lines.

There is a significant danger here, which Martha Nichols hit foursquare in a recent article for the *Harvard Business Review*.[24] Many successful entrepreneurs, as we all know, are rather egotistical, which contributes in no small part to their initial accomplishments. However, the ego inflation and sense of infallibility that often accompany material and creative success can easily lead these entrepreneurs to impose their view of the world, life, and business onto the organization they control, always under the banner of actualizing their personal vision. Thus they will appropriate the notion of "community" for their workplaces when, in fact, "such moralizing can disguise a paternalistic vision of what a company should be—a place where the good father expects his kids to uphold the 'family' work ethic and its 'shared' mission."[25] They can talk the usual politically correct talk about common goals and a work-life balance, "[b]ut winning in the marketplace is what underpins the entire 'family,' not concern for employees, suppliers, or other stakeholders. Such an intense work environment can thinly conceal the usual push for ever-increasing productivity."[26] And their hubris can open the way to serious ethical lapses, as Anita Roddick's well-publicized problems in recent years attest.

The trouble is that despite Maslow's clear insistence that self-actualizing work must *transcend* the interests of the self, we tend to see self-actualization in our culture as just the fancy version of "be all that you can be." Our heroes have always been cowboys, the old country song goes, and the entrepreneur is the modern equivalent. The problem is that many of our new cowboys (and cowgirls) are so self-absorbed that they show little interest in people or issues outside their business or else "confuse themselves—their goals, political beliefs, dreams, and considerable talents—with the companies they create and the people who work for them, [which] leads to both false humility and misleading assumptions about how their work translates to business as a whole."[27] In short, they confuse transcendent meaning with the personal drive for power and achievement.

I agree with Nichols that self-actualization can't be seen as just the road to personal success. Maslow would have flatly rejected any notion of an insular self that did not eventually grow to transcend its own narrow interests. But why? What of the self-made man or woman, the icons of American culture who pull themselves up by their own bootstraps? Well, have you ever considered that phrase, *pulling yourself up by your own bootstraps?* If you will think for a moment about the physics of that maneuver, you'll understand why the phrase has stuck in our language since the time when people wore bootstraps. It's physically impossible to do. You can't get your feet onto that next plateau without being pulled there from above.

This is the religious attitude of practically any of the world's believers. We differ in our views of how that pulling gets done, or by what power, or through which intermediaries, but we are all in agreement that our nature as men and women keeps us from being able to pull ourselves up totally of our own force and volition. To attempt to do so is the ageless sin of hubris—the desire to *be* the god of one's own little secure, tightly controlled world. That is why spirituality, as we've talked of it here, is so vitally important. It does not deny the desire and the need for human beings to develop themselves to their fullest potential. It does not even, in my judgment, preclude great material successes. But it does insist that we transcend our inherent selfishness, and thus become most truly ourselves, when we faithfully nurture a relationship with a God who makes no secret of his desire to pull us up by our bootstraps.

But aren't there people who live virtuous, ethical, and effective lives who don't even believe in a God? I suppose that's true, although

I confess that I don't see the abundant evidence for it that many people claim. I just believe that humanistic ethics, virtue, and a devotion to some vague concept of "humanity" is a thin reed on which to lean the gift of life.

I have taught ethics to college business majors for a number of years, and I can clearly state that I never saw a single thorny ethical issue that was satisfactorily resolved solely by reference to an ethical theory. People tend to untangle the most important problems that confront them by referring to their most deeply held notions about life, their place in the world, and the nature of Ultimate Reality. These are fundamental beliefs that spring primarily—perhaps even exclusively—from people's religious attitude and orientation. I mean by that not the creed they adopt nor the sect to which they belong but their more bedrock assumptions about the purpose for which they exist. Schopenhauer once said that if God does not exist, then all things are permitted. I think that is true, not because there is some cosmic scorekeeper in the sky who rewards rights and punishes wrongs, but because without God human actions lose their *significance*. However admirable or egregious they may be, human actions take place in flickering little lives lasting mere decades on a small planet in an obscure corner of a boundless universe. In that context, how much energy can we really put behind working for "humanity"? When, as Keynes observed, "in the long run we are all dead," what sense does it make to be virtuous solely for the sake of some abstract concept of virtue? No, for most of us our lives and actions can only draw meaning and significance from our connection to the ultimate source of significance in the universe—from our relationship to God. And from such a relationship a deep concern for the moral implications of our actions naturally flows.

Besides that, I have a healthy suspicion about those who tell me that their lives are devoted to serving "humanity" but that they don't have much use for notions of God. Nietzsche also said that he loved humanity—it was just people he couldn't stand. We tend to hide a good deal of disdain for others (Nietzsche didn't even bother to hide his) behind our facile talk of humanity. Like many of the other concepts we have touched on in this chapter, such talk is all too often a cloak for our egocentric pursuit of a lofty self-image. And thus quite the opposite of a genuine human spirituality.

Questions and Exercises for Further Reflection

1. How internalized (intrinsic) is your personal religion? One way to get a sense of this, if you can be honest with yourself, is to imagine for a moment that the country where you live is suddenly overtaken by a military force quite hostile to your personal faith. In fact, all religious expression is outlawed. Over time the new regime manages to convince the vast majority of the populace that no supreme being or beings exist, that all religions are a futile waste of human energy and time, and that all believers are simply ignorant people. There are no formal places of worship. It is distinctly passé and uncool to discuss one's religious beliefs, and to do so would be a severe impediment to social, economic, or career advancement. How strong would your personal faith be? How important would it be for you to continue to find ways to practice your beliefs? If there were nothing you could "get" from your religion, what would you still be willing to give? (A great many people in Communist bloc countries had little difficulty abandoning their religious traditions once it became unpopular or illegal to observe them. Do you think that Americans are somehow different?)

2. All college professors love pop quizzes, and I am no exception. Here is one for you.

a. You choose to wear on your lapel a Star of David that was given to you by your grandfather, a concentration camp survivor. A Christian and an Islamic coworker both complain that they are uncomfortable with this overt religious expression. Are they within their rights? [Answer: No. Personal expressions or symbols of religious belief, in and of themselves, do not violate the rights of others, even if they offend the particular sensibilities of others who have a different (or no) faith.]

b. Could your corporate employer prohibit you from wearing the lapel pin? [Answer: Yes, but only if all other religious expressions were similarly banned from the workplace.]

c. You and several coworkers wish to organize a group that will meet for prayer and meditation each morning before the start of the workday. The meetings will be on company property, and your employer has sanctioned the meetings to the extent of providing the facilities, donating refreshments, and allowing you to advertise the existence of the group in the company's monthly newsletter. Is the employer in danger of violating the law? [Answer: No (unless the employer is a government agency—in which case it's a bit stickier). First Amendment prohibitions do not apply, and the company has done nothing to create a "hostile work environment" for other employees.]

  d. The employer decides that the prework prayer meetings are such a good idea that all employees will be required to attend. Permissible? [Answer: No chance. Without a totally homogeneous workforce, the employer runs the risk of creating an offensive work environment for those of differing beliefs.]

3. Do you engage in any overtly religious or spiritual activities at work? Are there any visible signs or symbols of your religion in your office? Would you feel comfortable doing or displaying such things? What is the cause of any discomfort you have?

4. Have you ever thought about where our ethical values come from? Think about the last time you had a thorny but very important decision to make, preferably one where you were very proud of your choice and its outcome. Now perform the kind of regression analysis that you were asked to do in question 1 at the end of Chapter One. Ask yourself why you made that decision, then continue to ask yourself "Why is that important?" until you reach the bedrock ethical value that controlled that decision. Can you think where in your personal history you learned that particular value? What does your religious tradition have to say about that issue? What are the teachings of its greatest leaders and prophets that relate to the issue? Can you even pull up a line from the Bible, the Koran, the Upanishads, the Dhammapada, or other sacred scriptures that would seem to speak to it directly? What does this tell you about the origins of your deepest ethical beliefs?

Chapter Five

Why Go There?

In our era, the road to holiness necessarily passes through the world of action.
DAG HAMMARSKJÖLD

Along the Jersey coast, a man is trying to enjoy a long-postponed vacation with his children. There are plans to go to a nearby water park—a highlight of the week for the kids. All are up early to a cacophony of cereal bowls clacking, drawers and doors slamming, and rubber floats being patiently filled with air. But, before they can go, Dad has to "make a few calls" to the office. It's almost as if (he's come to think) his very loyalty to the company is tested every time he takes some time off. There will always be some meeting he simply must attend, or fire only he can douse, or customer only he can satisfy, that keeps him either back home in Maryland or constantly tethered to the pager and cell phone. Today it's the CEO himself who wants the 7:30 A.M. call to "get his input" on the crisis *du jour* and have him "touch base" with a few other members of the management team.

At 11:38 A.M. Dad finally hangs up the phone, the resort condo now all quiet. Despairing of ever getting to the water park as a family, the wife and kids have gone on without him. They will return well after dark, disappointed but not really angry. They've learned to expect this.

On the same day, down in the New South, a half-dozen middle managers gather around a lunchroom table. Their company, one of the international telecommunications giants, has recently announced the latest in a seemingly endless series of restructurings, rightsizings, divestitures, and early retirement packages. They gather to continue their discussion of a book they've all been reading together as their way of trying to make sense of the chaos around them and to find the strength to endure it. The book is Victor Frankl's *Man's Search for Meaning*—his personal account of survival and hope amid the horrors of a Nazi concentration camp. "There's more of a parallel than you might think," says the woman who organized the group.

And in the heartland of America there is a bright young college student, a business major, who with dogged determination (and more than a little obsessiveness) has posted a 3.65 grade-point average, checked all the right academic blocks, and is now poised to take a job with a Fortune 500 company that will likely run her young spirit completely into the ground. She never really liked the study of business, you see, and when she really allows herself to think about the horrific hours and travel expectations of her new job, she wonders where the time will come from for her painting or a social life—much less a family. But she is driven by an image that has stuck with her since high school and dictated her career plans. It's of her father sitting at the kitchen table in the middle of the day, aimlessly browsing the paper, months after simultaneously losing his job and his self-definition. This, she vowed, would never happen to her and her family—no matter what.

Three scenes from the New Economy. Three true stories. The boisterous bulls of Wall Street and the jubilant parade of economic statistics cannot drown out the fact that the relative prosperity enjoyed by some of us comes with a steep human price: the pandemic of workaholism and unrelenting stress, a pervasive feeling of bewilderment in the present and angst for a wholly uncertain future, and a deadening sense of purposelessness that makes mere survival the main career goal. Having passively accepted the instrumental view of work developed by our forbears (as described in Chapter One), we have layered on our own mythologies as well. You know them by heart by now: the global economy requires that we all work smarter (that is, harder) to maintain our place in world markets; competition at home requires that we all work more efficiently (that is, harder) in order to maintain market share; our market-driven economy requires that we all work more productively (that is, harder) to maintain shareholder value and avoid being spun off or be-coming the target of some hostile takeover. More hours, more stress, more looking over your shoulder, more wild cards for your work and career that you are absolutely powerless to control. And we have accepted and internalized these add-ons to our cultural view of work as surely as if they were penned by Adam Smith him-self—or contained in some other equally sacred text of American capitalism. They have become part of the prevailing myth.

All this is fundamentally affecting the way in which we look at our lives and jobs. More than two-thirds of us believe that the American dream of equal opportunity, personal freedom, and so-cial mobility has become harder to achieve during the decade of the 1990s.[1] Only half of us believe that our children will have a bet-ter life than we have had—down substantially from a mere ten years ago.[2] We may even be running up against the limits of the human organism itself. As one of my coaching clients puts it: "They can ask me to step up and sacrifice myself for this particular project or merger or performance goal. But what they're saying is that they want flat-out, superhuman effort from now until the day you die or retire. Nobody can do that and stay healthy."

There's evidence that he's right. Depression, the self-protective psychological response to the slings and arrows of life, has been on the steady increase during the whole of this century, but has sim-ply exploded during the past decade. More than thirty million Americans, the vast majority of them working adults, are suffering from its symptoms at this very moment, with another twenty mil-lion or so destined to experience a major depressive episode at some point in their lives.[3] Stress-related illnesses were the fastest-growing category of workers' compensation claims by 1990, and there is evidence that stress at work has only increased since that time.[4] More than two million employable working-age men simply *left* the workforce in 1996 rather than give the "flat-out, superhu-man effort" required of them ad infinitum—a true "dropping out" of unprecedented proportions. And, strange as the timing seems, as I write these lines the concerned coaching client I quoted ear-lier is attending the funeral of his company's fifty-one-year-old founder and CEO. He died while jogging—one of those physically exertive things we do to convince ourselves we're still healthy de-spite the craziness of our lifestyles.

Small wonder that the father on the Jersey shore has started a small business on the side and intends to go to it full-time within a year and that the manager who started the informal book club intends to retire as soon as she's offered a package. (And for what it's worth, I give the bright student three years in her new job before she bails out and does something completely different.) Welcome to the American Dream, New Economy style.

There's a sense of pain, loss, and separation in today's workplace from which practically no one emerges untouched. Peter Vaill has used the strong word *anguish* to describe it,[5] but it might just as well be called *spiritual pain,* for it grows out of the compelling awareness that some of the most important aspects of our lives are totally disconnected from our deepest sources of value and meaning. It is spiritual because it relates to those deepest wellsprings. It is pain because there seems no way to bridge the chasm between who we are expected to be at work and who we uniquely are as persons, between the community we yearn for and the "company" we keep.

We try to cope, of course. Societially, we apply the age-old balm of humor to the wound, elevating benumbed Dilbert to hero status and cranking out sitcoms like NBC's *Working* (motto: "Like your job, only funnier"). Individually, our coping mechanisms are more subtle—but more dangerous. We may mask the pain with intrigues and political maneuvering, often at the expense of both our colleagues and our ethical standards, in order to garner all the goodies we can from our organizations. We may dull the pain with workaholism, trying to feed the bottomless pit of our sense of inadequacy with ever increasing dedication to our jobs. We may vent the pain, as though we were some pathetic imitation of Dabney Coleman in the movie *Nine to Five,* with imperious badgering of our subordinates, petty conflict with our peers, and sexual harassment of our colleagues. Most often, and most tragically, the pain simply transmutes itself into indifference, passive aggression, and outright depression. In my coaching and consulting practice, I consistently find that even among the most successful executives there are one or more coping mechanisms hard at work, creating various dysfunctions in their families, personal lives, or interpersonal relationships.

A spirituality of life (and, hence, of work and business) offers what no coping mechanism can. By coping you can mask the pain, but the wound that caused it is still there. You can adapt and "succeed," but the dis-ease creating your un-ease remains. You can "win" the rat race and remain, as Lily Tomlin observed, very much a rat. It is in human spirituality—ancient and ever new—that we finally find the antidote, the cure.

A Credible New Mythology

The myths created by a culture are its self-descriptions, its own particular view of reality. They are containers into which cultures pour their collective hopes, fears, visions, and "eternal truths." They are thus, each in its own way, quite real. Quetzelcoatl tells us as much about the Aztecs as Theseus about the Greeks, and because of our common psychic heritage, both still speak quite clearly to us and our "modern" experiences. There may be much about the legends of Quetzelcoatl and Theseus that were not literally true, yet in form and ideation they both expressed and sustained the culture that gave them birth.

We have our own mythologies, of course, and many of them relate to the world of work. The notions of work and business that we explored in Chapter One—from Martin Luther to Adam Smith to Ben Franklin—were all mythologies that sought to explain the proper role of human enterprise and its relationship to the rest of life. So are the rhetoric of Milton Friedman ("corporate social responsibility . . . is a fundamentally subversive doctrine"), the radicals of the 1960s ("the conspiracy of the military-industrial complex"), and the popular movie *Wall Street* ("Greed is good"). The difference now is the plethora of myths, the exploding marketplace of forms and ideations vying for our allegiance and belief—a nightly competition for us to identify with the strong-willed Murphy Brown, the committed Dr. Doug Ross, or the irreverent Drew Carey.

Against this backdrop we place the arguments contained in this book, and their invitation. No government has decreed, nor religion insisted, that you must continue to look at your work and your life in the way you do. You are not sentenced to live by the same mythology as that of the prevailing culture or your parents or even your coworkers. And although it is undoubtedly possible for you to change your individual mythology about work and business, there are some unmistakable signs that a significant cultural reformation is also taking place in the larger society itself, one that provides a counterweight to the most dispiriting aspects of the New Economy and may actually come, in time, to outweigh them.

An important driver for this cultural reorientation is simply the sense of impermanence, the lack of anchors in a world that seems to swirl unpredictably around us. Our jobs are anything but secure, dependent on factors that are often completely beyond our control. The problems threatening our society—from the environment to the cities to AIDS to terrorism—seem immune to our persistent attempts at great social, scientific, or military solutions. Even our national leadership has been reduced to the intrigues of twenty-something interns and oddly stained dresses. In such an environment it is hard to find a stable handhold or a reliable moral compass. Add to this the fact that the baby-boom generation is reaching the age at which they are facing their mortality and entertaining their own midlife crises, and you have a readiness for a new mythology of life and work that is moored in values and principles that don't change with the swirling winds.

A search for anchors and answers is clearly afoot. Membership in evangelical and fundamentalist churches sharply increased during the past decade as more traditional denominations suffered diminishing attendance. Those eschewing conventional religions altogether flocked in increasing numbers to alternative "churches," whether New Age centers, informal meeting groups, or cultlike phenomena such as the Church of Scientology. An ever growing number of "recovery" groups, from Emotions Anonymous to Gamblers Anonymous to Adult Children of Alcoholics, find shelter in the twelve steps and the community of those practicing them.

Yet a spirituality of work and life, as we have described it in this book, offers the wearied searcher what these other movements by and large can't. You are not required to surrender your individuality as the price of community; rather, you are in fact encouraged to become the uniquely textured individual you are intended to be. You are not asked to leave your reason at the door or to adopt wholesale a credo that has been thought through for you by someone else; rather, spirituality finds in the interior life the answers that were there all along, together with your very human questions and doubts. Perhaps most important, a spirituality of life and work does not ask that you leave behind the religious tradition in which you were raised. As Jung so often took pains to point out, individuation most fruitfully takes place in a personality thoroughly rooted in the symbols and traditions of its cultural (including its religious) lineage, no matter how much the person has been broadened and deepened by exposure to other cultures. You grow best, in other words, in the soil where you were planted. In a world where stability, security, and predictability have gone the way of cheap gas prices, it is human spirituality that connects us to our most reliable and enduring anchor, without requiring of us our individuality, our intellect, or our religious heritage.

Our spiritual lives have become increasingly important in another way as well. There is an entire value system that underlies our notions of work, and particularly of business. We may be dimly aware of the values and behaviors this system promotes, but we fail to see the costs inherent in the loss of things it discourages. We value externality and extraversion, ever and always at the expense of the interior life. So we reward and promote those people who are the most gregarious, mile-a-minute interactors among us, in spite of the fact that they may have nothing of importance to say. At the same time, those who are reflective, studied, and careful with their words are often seen as withdrawn and unenergetic. We esteem objectivity over intuition, rationality over faith, and technique over purpose (something Jack Behrman calls the national disease[6]). In such tussles the values of the inner world are always the loser. A spirituality of work holds the promise of restoring a balance in a culture long out of whack. It recognizes the importance even in our commercial intercourse of the values attendant to the inner life—reflection, listening, silence, intuitive ways of knowing, seeking the purpose behind the task—and gives them their rightful place.

Spirituality also provides the antidote for the mind-set that Pope John Paul II calls economism, a view of commercial reality that measures all importance and makes all decisions on economic factors alone. Economism is certainly not a new phenomenon (as Dickens's Scrooge will attest), but its effects are now more stark. In Columbus, Ohio, for example, there is a building that houses the headquarters of the largest power producer on the continent, American Electric and Power (AEP). Spanning its entranceway is an enormous steel turbine taken from one of the company's early plants, a symbol to the eighteen thousand employees of AEP of the innovative advances the company has made over its ninety-year history in the production and transmission of electric power to customers in eleven U.S. states. There is a palpable sense of pride among the engineers I met there—a sense of accomplishment, service, and stewardship that could (and, for many, does) form the basis for a spirituality of their work.

But then there are the guys on the sixth floor, the "traders." Theirs is a new and lucrative line of business for AEP made possible by the deregulation of the power industry, in which kilowatts are bought and sold, positions taken, and fortunes made, just like any other commodity. And to the traders, in fact, all of AEP is a commodity. They ask, without cracking a smile, why AEP really needs power plants if they can buy all the power the company can use at competitive prices from other suppliers. All the company really needs, in fact, is *them*—and a few distribution wires. And as to the model of engineering ingenuity that guards the corporate gate: "A worthless piece of junk, when you think about it," says one trader. "We couldn't get a plug nickel for it." In a world ruled by economism, to have no value in the market is to have no value at all. Only a view of life and economic reality that admits of the possibility for a spiritual basis of work can stand over against the demeaning, dis-spiriting effects of the economistic mind-set.

A credible new mythology based on a spirituality of work is not as far-fetched as it might initially have seemed. It provides an anchor for the sense of aimlessness, impermanence, and economic insecurity that surrounds our jobs these days. It restores some sense of balance for our externally oriented, overly rational world of work by giving the important values of the inner world their place and due. It gives us a new yardstick by which to measure success and fulfillment, replacing the one that leads down the road to frustration, anxiety, workaholism, materialism, and spiritual starvation.

If such a new mythology were more afoot in the world, perhaps my friend Don Craven would still be alive. I first met Don in 1985, when he moved to my city with his wife and small children. After a successful stint as an Air Force fighter pilot, he had returned to school for an M.B.A. and was now ready for the next leg of his career as an officer of a large and very traditional manufacturing corporation. Before long he had moved on up the ladder and was sent to head the company's operation in a town some distance away.

No one will ever know exactly what went on in his mind the night he killed himself. After hosting a company function, he had been stopped by a highway patrolman and found to have a blood alcohol level slightly over the legal limit. Embarrassing, you say, but not the end of the world? It's likely that Don didn't see it that way. His highly visible position made such conduct anathema, and the highly conservative nature of the company for which he worked made it unlikely that all would be forgiven. This particular position would almost certainly have been lost to him, and the sequential, straight-line career he had envisioned would almost certainly be disrupted. Not the end of the world, but the end of something imponderably precious to Don Craven. As arrangements were being made for a relative to drive him home from the scene of the arrest, he reached into his glove compartment, took out a handgun, and turned it on himself. He left behind a widow, two young children, and a host of bereaved and puzzled friends.

I wish that our culture could have given Don Craven a different yardstick by which to measure his life and his career. How could this man—pillar of his community, deacon of his church, loving father, generous friend, decorated veteran—have come so to internalize our collective notions of success and failure that he would end his life rather than endure a hitch in its flow? Would but that our cultural myth was not largely about a "game of life" in which there are either winners or losers—the winners being those who make it to the "top of the ladder" or "die with the most toys." Rather that it were a tale about a purposeful life in which we learn and grow, struggle and triumph, move forward or fall back and regroup; and not only for the sake of our careers but also for that which imbues our careers with meaning and makes them into vocations. Of the sixteen thousand suicides that take place every year in the United States, how many, like Don Craven's, are sacrifices to the gods of our ailing mythology?

The Rising Tide of Expectations

There are seventy-eight million baby boomers in the United States, those born during the age of innocence that stretched from 1946 to 1964. They are now, if you will look around you, the emerging leaders of our organizations. They are the mid- and upper-level managers of our corporations, sometimes even the CEOs. They are at the helm of many of our nonprofit organizations. They preach from our pulpits, form the core leadership of our labor unions, and are the rising stars of our military. There is one in the Oval Office of the White House. And from research that began as far back as the late 1970s, we have come to understand that baby boomers operate on a perceptibly different set of values than those embraced by the previous generation. To understand this shift in priorities is to understand why talk of spirituality in the workplace has become much more acceptable in recent years.

In his highly influential book *The Third Wave*, written in 1980, futurist Alvin Toffler observed that there was a visible and growing difference in the attitudes of the generations when it came to work. Older workers, then still a majority, were "motivated by traditional incentives. They are happiest with strict work guidelines and clear tasks. They do not expect to find 'meaning' in their work."[7] But drawing on the work of opinion researcher Daniel Yankelovich, Toffler observed that there was an emerging young class of managers who were hungry for a larger sense of responsibility, wanted more challenging and vital work, and wished to commit to larger goals worthy of their talents and skills. To Toffler, it seemed clear that this would be the generation that would "seek meaning along with financial reward."[8]

As the twenty-first century begins, the shifting values first breaking ground in the 1970s have blossomed full. Where authority was once the watchword, autonomy now holds sway. Where positional power once ruled, *empowerment* is the buzzword of the day. The structure of command and control, imported into business from the last century's military successes as the unquestioned way to organize any enterprise, has given way to decentralization, the sharing of information and decision making, and teams. No longer does the successful manager need only two tools—a carrot and a stick. She (gender equality being yet another change) needs a toolbox full of incentives, recognitions, rewards, and motivators, administered with substantial expertise and interpersonal savvy. And it is no longer enough that we be given a job to do and be paid well to do it; our sense of well-being is predicated too on what Yankelovich refers to as "an overall sense of meaning and coherence in one's life," to which we increasingly expect our time at work to contribute.[9]

For a very significant number of people, the work-life split I have called the Great Divorce is no longer an acceptable part of either working or living.

This shift is not just a matter of the way people want to feel about their jobs, but relates fundamentally to how they want to be led in doing them. In most organizations the role of manager as straw boss and conduit of information is largely obsolete. In its place, the manager who avoids the downsizing ax is the one who values the energy and ideas that the autonomy and empowerment of his "team members" can bring and who creates the kind of environment in which personal growth—all *kinds* of personal growth—is valued because it makes for happier and more productive people. The emerging workforce values leaders it can respect and learn from in a self-directed environment, who provide the resources needed for people to grow to the full measure of their abilities, and who can provide at least the *space* for that very personal search for the sense of meaning and coherence that Yankelovich describes.

Do you start to hear an echo here? If the need for self-directedness, significance, coherence, and meaning have such ascendent importance in the world as it is being molded by this new generation of organizational leaders, is not human spirituality as we have described it supremely responsive to that need? As corporate consultant Steve Boehlke frames it, "A whole generation of baby boomers have hit mid-life. That's us. Many of us have been successful by some standard. In many ways, I would characterize our generation as a generation of seekers. In the '80s we externalized our success and meaning. We're now realizing that emotionally, spiritually we need a place to dwell. Where are our roots? Where can we sink ourselves deep into something because we really care? Where am I grounded?"[10]

For Boehlke the question is rhetorical and the answer obvious. What is new is that he and others are beginning to talk openly about those roots and the desire to more fully ground them in all the aspects of their lives, specifically including their work. The deeper issues and concerns of life, for which spirituality is a natural conduit, have become a far more common part of our discourse as a result of the baby-boomer search for roots.

I see the evidence for such New Breed values (as Yankelovich calls them) even in my thoroughly materialistic college students. True, they are much more focused on that first job than in meeting the world's (and their own) greatest needs. Yet there is a consistent sense that they have absorbed much of the New Breed attitudes toward work and leadership: the primacy of self-development, hierarchies based more on mutual respect than on positional power, the need for a more "balanced" or "integrated" life. These students are about to join a young workforce that, according to a recent survey of HR professionals, has unrealistically high expectations of what companies should provide and a low tolerance for unmet needs.[11] What remains, for many of them, is simply the midlife encounter with the need for roots and meaning of which Boehlke speaks. The boomers are not a historical anomaly that the next generation is destined to reverse. They have indelibly changed our view of the world of work in ways their sons and daughters seem happy to build on.

Little wonder, then, that a recent letter to the editor of a local newspaper fell on deaf (and probably amused) ears. It was written by a grand dame of the community, the widow of a businessman quite prominent during the 1960s and 1970s. She hated the popular comic strip Dilbert, she said, asking that it be "removed from our city's fine newspaper" as a result of the "lack of respect for authority" that it portrayed and seemingly encouraged. Indeed, even if presented in jest with pen and ink, the New Breed values of self-directedness, empowerment, and healthy distrust of purely positional authority must seem like a kind of heresy to those who grew up and prospered in the command-and-control culture of the past.

It seems to me that a certain critical mass is being achieved that may eventually allow for the expression of the full range of the human experience at work. Perhaps the best evidence of that notion is the fact that you are reading this book—and that there were several others on the bookstore shelf beside it. There is no doubt that the New Breed values of the baby-boomer generation have begotten such positive changes in our work environment as the empowerment movement, the decline of the traditional command-and-control system, and the rise of more humanistic values in management. Perhaps the next step in the evolution of our workplaces will be the most fundamental. Can we insist on the right to do meaningful work and to be true to our deepest selves while doing it?

Covenants Lost and Unfound

Much is said these days about the "new covenant" in business. No one denies that the old covenant—loyalty and hard work in exchange for job security—has been broken. But what has taken its place? If you listen to the corporate line as spoon-fed by today's management consultants and theorists, you'll hear something like this: "Give us your full effort and your loyalty while you're here, and though we can't guarantee you long-term employment, the skills you learn and the training you receive will make you equally employable elsewhere."

But is that enough? In your heart of hearts, in the deep of the night, are you really satisfied with the bargain being offered here? To you, the proffered contract probably sounds more like this: "I will work 20 to 30 percent more hours than I used to, under incredible and unrelenting stress, doing more with less resources, and you will offer me cross-training I have no time to attend and a somewhat larger severance package when you unilaterally decide to can me; I will then spend the next year of my life in a nerve-racking encounter with want ads, head hunters, and outplacement counselors—oh, yes, and a divorce lawyer." Sound like a good deal, or just the only one they're floating?

Let's face facts. What is required from you by your employer is not likely to change in the near future. No one is predicting that you will soon have to work less hard. According to the magazine *Business Ethics,* in fact, it's America's "dirty little secret" that increased productivity is largely bought at the price of your working ever increasing amounts of overtime for which you are, legally or illegally, not paid.[12] Nor is there any reliable data out there indicating that the external rewards and incentives from your employer are about to ratchet up—no sudden spike in corporate salaries, no glut of new hires to shoulder the workload, no pot of previously unused resources to shovel in your direction. The board isn't likely to vote you a nice fluffy golden parachute any time soon.

No, there is unlikely to be any real break in the *external* effort expected from you or any bump in the *external* motivators you can anticipate from your employer. The sense of equity we expect if we are to enter into a truly voluntary contract is thus wholly lacking— that is, unless we were to mix in an ingredient too long neglected by both organizations and employees alike: our *internal* motivations, rewards, and incentives.

Think about it for a moment, and let yourself idealize about a future way of being. What if a spirituality of work as we have described it in the last two chapters could come to be formed in you? What if the energy spent on work was in some way responsive to the need to acknowledge and align yourself with Ultimate Reality, was an active part of your attempt to cultivate God's presence in your day-to-day activities? Better yet (and perhaps more of a stretch for most of us right now), what if your employer accepted that desire in you, encouraged it, thought it to be a valuable part of your entire development, and gave you the space and permission to pursue it? What if such issues were actually talked about openly, comfortably, and in the same breath with skills training and leadership development? What if, without being the least bit sectarian or parochial, senior leadership demonstrated their alignment with Ultimate Reality as they saw and experienced it? What if they themselves were valued and respected in the organization not so much for their financial acumen, political savvy, or glibness but for the depths to which their roots had sunk and the consistency with which the sacred and the secular coincided in their commercial lives?

If you could be possessed of such a working spirituality in such a place of work, what would that portend? Could you commit yourself to that business wholeheartedly in the knowledge that you were serving far more than your own interests? Could you work with a sense of loyalty toward the company that has provided you momentary security and an outlet for your skills, ever mindful that your ultimate loyalty (and source of security) lies elsewhere? Could you render unto Caesar, content in the knowledge that you were at the same time rendering unto God? Would you then be more able to see a downsizing or consolidation of functions—even an outright firing—more as the temporary glitch and future opportunity that it is, rather than as the end of your self-constructed little world?

The old covenant is indeed lost, and it will not return. Moreover, to quote one of my clients, "Lifetime employment should not even *be* the goal for any of us anymore. It's not just unrealistic; it stunts most people's growth." Indeed, to stay with one job or one company for all your life probably wastes a vast portion of your talents and potential. But what has been lost can be replaced. The equity and fairness of the covenant can be restored. In place of the external motivators of the old covenant we can begin to imbue our work with the powerful personal incentives of human spirituality, which can produce initiative and commitment far beyond what mere "job security" ever yielded.

Our organizations, from their side of the equation, must respond in two ways. They must provide a workplace that not only is open and tolerant of spiritual aspirations and concerns but also encourages them as part of an atmosphere of growth and development of the whole person at work. What's more, they must operate from a set of values that invites alignment with the core beliefs of those who work there, making it possible to remain true to one's deepest self while at work. Those companies that do will inevitably find that in balancing the scales of the "new covenant" they have also increased employee trust, loyalty, initiative, and the capacity for genuine creativity.

There are places where such efforts are being made, right in the mainstream of American business. Boeing, AT&T, Lotus, and Medtronic were among the companies singled out by *Business Week* for "hitting the road less travelled" with a variety of initiatives related to spirituality and "soul" in the workplace.[13] The World Bank, of all places, has a position called "values coordinator," has sponsored conferences on spirituality and the work of the bank, and gave its tacit approval to an internal group called the World Bank Spiritual Unfoldment Society, which held well-attended weekly meetings of a broad cross section of bank employees. The founder of the World Bank group, Richard Barrett, has gone on to join a growing number of consultants who work with companies on issues of spirituality in the workplace, often with demonstrable, bottom-line results. Says Barrett: "Over the next few years, we're going to see the rapid development of the practical side of these ideas. It's going to be huge, this questioning of beliefs and assumptions. This is all going to happen."[14] As leaner, downsized companies reduce the tangible rewards of organizational life, and the expression *job security* becomes another quaint anachronism of a bygone era, the lure of work's inner rewards becomes more practical indeed.

The Rise and Fall of the Management Fads

Let's begin with a multiple-choice question. Which of the following, given the option, would you prefer: (1) a sharp stick in the eye, (2) hemorrhoids, (3) forced early retirement, or (4) introduction into your company of the latest revolutionary management technique that is supposed to change everything?

The sharp stick, right? You are forgiven if, like the rest of us, you have lived through one too many quality circles, team bonding experiences, and well-intentioned HR initiatives. We've all been numbed by the parade of quick fixes and simplistic solutions that promise grandiose results but deliver, at best, only a momentary feeling that we're out there on the cutting edge "doing something" about our most stubborn problems. We've been TQM'd, reengineered, rightsized, flattened, and empowered. We've experienced participative management, strategic management, visionary management, one-minute management, and management by walking around. Not that these concepts and techniques haven't had value, of course (some much more than others); but our skepticism comes from the fact that they each claim in the abstract to have great promise for solving the most insidious ills of our organizations and end up delivering far, far less. We now paint them all with the same brush, hoping that we get to retire before the next innovation rears its ugly head and we're sent off to a new round of seminars, training sessions, and motivational speeches by supposed management gurus.

You will also be forgiven if you worry that the notion of spirituality in the workplace might be just another flash in the management pan. I worry about that, too, and can't think of a worse fate for the ideas here proffered than that they should become faddish and popular. But the reason why the management fads of the past three decades failed or were only moderately successful is precisely the reason why human spirituality is different. Management techniques have come and gone because they have confused motivation with meaning, because they have relied on surface manipulations rather than connecting to life's deeper dynamics. At best, they have tapped the *immanent* motivations for our work that we discussed in Chapter Two but have left any notion of work's *transcendent* meanings to the more "appropriate" religious realm (which, as we have seen, has largely ignored the problem). They have sought to engineer valuable change by tinkering at life's edges, rather than exploring what transformative powers might be at life's core.

What spirituality does in our lives is to connect work to our deepest sources of meaning and thus to the most powerful motivator of all. It is not the latest in the series of slogans designed to manipulate the motivations of employees in the service of management, but a concept at the very center of meaning and motivation itself. When you engage an employee or an entire workforce at the level of their deepest affections and strongest sense of purpose, you need no flashy slogans or fad of the month to render you the commitment, productivity, or creativity that will quite naturally flow from their work. Management techniques can help channel and organize such energy, but they can't create or sustain it. Spirit is the engine; the best thing management can do is steer.

The management fads rise because they appeal to our sense of optimism and our need to feel that we are proactively "doing something" about a problem. It's management's version of the scientific fallacy, which holds that all human problems can be resolved if only we apply our technical knowledge to them. These fads also, in the early rush of implementation, produce just enough observable results that we can excitedly anticipate there will be more. Perhaps there are, more or less, but the sum never seems to be as great as its parts. But when an innovation or technique falls out of favor, it is usually because, in the press for ever greater results, we push the idea so far that it becomes a parody of itself.

Consider the case of reengineering. Beginning in the late 1980s, such theorists as Michael Hammer and C. K. Prahalad helped popularize the planning and structural concepts we now know by that name. Obvious and immediate financial results could be achieved by reorganizing functional roles, flattening out hierarchies, and making "salary expense reductions"—that is, firing people. Terms like *downsizing* and *rightsizing* became part of our common parlance, not surprisingly about the same time that *outplacement* and *going postal* came into vogue. Wall Street loved the idea, and soon the merest rumor of a major layoff or divestiture could guarantee your company's stock price an appreciable bump. Companies like AT&T, in fact, so perfected the art that it became next to impossible to determine the true value of the corporation from its oft-manipulated stock price.

Yet the supposed reason for reengineering in the first place—long-term productivity and cost-efficiency—largely never materialized. No more than about 20 percent of the companies that jumped on the reengineering bandwagon ever realized the gains they had anticipated. And, of course, such gains as were seen came at an incalculable cost to the millions of American families who had suffered through a job loss and the countless others who had endured the very real threat of one.

Enter, stage right, the parodic version of reengineering in the person of Albert J. Dunlap. Chainsaw Al, as he liked to be called, became the darling of the "shareholder value" crowd by dismantling Scott Paper, firing thousands of employees, and selling the carcass to Kimberly Clark for a tidy profit. He proudly wrote of his slash-and-burn exploits in his book *Mean Business*, which we all then participated in making a best-seller. When lured to proud Sunbeam in 1996 by two of the company's investors, Chainsaw Al's one-note management style soon produced the firing of almost half of Sunbeam's twelve thousand employees and the sale or consolidation of three-fourths of its facilities. By 1997 Dunlap was declaring victory and looking for a buyer. But there was trouble, it seems. Sunbeam's 1997 profit figures had been exaggerated by a couple of accounting tricks and were not nearly so rosy as Dunlap had led Wall Street and his own investors to believe.[15] In addition, the notoriety he had achieved was resulting in some unwanted revelations about just who this poster-child of downsizing was at his core. It seems that the man who had promoted himself as the new paragon of American business had been too busy to attend the funerals of either of his parents, had denied his sister either emotional or financial support to deal with her daughter's leukemia, and had refused to contribute to the college education of his only son.[16] By mid-1998, Sunbeam's stock had lost 75 percent of its value, and Dunlap himself was finally fired, "his reputation shot and his stock options underwater."[17] Live by the chainsaw, die by the chainsaw.

It is this tendency of both the best and worst of the management fads to become caricatures of themselves that concerns me. If we take the notion of spirituality in the workplace for the inherently powerful motivational force that it is and give it room to grow in ourselves and permission to grow in others, we will see results very different from the motivational manipulations and superficial tinkerings of the typical management fads. But if we should ever consider spirituality to be a "tool" of greater productivity, I hate to speculate on what the equivalent of a "spiritual Al Dunlap" would be. To ever think of spirituality this way, or even start down that path, is to ask the wrong question. Seek *only* the narrow ends of efficiency, productivity, cost-effectiveness, and the like, and you may or may not get them. Moreover, the lesson of the last three decades is that you won't get them in a way that can be sustained long-term. But ask the right question—seek the higher purposes of transcendent meaning in what you do—and you not only will find the immense satisfactions that come from a more spiritual connection to your work but also may achieve those perfectly valid "business" goals as well. The chapters that follow will show you why.

If Not Here, Where? If Not Now, When?

The late Joseph Campbell had a wonderfully evocative image of the changes that have taken place in our society since the time of the Great Divorce. Imagine, he says, that you are on horseback approaching a city of the seventeenth century. You round a bend in the road, and there stretched before you is the outline of the city silhouetted against the setting sun. What do you see? The steeple of a church? The turret of a castle? The spire of a government hall? The institutions that dominated the skylines of our past also ruled our cultural psyche. The lives of the people who lived in that town would have revolved around, and been lived in fealty to, the church beneath that steeple, the government beneath that spire, and the powers of the existing social order.

When we approach the city of today and catch a first glimpse from the wheel of our automobile or the seat of our airliner, the landmarks of old are all but invisible against the skyline of our "gleaming towers of commerce," the temples of our modern lives. The skyscrapers of today's village—our corporations—have all but eclipsed the institutions of religion and government as the primary architects of cultural values. They don't simply provide us with our livelihoods; they give us our sense of security and coherence. Just listen to conversations these days, and see if talk of 401(k)'s, retirement plans, the economy, and the stock market hasn't supplanted talk of religion, government, or any other social institution as our sense-maker for the present and hope for the future. Our gods live in those towers.

Business today enjoys a status we once afforded only to political leadership, religious authority, or the social elite. Our icons are more likely to be Bill Gates or Warren Buffett than Dick Gephart or Billy Graham. The nonfiction best-seller list is full of books for and about business; whole sections of our daily newspapers and at least half a dozen cable channels provide an endless stream of news and views of our commercial life. The language of business has seeped into every pore of our intercourse, and its "bottom line" values (or perversions thereof) now rule significant aspects of even those churches, government bodies, and social organizations whose influence it displaced. Not to mention, of course, the *time* we are required to give to this all-powerful ruler of our modern culture—time spent in our working environments that used to go into the other institutions of our social and community life.

With this as our current reality, I am led to a conclusion that I cannot escape: *for any fundamental change in our society to occur—including a spiritual renewal—that change must go into and through business.* Our work and the institutions in which it is performed are simply too central to our lives and values for deep-seated cultural change to evolve without them. As M. Scott Peck has asserted, a better society is simply not possible unless the search for it is "instituted through our largest, best-organized, everyday institutions."[18] Real and enduring change must take root within those institutions that command our greatest respect and dominate our cultural psyche. Where we must begin is right where we are—not for two hours on Sunday or on the third Tuesday evening of each month—but day to day.

For those already attending to their spiritual lives in the workplace, or trying to, this point is old hat. It is apparent to them that the place where the bulk of their productive time and energy is spent would be an important, perhaps the most important, place for spiritual growth. If work does not provide that opportunity for them, then they would agree with James Autry that "we're wasting far too much of our lives on it."[19] For these individuals, the notion that God is not present in the workplace (or at least not one's own), or that a connection to such a higher power is not possible there, or that, if anything, we must tightly package our spiritual "leftovers" from some more religious environment and take them into the workplace like a bagged lunch, is simply a pernicious and heretical assumption that has ceased to work for them. Business, whose stock in trade is change, is of necessity the place where a transformative change in these attitudes must take place.

If Not You, Who?

The image of the hard-boiled, no-nonsense, wholly insensitive business executive is beginning to fade into memory. Not that there aren't a good many of them still around, of course, but in my consulting practice I will encounter managers like Steve and Anne (whom we met in Chapter Two) with much more frequency these days than I will the fire-breathing authoritarian who lumps religion and spirituality in there with other "touchy-feely stuff." To date, this change in the prototypical executive has manifested itself mostly in terms of outer behaviors: managers who are more approachable than elitist, more encouraging than critical, more adaptable than dogmatic. But there's quite a chasm between exhibiting outward behavior and truly bringing one's authentic self to work, the bridging of which consists principally in (1) seeing the benefit of doing so, (2) giving oneself permission, and (3) overcoming the accumulated cultural learnings of the past few centuries that lead us to think that bridging that gap is somehow wrong. There is some evidence, however, that executives in business and not-for-profit organizations might be just the people most capable of accomplishing this task— a field ripe for harvest, in biblical terms.

In the first place, as surprising as it might seem, executives are significantly more religious than the general population, according to a survey by *Forbes* magazine.[20] More important, their religious orientation seems to be more active and internal, as opposed to the "see and be seen" motivations of typical extrinsic religiosity.[21] To what this may be attributed is not entirely clear, but it is evident that many of the brightest, best-educated, and financially secure among us have turned their attentions inward, where they have found that a true spirituality of work may blossom.

Business managers are also notoriously committed to their own growth and development. If they are lacking a skill base, they're the first to take a course. If their performance is subpar, well, they will immediately take corrective action. Should they find themselves with a few extra pounds or their HDLs too low, they're the first ones to the health club, whether or not they really enjoy exercise. Don't misunderstand; this is not about using the spiritual life as an aid for climbing the corporate ladder. But it does mean that if business executives can see the benefit of the Congruent Life, they are more likely to give themselves *permission* to make that a personal priority and will tend to put more energy behind it than others would. What's more, business executives tend to have more disposable energy to give—not time, mind you, but the psychological energy that allows them to use the time they have to the maximum productive extent.

What heartens me about the future of spirituality in the workplace is the knowledge that if executives can truly understand its implications, see its potentiality, and give themselves and others permission to live the Congruent Life more fully, then we will see one of those situations, wonderful and rare, in which a change in only a few people can work a change for a great many others. The most powerful people in our corporations, after all, control 70 to 80 percent of the *productive* time of the vast majority of working-age adults and all but a small percentage of the world's economy. The exponential effect of such a change of heart—or spirit—could be profound.

And a sea change has indeed begun. It's visible in the writings of retired business leaders such as Max De Pree and Rolf Osterberg, and in the enlightened management style of such executives as Lynn Draper of American Electric Power and the late Wayne Calloway of Pepsico. You can see it in the managers and executives who flock to the High Impact Leadership Seminar of Staub-Peterson Leadership Consultants, which explicitly emphasizes the spiritual side of leadership. It's evident in the Shalem Institute's two-year study program called the Soul of the Executive, which drew to its very first class in 1998 some thirty senior people from organizations around the United States and Canada seeking a long-term spiritual framework for their organizational leadership. Says Shalem's Carole Crumley: "Many of our executives are looking for ways of deepening their own soul's growth, knowing that this is what they take into the working environment; others are seeking practical ways of being spiritual at work. Whatever needs they bring to the program, there is a strong desire to be with others who understand the many demands made on executive leadership and yet share their yearning for the things of the spirit."

For this nascent brand of executive, our traditional understandings of organizational leadership must seem almost comically naive. We teach "managerial competencies" in our business schools, as if anyone with enough brain power to learn a set of skills has the wherewithal to run an organization. We preach "visionary leadership" without asking from whence one gets a vision in the first place. We speak of "emotional IQ" and of bringing the heart as well as the head to the task of effective leadership, yet we remain reticent to talk of a still more powerful and integrative part of our humanity. The poverty of our ideas about leadership, and the way to enrich them, is forcefully put this way by Peter Vaill:

> The pervasiveness of spirituality means that the ideas we have about leadership, management, organizing, and facilitating change are *incomplete* to the extent that they do not recognize the spiritual basis of working with human beings. They are *inadequate* in times of change to the extent that they do not recognize this spiritual basis, and they are simply *wrong* if they try to argue that the spiritual condition of the people involved is of no importance to the way things proceed. And . . . I mean wrong for all time—wrong as long as there have been human beings involved, because spiritual *feeling* is such a significant part of what it is to be a human being.[22]

In-Spired Leadership

There are qualities essential to leadership that are not learned, at least in the way we commonly conceive of learning. Vision, commitment, creativity, enthusiasm—such qualities are not determined by what a person knows but by who that person *is*. And it is the connection to the life of the spirit—what we are calling the Congruent Life—that molds and shapes who we essentially *are* at our core.

We have seen how the realities of life in the New Economy, the need for a credible new mythology of work, the rising tide of employee expectations, and the need for a new species of work incentives have readied us for a redefinition of our relationship to work, business, and organizational life—one that takes into account our widest circles of meaning and our deepest wellsprings of purpose. And we have seen that it is the institutions and people of business that stand best able to lead this cultural reorientation. What remains, both to encourage the seeker and convince the skeptic, is to show how *a genuine spirituality seems to produce, over time, characteristics that are not only desirable personal qualities but traits highly valued in today's business environment—the "fruits" of a spiritual life.* Such is the task of the next three chapters.

Questions and Exercises for Further Reflection

1. Do you watch much television? If you do, think about the characters in the shows you enjoy (or perhaps characters in movies to whom you find yourself relating) and their relationship to their jobs. What do they say about your own personal mythology of work? What do they say about your coping mechanisms related to work?

2. Think about your own work environment. What are the ways in which it values externality and extraversion at the expense of the values of the inner life? How well are such behaviors as reflection, listening, silence, intuition, and the like encouraged or fostered? Are you yourself guilty of discouraging them—in yourself or others?

3. Where does economism rule supreme in your life? What decisions do you make or support based on consideration of economic factors only? What other factors could you take into account in those situations if you were so disposed? Is there something in your mythology of life and work that tells you that you shouldn't consider those factors?

Part Three

Psychospiritual Growth and Organizational Leadership

Chapter Six

The "Fruits of the Spirit"

By their fruits you will know them.
MATTHEW 7:20 (NKJV)

We have accumulated many sayings over the years that stand for the basic notion that the behaviors we exhibit are more important than high-sounding words or pleasing appearances. You know the ones I'm talking about: "You can't judge a book by its cover," "Actions speak louder than words," "Pretty is as pretty does," "The proof is in the pudding." You could doubtless add many more. But none is more direct than the admonition Jesus had for his disciples. His consistent message was that you could tell the quality of people not by their rank or title nor even by their status in the community. No, you would know them by their "fruits"—the observable results of the kind of assiduous devotion to God's will that Jesus preached and seemed to live every day, even unto death.

In this and the next two chapters we are going to explore the modern context for that advice. We know, after all, that there are tremendous differences between people in their capacity to exhibit love, patience, forgiveness, and a rainbow of other admirable human traits. Even more clearly, we can see in our organizational lives vast differences in the ability to model important qualities such as tolerance, empathy, and creativity. What we will find is that such traits and characteristics are largely the fruit of a process of growth and maturity that has been scientifically studied and given conceptual form in such a way that we can now understand it.

Moreover, the development of a strong interior life, as we have described it in the preceding chapters, can deepen and accelerate this process of growth and maturity in substantial and identifiable ways.

In one sense, this but confirms what our religious traditions have been telling us for centuries: that the dynamic process of spiritual growth can, over time, literally produce "new" men and women possessed of heroic human traits they may scarcely have thought possible before. It also echoes what depth psychology has been telling us over the past century about the process of individuation (discussed in Chapter Three). Jung called this process "a religious orientation" for good reason: spiritual growth and individuation are, if not two words for the same thing, closely interrelated. And with both there exists the potential for remarkable personal transformation and the development of exceptional human character.

What is different, now, is that we might just be ready for the first time in our history to apply what we know about human growth and development to business and organizational life. We can observe that people in business and elsewhere who are committed to a genuine spiritual path and who make honest (if faltering) attempts to bring its wisdom to bear on their work and relationships, exhibit behaviors that distinguish them from many of their peers. The need has never been greater than it is right now for us to understand why that happens, and how we can apply that understanding to our own lives and organizations.

Growing Up After You're a Grown-Up: Adult Developmental Theory

Although it may seem apparent that adults vary widely in their psychological and emotional maturity—and thus in their behavior—our scientific understanding of the reasons for those differences has lagged behind. Until very recently, the mention of the term *human development* to a trained psychologist would conjure up only his learning on childhood and adolescent development, as if observable human growth ended when one reached physical maturity. As late as 1990, there was still no journal devoted to lifelong development, no integrated body of research, and no accepted place for the topic in most university psychology departments.[1]

This dearth of knowledge on so important a topic began to change, if slowly, with the work of American psychologist Lawrence Kohlberg. Along with a handful of other researchers, he began to expand on the ideas of influential Swiss psychologist Jean Piaget, who had posited identifiable stages of development in children and adolescents. Kohlberg went significantly beyond Piaget's framework, however, by advancing a theory of human development that extended (or at least *could* extend) well into adulthood. Kohlberg's approach was cognitive; it focused on differences in moral reasoning ability rather than on issues of behavior. Yet despite the admitted limitations of the theory (which all theories have), it gave us a credible way of seeing human growth and development that helps explain the differences we *know* are there. Moreover, Kohlberg's "way of seeing" (which is what *theoria* means in Greek) adult development provided the conceptual framework for the more generalized research by others that followed.

There have since been a number of proposed modifications to Kohlberg's original theory, many of which have gained wide acceptance, and his framework of developmental stages has continued to undergo refinement as warranted by subsequent research. A number of theorists have also proposed quite different terminology for the identifiable stages. For our purposes, however, we will stick largely to Kohlberg in order to gain a broad understanding of the process of "growing up" as a grown-up.

Kohlberg identified three levels of cognitive development, each containing two stages. Now, a word of caution before we start throwing around words like *level* and *stage*. Human development is a dynamic process that follows a unique course within each individual. It is anything but predictable, subject to life situations and traumas that can arrest the process as well as graced moments of insight that can accelerate it. The six billion or so individuals who inhabit our planet each cannily avoids absolute classifications and is quite unlikely to consistently exhibit only the characteristics of one particular stage.

That said, it is still possible to make generalized statements about the differences between people at various levels of development.

Moreover, enough research has now been conducted that we can confidently state that the stages are, as postulated by Kohlberg, "sequential and invariant." That is, we do approach the stages of human development in a certain intractable order, and it is impossible to skip one along the way. Perhaps it would be better to call them frames of reference, for with the passage of each stage our world gets progressively bigger. Like the concentric circles we discussed in Chapter Two, each succeeding frame of reference contains all the possibilities of the previous stages but also all the new alternatives of the next.

In stage 1 in Kohlberg's scheme (sometimes called the Impulsive stage) one sees the world in terms of the gratification of one's own basic needs and the avoidance of personal harm. This is the stage of the very young child, who obeys rules and authority solely as a means of avoiding punishment. It is extremely egocentric, focused almost exclusively on personal needs and wants at the expense of the interests of others. If one were to arrest at this stage, as have many of the inhabitants of our jails and penitentiaries, one would be practically incapable of having a normal social and organizational life.

People at stage 2 become capable of assessing the needs of others and will occasionally satisfy them, but usually only as a means of getting what they want themselves. It is a sort of "you scratch my back and I'll scratch yours" mentality, where an instrumental and "fair" exchange trumps any consideration of altruism or duty to others. Although this stage is usually negotiated between ages seven and twelve, we will find that there is a small but disturbing percentage of business managers who score within this level of development. Together, stages 1 and 2 constitute Kohlberg's Preconventional level of development. Incapable of either self-reflection or insight into others, people at this level live in a world that typically extends no farther than the limits of their own self and its needs.

The Conventional level, so named because it comports with our normal societal expectations of others, begins with stage 3, or the Conformist stage. Exhibiting the typical adolescent mentality, the person at this stage becomes concerned about other people and their feelings and expectations. Relationships become all-important, involving the person's family, one hopes, but inevitably (as all parents of teenagers know) with a relatively small peer group whose opinions are highly valued. The norms of family or peers become internalized, and what is "good" or "right" is largely measured against that standard.

As the concentric circles continue to widen, a person who progresses to stage 4 (sometimes called the Conscientious stage) begins to internalize the values of the larger society in which he or she lives. Relationships with peers continue to be important, of course, but they are supplanted in their primacy by the person's conception of his or her role and duty in society. There is an emphasis on laws, rules, and perceived obligations. Kohlberg felt that no more than 20 percent of the American population ever progressed beyond stage 4, but subsequent research paints an even less optimistic picture. In a study of nearly two thousand subjects ranging in age from eleven to eighty-four, 91 percent scored at stage 4 or *below* on a frequently used indicator of developmental level.[2]

Those who do move beyond a Conventional to a "Postconventional" mentality experience a qualitative leap in their personal frame of reference, a radical widening of their world. The values of society remain important, but an increased capacity for reflection allows the person at stage 5 to step back and critically examine both his or her own values and those of society. Inherent in this stage is the possibility of going beyond a duty-oriented mentality to become a truly autonomous moral entity. "The crucial new element," according to one researcher, "is generativity, the commitment to generate a meaningful life for oneself through self-determination, self-actualization, and self-definition—the hallmarks of an autonomous person."[3]

Kohlberg himself never fully articulated the qualities of a stage 6 individual, perhaps because there are so few of them, perhaps because we find it difficult to describe that which we do not personally know. We will come back to this stage—considered by some to be the terminus of adult development—later in this chapter. Suffice for now this description from James W. Fowler's book *Stages of Faith:*

> Stage 6 is exceedingly rare. . . . Living with felt participation in a power that unifies and transforms the world, [people in stage 6] are often experienced as subversive of the structures (including

religious structures) by which we sustain our individual and corporate survival, security and significance. Many persons at this stage die at the hands of those whom they hope to change. [They] are often more honored and revered after death than during their lives. The rare persons who may be described by this stage have a special grace that makes them seem more lucid, more simple, and yet more fully human than the rest of us.[4]

Kohlberg's research experience led him to believe that we become attracted to the next level of development as we begin to move toward it. We've probably all had the experience of greatly admiring someone with whom we work or otherwise interact—the person just seems to "have it all together." Chances are, that person embodies for us the qualities and outlook of the next stage of adult development, and through emulation of his or her example we have already started on the path toward the next step. Interestingly, however, Kohlberg also found that we could not comprehend the reasoning of a person more than one stage beyond our own. That person's worldview and ours are just too different. Perhaps this partially explains our historical knack for killing those people who attain the highest levels of human growth.

Once we have achieved a broader frame of reference, there is no way to go back to a prior stage—our world has been unalterably changed. However, although our perceptions of ourselves and our environment may have been broadened, that does not always translate into our observable behavior. In this sense, we are subject to "regressions" all the time. This is just part of the nature of these concentric circles of growth—each succeeding stage transcends, but includes, the concerns, qualities, and point of view of the preceding stages, and we are simply incapable in our humanity of acting consistently and invariably from the highest place within us. More frighteningly, studies suggest that developmental level is a better predictor of behavior in personal and family settings than it is in the work environment.[5] Apparently, one of the enduring effects of the Great Divorce is that many of us feel the need to "dumb down" our level of maturity in order to succeed in organizational life.

And what are the factors that prompt us to move from one stage of development to another? Kohlberg observed that movement takes place only after our prevailing worldview becomes inadequate to deal with the challenges life presents us. Striking examples can probably be found on kindergarten playgrounds every day, as egocentric children who have never had to share anything in their lives get decked by the classmate who won't take "it's *my* toy" for an answer (striking indeed!). The selfishness of the stage 1 Impulsive soon gives way to the marketplace mentality of the stage 2. More tragic, how many stage 3 Conformists, whether adults or teenagers, find out only too late that unquestioned loyalty to the values of a small group can get you arrested, or worse?

In understanding how movement to a higher stage takes place, perhaps we can better understand why so few people ever transcend the Conventional level of development: society and its institutions provide little incentive for people to go beyond their vested interests, and certainly no penalty for failing to. Absent the moral upheaval of a Vietnam War or national desegregation, individuals must find within themselves the will and the need to grow beyond the conventional norms and expectations of the larger society—to fully individuate. Fortunately, there are some who do.

A Developmental Model of Work and Leadership

As we might expect, the frame of reference in which we find ourselves at any given point in life can profoundly influence our approach to work and our abilities to manage others. An organization run by a Mother Teresa would be expected to be very different from one run by a slash-and-burn downsizer like Chainsaw Al Dunlap. *M*A*S*H*'s* "Hawkeye" Pierce would make a very different colleague than Archie Bunker. Adult development theory helps us understand why.

William Torbert of Boston College, along with his colleague Dalmar Fisher, has given us the clearest explanation yet of the work-related traits and characteristics endemic to each developmental stage.[6] Although much more research needs to be done in this area, I find their conclusions compelling. I also find them enormously useful in my work with business executives, not only because they provide valuable insight into the reasons for certain work-related behaviors but also because they provide a reliable map for the future growth and development of people for whom such growth becomes a priority. With that in mind, let's look at the work and leadership behaviors associated with the identifiable stages of development.

The Impulsive

Torbert and Fisher spend very little time talking about the stage 1 Impulsive, mostly because their research focuses on people at management and supervisory levels, and no Impulsives were found there. It is certainly true that genuine Impulsives would find it difficult to survive for very long in most mature corporations—their behavior is just too self-serving. But there are probably more Impulsives populating our workforce, and even running entrepreneurial companies, than we would like to admit.

Impulsives are primarily interested in fulfilling their personal needs, either directly or through the agency of others. They may be adept at using power and coercion to meet those needs and are largely heedless of the effect. They might be quite pleasant and charming to talk to, but invariably the subtext has to do with meeting some immediate personal desire. Their time horizon is exceptionally short, and they are almost incapable of self-denial or sacrifice in order to achieve some longer-term good. They reject negative feedback out of hand and are usually adept at avoiding even self-criticism, preferring instead to ignore or rationalize past failures. As one researcher has pointed out, they may be able intellectually to talk like those at higher stages, but their automatic and unconscious responses are still governed by their exceedingly narrow frame of reference.[7] Impulsives view work only as a necessary evil, and they would certainly not work if they could help it. If the picture of Archie Bunker propped up in his recliner comes to mind, you are not alone.

The Opportunist

This is the name given by Fisher and Torbert to the person at Kohlberg's stage 2. Opportunists share with Impulsives a focus on self as the center of the universe, but they can also develop a pronounced manipulative quality as they seek to get ahead in the zero-sum game that is their version of life. The 5 percent or so of business managers who are at this stage must be very difficult to work for. They are exceedingly concrete and rationalistic, which can make them quite capable in dealing with financial concerns and issues of productivity and efficiency. They may also be good at understanding and wielding hierarchial power. But they pay a heavy cost for the narrowness of their frame when it comes to issues requiring the delicate weighing of other important values or an appreciation for shades of gray. Their proposed solutions can thus sometimes be overly simplistic. If something goes wrong, they will generally find a way to blame something other than themselves (subordinates being a favorite target) and will reject negative feedback about their performance. They will be objectively "fair" in their dealings with others from whom they expect the same kind of treatment—indeed, this is *the* stage of the quid pro quo. But woe be unto you if the Opportunist does not see you as a potential trading partner. Then anything he or she can get away with is viewed as both legal and moral. Opportunists see the workplace as a highly competitive, cutthroat place where they must gain as much hegemony over others as possible in order to control their future security and meet their needs. Work is self-sacrifice, something that one must do in order to get something in return.

Notice something very basic here, which will be applicable throughout our discussion. It is not that decisions are not sometimes black and white or that in the context of business, decisions must sometimes be made solely on financial or other objective considerations. The difference is that the Opportunist's frame of reference is so delimiting that he or she has no other basis on which to make such a decision. Later stages may aptly be called *higher* for precisely this reason: the person at a subsequent stage of development can appreciate the concerns and the logic employed by the Opportunist but has the capacity to *choose* to act from a broader perspective when the situation calls for it. Dilbert's pointy-haired boss, in contrast, can't seem to help but be the way he is: his small view of the world gives him no real choice.

The Diplomat

Corresponding to Kohlberg's stage 3, the Diplomat has made a significant advance in his or her frame of reference. The values and opinions of others have now become important—so important that Diplomats will largely fashion their self-image around the approval of a certain core group. As the name implies, interpersonal skills now move center stage, with the emphasis being on those that lead to harmony, civility, and social approval. The studies reported by Torbert and Fisher indicate that 5 percent of the senior managers, 9 percent of the junior managers, and fully 24 percent of the first-line supervisors surveyed fall into this category.

Taking nothing away from the Diplomat's advancement beyond pure egocentricity, this frame is fraught with potential dangers. Conformity to group values and demands is the chosen currency of this stage, and Diplomats will go to great lengths to avoid both inner and outer conflict. They are also unlikely to seek out negative feedback, which makes them quite blind to contrary opinions lurking beneath the placid environments they seek to create around them.

This stage is typified by a young go-getter friend of mine who had just begun his first job. When he announced over lunch one day that he had decided to vote for a particularly sleazy political candidate, whose views I knew to be at odds with his own, I asked him why in the world he would do such a thing. He replied, almost boastfully, that his boss was an ardent supporter of the scumbag. At this stage of development, loyalty overcomes principle with disturbing regularity. I think we can speculate that much the same mentality was afoot on the trading floors of Drexel Burnham Lambert and the laboratories of Phillip Morris when they made their determinations that Mike Milken was terrific and cigarettes were safe.

The Technician

The Technician is in a transition phase between Kohlberg's stages 3 and 4. People in this frame of reference have ceased to define themselves solely in terms of the norms of a small group but are not yet embedded in the norms of the larger society. In fact, Technicians tend to define themselves—often with a vengeance—in terms of what makes them stand out from the group. They commonly accomplish this by developing an area of skill or expertise in which they feel they can excel.

You might anticipate that there are some people in businesses and organizations who have arrested at this level of development.

What might surprise you is that in the several studies done by Fisher and Torbert there are always more Technicians among the managers and supervisors surveyed than any other type. You can doubtless think of a number of your colleagues who exhibit a predominance of Technician characteristics. Dogmatic, perfectionistic, and rigidly logical, Technicians generally feel there is only one right answer to any problem. Owing to their need to stand out from the crowd, they can be disdainful of authority and bureaucracy but will be unswervingly obedient to those whom they see as having superior skill and know-how in their chosen area of expertise. They are unlikely to be good team players because of their perfectionism and their tendency to be hypercritical, and when placed in management positions they can often foster cultures that are full of stress and unproductive competition. They can be quite competent in the performance of their objective tasks but encounter trouble when asked to manage others for the first time.

Judith, one of my favorite coaching clients, tested at this level when she was first referred to me. Bright and experienced, she had been brought in by a very large and conservative regional bank to head their credit card marketing operation. She was technically a wonderful fit for the job and was personally responsible for adding several million dollars to the bank's bottom line in her first year. But problems soon arose in her relationships with subordinates. The high standards she set for herself and others were often unachievable, and her way of communicating her dissatisfaction must have seemed like a thermonuclear explosion when compared to the staid, civil environment that had always been the norm. "Judy just runs over people," "It's her way or the highway," and "We just don't treat people like that around here" were typical of comments I'd hear from her subordinates. To make matters worse, her superiors saw her as disdainful of established procedures and protocols—the "way things are done around here." The end result was that despite her considerable abilities and financial successes, she was failing as a manager.

Employers are always interested, first and foremost, in having executive coaches "fix" the behaviors of their managers, but it was clear from the outset that Judith's situation was not that simple. Hers was not just a behavioral issue but a developmental one. The staid, civil, and conservative environment in which she operated was that way primarily because it was heavily populated by Diplomats.

It was quite apparent that she was practically surrounded by people for whom conflict was anathema and politeness the ultimate virtue. Her style, both creative and disruptive at once, was clearly not welcome there. With awareness and practice she could (and did) modify those aspects of her behavior that truly ran counter to the goals she was trying to accomplish. But for her to be authentically herself *and* truly succeed in that environment would require a long-term developmental process that would begin to move her toward the next stage. As I write this, Judy is well along that path, albeit with another employer.

The Achiever

For Judith, progression toward the next level of adult development holds the promise of resolving some of her current work-related issues. Achievers are very goal oriented but are capable of taking a much more long-range view than those at prior stages. They value effectiveness in the pursuit of goals and results much more than mere technical efficiency and are able to recognize and allow for exceptions and contingencies. They have a deep sense of responsibility, which can sometimes make them appear excessively duty bound, but they are keenly aware of the consequences of their actions and may go to significant lengths to avoid hurting others. They are conscientious, they show initiative, and they think of themselves as originators rather than pawns. In their interpersonal relationships they encourage mutuality rather than hierarchy, foster the creativity of others, and are accepting of personal feedback, at least where it's seen as helping them toward their goals.

Although very few first-line supervisors score at this level, somewhere around 40 percent of managers and executives do. As you can tell from the preceding description, that is largely a good thing, both for the Achievers and the people who work for and around them. But there is a catch. Most Achievers are so ensconced in their frame of reference that they are incapable of seeing it as a frame at all—it's just "the way the world is." They are rather like the fish that doesn't "know" it's in water unless and until it's pulled out of it. Achievers therefore believe their view of the world to be wholly objective and rational and are unable to see how individual and subjective it really is. Thus the dual nature of their response to negative feedback from others: they will readily accept it if they can acknowledge fault and can see corrective action as something that will further their goals; they will reject it or rationalize it away if it threatens their well-constructed view of themselves and "the way things are."

An experience that takes off the Achiever's blinders and exposes the narrowness of his or her worldview can be thoroughly disorienting. I've seen that happen any number of times at good, process-oriented executive development courses. But while such experiences can be unsettling and unpleasant, they may just be necessary for someone to advance beyond the Achiever stage. After all, with so few managers going beyond this level of development, there aren't many role models out there. Studies say that no more than 10 percent of even the most senior people in organizations, and less from lower levels, move beyond the Achiever stage.[8] And that fact, for any person interested in the future of our business and nonprofit organizations, is perhaps the most disturbing aspect of this line of research.

The Strategist and Beyond

In his classic book *Leadership,* historian and political scientist James MacGregor Burns postulated that it was from among those individuals who moved to Postconventional levels of adult development that our future political leaders would be recruited.[9] Twenty years after that book was written, we can go further and say that if our organizations are to profit and prosper in the twenty-first century, their leadership must be recruited from among those ranks as well. The reasons have to do with the substantial and fundamental differences in the way Postconventional personalities view themselves, others, and organizational life, and with their ability to grasp and actualize the transcendent meanings of work and leadership of which we first spoke in Chapter Two.

The Strategist is the name given by Torbert and Fisher to a person who has attained a Postconventional, stage 5 level of development. It is only at this stage that a manager begins to see that his or her frame of reference is but an outgrowth of personality and life experiences and that there thus may be other, equally valid points of view. Aware of their own frames as well as those of others around them, Strategists can develop the ability to "speak the language" of others they encounter in the workplace, understanding their individual perspectives. Strategists do not avoid conflicts but creatively manage them by honoring disparate points of view while still accepting the role they may have as a decision maker. Strategists are process oriented as well as goal oriented and can slide in and out of a variety of workplace roles with relative ease. They understand and accept paradox and contradiction as part of the fabric of reality rather than as ambiguities to be stamped out. Strategists still have dark sides, of course, but their increased capacity for self-reflection allows them to be aware of their shadows—perhaps even to modify them.

The shift in center that goes on at this stage is perhaps even more dramatic than the earlier shift from the pure egocentrism of the Preconventional level to the outer orientation of the Conventional. Although the concerns of the self, group, and society remain important, the Strategist's center of gravity shifts from conventional rules and roles to self-chosen principles and values. Strategists, perhaps over a period of years, become autonomous people with individually adopted value systems that help them give shape and meaning to the world around them. Unlike people at earlier stages, however, Strategists understand this adopted frame of reference to be just that, and they control that frame, rather than the other way around. Strategists see that they *have* a frame of reference, but they are not so embedded in it that they cannot see past it.

It is primarily at this stage that people move beyond achievement and ambition to more transcendent meanings of work. The single-minded pursuit of goals gives way to the need for personal fulfillment; the striving for linear progress is modified by insight and self-acceptance; the commitment to career may continue, but Strategists no longer measure themselves solely with that yardstick. The center is now occupied not by self or others but by the values and principles that are "the ultimate" in that person's life, by whatever religious or philosophical terms those values and principles may be described.

The importance of people at this level of development to modern organizations cannot be overestimated, regardless of where in the hierarchy they may be found. These are the people capable of developing the skills critical to the future of any enterprise. Prime among these are the ability to react flexibly and fluidly to a rapidly changing environment, the ability to reframe and reconceptualize issues, and a preference for empowerment and collaborative solutions. These were just the managerial and leadership skills that distinguished the Strategist from all other frames in a 1987 study.[10]

We all know that in the turbulent world of the New Economy, what made for success and stability in the past no longer works for many companies and organizations. "Nothing fails like success," the adage-turned-on-its-ear now goes, meaning simply that businesses that insist on walking into the future with the same strategies and assumptions that served them in the past may be walking off a cliff. Just ask the management of any of the thousands of companies that, in only the last few years, have failed, been acquired, or forced to radically restructure in order to stay afloat. Such dinosaurs have what Fisher and Torbert term *systematic productivity:* they take their standards, structures, and roles for granted, have highly normed procedures for accomplishing predefined tasks, and typically measure their success in terms of quantifiable, short-term results. Systematic productivity is no longer enough.

In practically all segments of our society, even in nonprofit entities, there is a growing realization that organizations run in this way cannot adequately predict or plan for future trends, cannot creatively locate and exploit market advantages, and cannot successfully negotiate the turbulent times that inevitably lie ahead. As we will discuss more fully in Chapter Nine, the organization of the future must find its identity "less in its current structure than in its capacity for restructuring."[11] Its measures of success must go beyond the quantitative to embrace both the short-term profitability and long-term legitimacy of the company, and its strategic process must become more open, explicit, and truly empowering of others in the enterprise.

Achievers can operate very effectively in an organization that has developed to the stage of systematic productivity. Their goal orientation, sense of responsibility, interpersonal skills, and focus on results make them perfectly adequate managers in many mature, stable companies. But only Strategists have the capacity to develop the skills necessary to take a company beyond systematic productivity to become the organization of the future. Only Strategists have the ability to reframe themselves as they are reframing the organization's mission, strategy, and structure. It is the Strategist who has the far greater capacity for ambiguity and stress, a greater desire for collaborative action and empowerment, and a greater facility for seeing multiple perspectives and applying multiple logics. Most important, perhaps, the Strategist's center is located in something far more immutable than our human groups or our own egos, which gives to the Strategist an uncommon strength in turbulent times. They are as essential as they are rare.

Business Managers as Developing Human Beings: One Company's Experience

June Jackson is just one of those people who intuitively understands developmental theory. A mid-level manager with a division of a major telecommunications company, she had been selected to participate in its Future Leaders program, essentially fast-tracking her for a potential leadership role. But her interest in the whole process of executive development was so clear to her superiors that she was soon given the task of examining and evaluating the whole program, looking for ways in which it might be improved.

This led to our meeting in 1995. She had done a lot of reading on leadership and, like many others, was a bit bewildered by the numerous definitions of leadership and the countless traits and qualities that were supposed to embody it. Yet she knew what she knew: there were vast and identifiable differences in the people around her in terms of their abilities to move the company and its people forward in a positive direction. There just seemed to be no way to capture what those differences were.

When we began to work together, we started with an exhaustive list of the qualities and traits that the company itself, in one pronouncement or another, had indicated were valued work-related characteristics. These ranged all over the place, from respect for others to strategic thinking to continuous learning. But on closer examination there emerged three distinct categories. There were "organizational" skills and competencies—such things as understanding technology, being results oriented, accepting responsibility, and being dedicated to customers—which were very important if you hoped to be successful at practically any job in the company. There were probably an equal number of "interpersonal" abilities, such as listening and communication skills, team-building abilities, diplomacy, empowerment, and the capacity to motivate others. These were particularly important if your role in the organization called for you to manage others.

But then there was a third category, which for lack of a better term we labeled "inner-personal." This category included such qualities as integrity, self-knowledge, optimism, vision, courage, and creativity. They weren't directly related to task competency or even to the technical aspects of managing other people. They were simply qualities that set that person apart from the normal run—the kinds of traits that would make you admire that person, want to work with her, be willing to be led by her.

Against this backdrop, a pattern began to emerge. Everyone at June's level in the organization, whether they managed people or worked alone in some highly technical area, had the organizational skills we had listed. If they didn't, they were pretty quickly gone. But there was much less consistency within the company when it came to interpersonal skills. Some people were truly masters at dealing with coworkers and subordinates, exhibiting most or all of the characteristics on our list. Others were clearly less adept. Some of those with weak interpersonal skills were older, more tenured managers who ruled their areas through fear and intimidation; others were younger employees who had excelled in some technical field but were now struggling when put in positions of authority over others.

The reason for the disparity soon became clear: in reading the descriptors of managers at early stages of adult development, one could see that they corresponded very well with many of the traits and characteristics of June's colleagues who, although technically proficient, were perfectly lousy in their interpersonal skills. By the same token, the more the manager seemed to match the traits of the Achiever, the more their 360-degree feedback results revealed harmonious and constructive relationships with subordinates and others. Without intending it, I had just replicated the results of the budding research in this area, which seems clearly to stand for the proposition that dependable task accomplishment (our "organizational" skills) is accessible to any level of adult development but that collaborative and interpersonal skills are significantly more prevalent in those who have attained the higher, Conventional levels.[12]

The next logical step was not a difficult one to make. It was true that those qualities in our inner-personal category were not the exclusive province of any one person or group in the corporation. But it was also abundantly clear that there were a few managers, whom June could call by name, who seemed more consistently to embody those traits and whose lives, both in and outside the work environment, seemed permeated with those qualities. They were mature, seasoned, balanced individuals who garnered not only the respect of those around them but their admiration and even their affection. They seemed a little more wise, a little more caring, and a little more authentically themselves than the rest of us. And the various descriptions in the literature of the personality at the Postconventional level—the stage 5 Strategist and beyond—fit these individuals to a tee. The model of leadership development that thus emerged looked something like Figure 6.1.

Movement along the continuum toward higher levels of adult development results in at least an increased capacity for the maturation of skills and competencies beyond the organizational. Moreover, just as more advanced developmental frames subsume and include the concerns and perspectives of the less advanced frames, so too do they subsume the work-related traits and characteristics of those lower frames. So, while a stage 2 Opportunist

Figure 6.1.

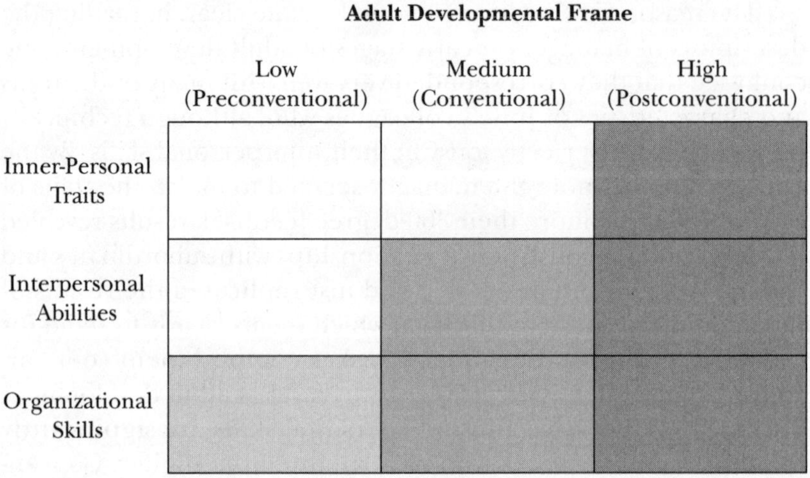

Adult Developmental Frame

	Low (Preconventional)	Medium (Conventional)	High (Postconventional)
Inner-Personal Traits			
Interpersonal Abilities			
Organizational Skills			

might be able to develop only the organizational skills valued by the company, the stage 4 Achiever could be expected to have some capacity for competency in both the interpersonal and organizational realms. But it is at the higher stages of development, the Strategist and beyond, that we would begin to experience the full spectrum of traits and characteristics essential for leadership.

In 1995 the implications of this understanding for June's corporation were large indeed. If there were ever a monolithic company locked in systematic productivity, this was it. Hierarchial, bureaucratic, slow to react, and hard to steer, this company was facing unrelenting pressure from a variety of new and old competitors, was up against an uncertain regulatory (or, more aptly, *de*regulatory) environment, and had uneasy shareholders clamoring for more aggressive actions to bolster market prices. Yet, as subsequent testing would show, the company's management was heavily populated with stage 4 Achievers. Although several fairly young managers seemed clearly to be in transition toward stage 5, less than 8 percent of the total sample tested conclusively at that level. The management team for June's division clearly saw that a viable future lay only in progressing from systematic productivity to a more fluid and strategic style. The company's task now was to give the next generation of the company's leadership—people like June Jackson—the support and resources necessary to provide them with every opportunity to grow into the Strategist frame of reference. Without a critical mass of them doing so, the day would surely be lost.

The story does not have a happy ending. Four months after we began our project, the company's CEO announced a massive corporate reorganization, complete with the divestiture of major parts of the company's core business and an accompanying loss of thousands of jobs. The typical angst and uncertainty soon set in, along with the inevitable funding cuts for "nonessentials" like executive development. Today, more than 80 percent of the managers we worked with in June's division are gone, lost to early retirement, reorganizations, or spin-offs. June Jackson's insights and the determined support of her management team were not enough to stop the death and dismemberment of this particular dinosaur. It will be up to companies a little more ahead of the curve to pick up where they left off.

The Role of the Inner Life

Research over the years has shown us that individuals at later stages of adult development are indeed capable of behaviors that we associate with good management and leadership skills. They have better conceptual tools for making sense of the world and a more developed sense of conceptual complexity.[13] Their thinking is more abstract but also more precise and specific.[14] They are more likely to accept responsibility for their actions, empathize with others, and tolerate higher levels of stress and uncertainty.[15] They are simply more *aware:* of themselves, of their assumptions, prejudices, and shadows, and of the differing perspectives and interests of others.

But higher-stage individuals also share an attribute that is both an effect and a cause of the integration they have achieved in their lives. To stay with the metaphor of our chapter title for a moment, it is an attribute that is both the "fruit" of their higher development and a force that helps to "ripen" them in their growth and maturity. It is the inner, spiritual life of which we spoke in Chapter Three. Remember what we said there: the Copernican revolution that takes place within us dislodges the ego from its central place in our private little world as we *open* ourselves to a higher influence and *acknowledge* its primacy. This is precisely the process that takes place as one moves to a Postconventional frame of reference. In the words of one researcher, the awareness achieved at the later stages "includes the expectation and experience of transcendence" as one's worldview goes from merely "logical" to "metaphysical."[16] To use the language of more traditional religion, when our personal center becomes grounded in Ultimate Reality, we become open to its influences and even to a much more real and direct experience of it. To move beyond the Conventional view of the world is to embrace a fundamentally larger view of reality that, at least for a great many people, includes the idea of a transcendent force alive and at work in the universe. And with that realization—that acknowledgment—comes the desire to *align* ourselves more fully with its purposes and to *cultivate* its presence in our life. In other words, we develop a strong spiritual life.

It isn't that the rewards of an inner life aren't available at earlier stages of development. The experience of transcendent reality is open to all who will open to it! But research does support the notion that those at higher stages are more likely to have religious, even mystical, experiences.[17] In my own view, this is so because earlier frames tend to view the world in terms that are much more concrete and linear, which can provide significant barriers to an in-breaking of spiritual reality. In later stages, and particularly those at the Postconventional level, people's natural openness joins with the lessening of their earlier egocentrism to provide fertile ground in which the spiritual life can grow.

Probably without knowing much about adult developmental theory, E. F. Schumacher employed much the same continuum in his engaging exploration of business and life called *Good Work*. He describes mankind's task and purpose on earth in a way clearly parallel to that of Kohlberg:

> The human being's first task is to learn from society and "tradition" and to find his temporary happiness in receiving directions from the outside. His second task is to interiorize the knowledge he has gained, sift it out, keep the good and jettison the bad. This process may be called "individuation," becoming self-directed. The third task is one which he cannot tackle until he has accomplished the first two, and for which he needs the very best help he can possibly find. It is dying to oneself, to one's likes and dislikes, to all one's egocentric preoccupations. To the extent that a person succeeds in this, he ceases to be directed from the outside, and he also ceases to be self-directed. He has gained freedom or, one might say, he is then God-directed.[18]

To be inner directed (or God directed, in Schumacher's language) comes naturally to those at later stages of adult development. At the same time, to be inner directed is to cultivate and perfect the fruits of that inner orientation as they are manifested in the world. "The soul will bring forth fruit exactly in the measure as the inner life is developed," says Charles de Foucauld in his *Meditations of a Hermit*,[19] and the truth of that axiom is borne out daily in the actions and behaviors of those for whom spirituality has become a way of life.

The research of Allen Bergin and others is particularly instructive here. Building on Gordon Allport's distinction between intrinsic and extrinsic religion (see Chapter Three), Bergin was able to show that the intrinsically religious rated significantly higher in a variety of very positive social and psychological traits. These included self-control, tolerance, low anxiety, responsibility, a sense of well-being, sociability, intellectual efficiency, psychological-mindedness, and flexibility.[20] Obviously, these are many of the same traits that distinguish the higher levels of adult development, giving credence to Bergin's assertion that personality development is "intertwined" with the development of a religious orientation.[21]

This link between the inner orientation of the intrinsically religious and such positive personality traits both confirms the body of research growing out of adult developmental theory and *extends* it. The dual conclusion we reach is that (1) the higher stages of development produce the capacity for a variety of very positive traits, characteristics, and behaviors not consistently accessible at lower stages, and (2) as our spiritual traditions have long taught us, consistent devotion over time to the inner, spiritual life produces fruits of much the same character. What remains for science is to "show" us what we already know: that points 1 and 2 are interrelated—that progression to the higher stages of adult development opens us more fully to the potential of a strong inner life and that the spiritual life in turn deepens and accelerates the process of growth while ripening its fruits.

The role of the inner life is one of the "leading edges" in developmental theory and research. Before his untimely death in 1987, Kohlberg himself had begun to theorize about the existence of a stage 7, which was marked by "a sense of unity with the cosmos, nature or God."[22] For him the doorway to such an expanded perspective could come from the experience of despair or from great beauty, but was always experienced as a "nonegoistic" oneness with a larger reality. Kohlberg solidly aligned himself with James Fowler's thesis in the book *Stages of Faith* (quoted earlier) and adopted Fowler's description of the highest level of faith as the description of his metaphorical stage 7, characterized by such people as Gandhi, Mother Teresa, Dag Hammarskjöld, and Thomas Merton. Other researchers, though not proposing a wholly new stage of development, would agree that transcendent experiences do accelerate the process of growth by providing both the "disequilibrium" that can force the reconstruction of one's worldview and the grist for serious reflection about one's self and one's place in the universe.[23] Whatever their differences in theoretical perspective, all would agree that the highest levels of human development seem accessible only to those who are open to the experience of a transcendent reality and live lives consistent with its universal truths.

Probably the most exhaustive attempts to explore the convergence of adult development and spiritual growth have been undertaken by Ken Wilber and Jack Engler in what they term a *full-spectrum model* of human growth and maturity. Focusing on contemplative and meditative disciplines from around the world, they point out that "the major traditions we have studied in their original languages present an unfolding of meditation experiences in terms of a *stage model.*" They cite the Tibetan and Pali Mahayana Buddhist traditions as well as Hindu, Kabalah, Sufism, and Christian mysticism, among others. "The models are sufficiently similar," they write, "to suggest an underlying common invariant sequence of stages, despite vast cultural and linguistic differences as well as styles of practice."[24] Wilber has gone farther by examining the structural models of Freud, Jung, Piaget, Arieti, and Werner, and comparing them with the frameworks presented by a number of the world's contemplative traditions. From this study he has constructed a "master template" of psychological and spiritual growth that combines the best of both Eastern and Western traditions.[25] This is the frontier, if you will, of developmental theory, where the world's wisdom traditions meet our recently acquired knowledge of adult growth and find that there are fundamental and marked parallels.

Much work remains to be done in this area. But I am willing to let faith and the sense of the world's great religions suffice for now. It seems clear that adult development and spiritual growth support and further one another. *They may even be, at bottom, different ways of looking at the same thing.* The dynamics of such fundamental human processes do not always fit into the discrete little boxes that our meager concepts fashion for them.

The implications of all of this for businesses and other organizations are enormous. We have seen earlier how the psychological process of individuation is closely linked to spiritual growth. Now we see that the dynamic process of adult development is fostered by the spiritual life and produces certain qualities—the fruits of the spirit—as part of the interplay between them. For our ideas about managing and working with others now to fail to take account of these linkages would be folly. For our discussions of organizational leadership to neglect the spiritual element can now be rightly said to omit a most integral part of the whole—an essential piece of the puzzle. We have long ago dispensed with the notion that leadership is a set of competencies to be learned, just so many blocks to be checked. Admitting instead that, as Warren Bennis has said, it is the "integrated human being" among us—the individuated, mature, and developing man or woman—who is most fit for the task of leadership, we must look more carefully at the role the inner life plays in *becoming* that person. We may find that the fruits of which Jesus spoke two thousand years ago have simply assumed a modern garb and appear among us as the traits and characteristics of our most effective organizational leaders.

Questions and Exercises for Further Reflection

1. Think of three people who for you epitomize good, ethical, and effective leadership. They can be people you have known or simply read about. They might have exercised their leadership in the context of organizations, families, or politics. What are the essential traits, qualities, or characteristics that these three seem to have in common? Of the leadership styles described in this chapter, which description seems best to fit these individuals? Are there significant areas of their lives, which we might call dark sides or fatal flaws, that kept them from consistently operating at that frame of reference? What factors seem to have been at work in their lives that prevented a total congruence of image and actions?

2. Think of three people whose leadership you would characterize as bad, unethical, or ineffective. Where would you place them along the continuum of leadership styles?

3. Take a look again at the leadership style descriptors. Where would you say that you "reside" most of the time? Are there characteristics of the lower stages that you still often exhibit? Are there characteristics of the next stage to which you aspire? Toward which you feel yourself moving? Are there people with whom you work

or otherwise interact whom you admire for their possession of these qualities?

4. Is the frame of reference out of which you operate more or less the same at home and at work? If there is a difference, why does such an incongruity exist? What effects do you think that living with such an incongruity might have on you in the long run?

5. Think about the "culture" of the organization in which you work. What do you believe the developmental frame of reference of the typical manager to be? Which of the leadership styles do you think is most likely to be rewarded? Discouraged? Now forecast ten to fifteen years into the future—how do you think life in your particular business or industry will have changed? Will the leadership behaviors honored by the current culture still be those that bring success in the future as you envision it? What will have to change?

6. Who are the people, past or present, whom you would place at Kohlberg's stage 6? From what you know of them, what are the life experiences that caused them to move beyond the frames of reference most of us employ? Do you see evidence in their lives of the type of the opening, acknowledging, aligning, and cultivating that we have called spiritual growth? Think back over the course of your own life. What are the most important events and experiences that have brought you to the frame of reference you now employ? What about your life seems to have accelerated your process of growth? Delayed it?

Chapter Seven

The Personal Fruits

There are one-story intellects, two-story intellects, and three-story intellects with skylights. All fact collectors, who have no aim beyond their facts, are one-story men. Two-story men compare, reason, generalize, using the labors of fact collectors as well as their own. Three-story men idealize, imagine, predict; their best illumination comes from above, through the skylight.
OLIVER WENDELL HOLMES

The apostle Paul of Tarsus purported to enumerate the fruits of the spirit in his letter to the Galatians: "love, joy, peace, patience, kindness, generosity, faithfulness, gentleness, and self-control" (Galatians 5:22). I doubt that the list was complete, even for Paul's time (and, for what it's worth, Thomas Aquinas agrees). But focus for a moment on what those timeless old words say, as well as what they don't. Nowhere does he mention efficiency, competency, task orientation, or the myriad other qualities that make for success in our working lives. Those things were important, at least to a degree, even in 50 A.D.; but such organizational skills have always been just as available to "one-story" men and women as to those with richly cultivated spiritual lives. What Paul describes instead is a combination of those qualities that make us most fully human as well as those that make it possible for us to be most fully in community with others—the inner-personal and interpersonal traits of which we spoke in Chapter Six. It is those characteristics that most represent the fruit of growing, individuating, maturing inner lives.

At its best, the process of choosing organizational leaders involves identifying, developing, and encouraging those among us who are possessed of the inner-personal and interpersonal qualities that together are the signs of an integrated human being. If, as has been observed, leadership is both a relational and an attributional phenomenon,[1] our business and nonprofit organizations must come to pay a good deal more attention to the inner maturity and relational abilities of their managers and future leaders, rather than focus so single-mindedly on their organizational skills. And we must somehow quit trying so hard to escape the inevitable conclusion that such inner traits and outer qualities can be the fruit of the kind of genuine spiritual orientation we described in Chapter Three.

In this chapter, we will look more closely at the attributes—the inner-personal qualities—associated with a deep inner life and the higher stages of human adult development. Yes, I am aware (there being so few saints among us) that even where those qualities appear they often do so in degree and without perfect consistency. Moreover, at least some of the traits we will describe can at times be seen in individuals having little discernable spiritual life. But I for one am tired of our overrationalistic tendency to try to disprove perfectly obvious truths by finding an occasional exception to them. That's like saying that dogs don't have four legs because you find one who is able to hobble around on three. The truth is that a spiritual orientation can nurture and develop, as it has for many centuries, the highest and best qualities within us—and those that are most essential for life and leadership in our modern organizations. Let's look at those personal qualities that can rightly be called the fruits of the spirit.

The "Flexible Flyer"

Some years ago, management theorist Peter Vaill coined the colorful phrase *permanent white water* to describe the world of business management as it was coming to be practiced in the last of the twentieth century: no anchorage, few protective harbors, a chaotic and fast-paced world in which the speed of change is ever increasing and our common coping mechanisms are outmoded. What does it take to work effectively in such an environment? Better yet, what does it take to manage and lead and strategize in a world where your most basic assumptions about your business today may be the fallacies that put you out of business tomorrow?

The prime trait of those who prove able to negotiate those churning rapids is *flexibility*—having tremendous tolerance for the stress, uncertainty, and surprise that permeates their environment, without either burning out or becoming paralyzed. This was just the characteristic found in abundance by Fisher and Torbert in their study of several organizational leaders at the highest levels of adult development.[2] Fisher and Torbert observed that these leaders share the ability to live at once "symphonically" and "chaotically," moving effortlessly between roles, interacting with dozens of people in a single day and wearing several hats while doing so. They interweave work and leisure seamlessly, and often have such a sense of lightheartedness—even playfulness—about their work that it is hard to tell the difference between the two. It is as if they see change and fluidity not as anomalies to be controlled or stamped out but as the way reality is truly structured. As a result, they touch things lightly, never grasping too tightly at ideas or solutions, as they might be called on to reframe them at a moment's notice in response to some changing reality.

As we saw in Chapter Six, research has shown that individuals at later stages of adult development can tolerate higher levels of stress.[3] Studies have also shown that those with the kind of deepened inner life that is characteristic of the intrinsically religious are less anxious than other people,[4] supporting our conclusion that adult development and spiritual growth are intertwined. But why *are* such people less anxious? What is it about spiritual and psychological maturity that gives one the ability to become a "flexible flyer"?

St. Paul gave the name *peace* to this particular fruit of the spirit. John of the Cross called it tranquility. By whatever name called, it is finding your anchorage, not in the swirling torrents of organizational life nor in the ephemeral approval of others, but in a much larger reality that gives perspective to the craziness around you. It comes from letting go of your feverish and maddening attempts to control your environment (more on that later), realizing instead that true control lies beyond your grasp. Fortunately, however, the inner life brings with it a certainty that ultimate control does lie in the hands of an organizing principle that creates eternal order out of momentary chaos, is reliably benevolent, and seeks our good and our growth.

In the National Gallery in Washington, D.C., there hangs a painting by Thomas Cole, the third in his series of works called *The Voyage of Life*. It depicts a young man adrift in a boat at the headwaters of a roiling rapids, his hands clasped in prayer. Perilous rocks await below, and one can only barely glimpse the placid, tranquil sea that stretches out on the horizon, where the river ends its run. An angel looks on from a cloudy perch but well hidden from view. Like this young man, most of us cannot avoid the permanent white water of our organizational lives. It's not an option for us to rechannel the river, stop it, or slow it down, as much well-intentioned advice would have us do. The solution lies more in our own inner attitude toward the turmoil—having the security to live in insecurity. We use the tools and talents we've been given to help us negotiate those rapids; but, more important, we must find within ourselves a *faith* that the universe is inherently trustworthy and a *knowledge* that the exigencies of life and work will not ultimately defeat us. Flexible flyers successfully shoot the rapids not so much because they are smarter or better trained or more efficient; their success lies in the fact that they are grounded in a view of themselves and of reality that allows them to see their actions as a part of the much larger actions of a trustworthy God. Anchored in that reality, flexible flyers can function with great effectiveness in even the most looney-bin of environments, free to work, strive, risk, and even fail, in the knowledge that their ultimate security lies deeper than the uncertainties of the workplace can reach. Remember that in a fierce storm, only the tree with *both* deep roots and flexible branches survives unharmed.

Perspective: Big-Picture Thinking

Have you ever seen one of those pictures of the earth taken from outer space? On that beautifully mottled ball, swirling hurricanes are but dime-size white clouds. Whole countries ravaged by revolution are just richly colored shapes against a sea-blue background. Placid and serene from this vantage point, the planet gives no hint of the tragedy, strife, and anxiety that seem to permeate every nook and cranny of the terra firma. What's more, from this vantage we see the earth as it truly is: an interconnected and interdependent whole, without the artificial boundaries that humankind has created for itself.

Just as physical distance provides a larger perspective, to get mentally or psychologically "above" a problem or situation allows us to see it more clearly and objectively. By being able to see the forest as well as the trees, we can abstract a general meaning from what we are observing and see it as a particular example of a much larger issue. So, to take a simple example, the proprietor of a computer servicing company who tries to address declining sales through more advertising and quality improvement might eventually fail altogether, while a competitor who sees this problem as but a symptom of a consumer movement toward buying new and ever cheaper computers (rather than repairing old ones) might survive and prosper by diversifying his business. Perspective is what allows us to rise above the entanglements of the immediate problem to see the big picture this problem may portend. Trends, movements, interconnections—these are the stock in trade of the organizational leader with a sense of perspective.

What we know about human growth and maturity tells us clearly that the higher a person's level of adult development, the larger his or her realm of experience and thought. By the time people become embedded in a Postconventional frame of reference, they have come to understand clearly the boundedness of their own ego and are able freely to step outside their individual perceptions to take a more truly objective perspective. Postconventional development gives one the capacity for a greater abstraction of thought, which research has shown leads both to a greater inclusiveness of concepts and ideas and the creation of more "processing loops" beyond one's immediate perceptions.[5] In short, those at higher developmental levels know that their perceptions are limited and prejudiced by their own constructed egos and are able to adopt much larger perspectives that take into account the differing viewpoints of others, the larger demands of organization and society, and even the ongoing historical context. This process of continually transcending one's own perspective is what big-picture thinking is all about.

To have a higher perspective does not mean, of course, that you are oblivious to the details on the ground. It should, in fact, give you the ability to understand and manage those details more creatively. Just like the view of earth from outer space, your view from above should allow you to see the relationships between problems and to know which of the fires you are fighting are really important in the larger scheme of things. Not all details are created equal; to have perspective is to have the ability to determine wisely which details are deserving of your attention.

One important advantage of big-picture thinking is the ability to reframe and reconceptualize problems. A striking example of this dynamic emerged from a study done several years ago involving M.B.A.'s who worked in a variety of organizations.[6] The subjects were given thirty-four in-basket problems to handle or solve in a simulation in which they assumed the role of a newly appointed director of a community volunteer organization. The researchers designated as a first-order response any attempt to treat the problem as an isolated incident, acceptance of the given definition of a problem, or failure to detect the problem's underlying cause. The subjects gave a second-order response any time they questioned underlying assumptions, reframed the problem, or treated it as only the symptom of a deeper issue. Those members of the sample who tested at Postconventional levels of development chose second-order responses almost *twice as often* as those at Conventional levels. The acquiring of a broader perspective seems to lead, quite logically, to the ability to reconceptualize problems in terms of that broader perspective.

"We all know that leaders should help people see the big picture," writes Peter Senge, "[b]ut the actual skills whereby leaders are supposed to achieve this are not well understood."[7] Senge goes on to say that successful leaders are "systems thinkers" who understand trends, interrelationships, and the forces of change, but even he doesn't tell us how leaders actually acquire those skills. The truth, of course, is that *skill* is entirely the wrong word. Systems thinking is more a way of being in the world—it can't be learned like a skill any more than a cutting from a peach tree can be grafted onto an apple tree.

Intersystemic thinking is the fruit of a particular kind of tree. Basseches was able to illustrate this through a study in which he identified a number of different schemata (ways of thinking) that were shared by those at the higher levels of adult development. These included the tendency not to identify with a particular closed system but instead to see the relationship between systems and to be cognizant of the whole process of systems formation.[8] Rather than being a developable skill, systems thinking simply comes naturally to such people. It is the way their world *is*.

Polarity, Paradox, and Equanimity

Organizational leadership has been said to require, above all else, "a taste for paradox, a talent for ambiguity, a capacity to hold contradictory propositions comfortably in a mind that relishes complexity."[9] Most of us are not really wired up that way. Human thought processes are notoriously dualistic—we seem to be able to make sense out of our world only by splitting things into opposites. We like our political concepts either right-on (if we support them) or boneheaded (if we don't), our criminals either guilty as sin or wrongly accused, and our gods as light as our demons are dark. It's as if our preferred mode of processing is to define things in terms of polar extremes and then to identify with one or the other. And the failure to do so is all too often seen as ambivalent, indecisive, or wishy-washy.

At the lower levels of adult development this is consistently the way "truth" is organized. The opposite of that which is true cannot possibly also be true, and thus contradiction and paradox must be stamped out wherever they appear. In certain pathologies that are endemic to the lower stages (such as narcissism and borderline personality disorders), individuals engage in exaggerated attempts to see all concepts and persons (including themselves) as either all good or all bad. Pathology is the extreme, but we might observe that many of those with fundamentalist religious orientations seem to do the same thing.

Psychological and spiritual growth seems clearly to work a change in this way of looking at the world. As people progress to the larger frames of reference represented by the higher stages, they come to realize that contradiction and paradox are inherently a part of reality and can't be managed merely by rejecting one extreme or the other.[10] They don't feel threatened by contradiction or compelled to resolve it at all costs; rather, "the orientation seems to shift to the relationship between poles in a paradox rather than a choice between the poles."[11] Opposites are seen as two sides of a single concept, with the tension between them a potentially healthy and constructive dynamic.

Spiritually, this growth manifests itself as a loosening of our need to so exclusively possess "the truth." We come to a place where we can admit that the truth as apprehended by others might be as valid as our own and that all truth is textured by our life experiences, our personalities, and our naive images of God. This understanding is not a relativism, mind you, that accepts any conceivable viewpoint as valid—that would simply be the opposite of fundamentalism and equally immature. It is, instead, an acceptance of our fallibility and the limitations of our human awareness.

This understanding has important implications for life and leadership in organizations. In the real world—that is, the world that exists outside our dualistic frameworks—problems are almost never black and white. In insisting on a solution that satisfies your need for absolutes, you may set yourself up to make a costly mistake. Many managers in the Diplomat or Technician mode have found their careers derailed when they were unable to appreciate the complexities and hues of the business issues they faced. Far from wishy-washiness, the ability to hold the tension between opposites and manage the vagaries that live there is one of the distinguishing marks of a truly mature person. Decisiveness and confidence are fine qualities to possess; but when combined with an arrogant possession of the one right answer and a damn-the-torpedoes attitude, the result can be disastrous.

When we give up on our need to dichotomize the world, we acquire a largeness of spirit that can be very beneficial in managing and working with others. We become more open to the ideas and proposed solutions of those around us, even if very different from our own. I have even observed that the real breakthroughs come *especially* from those whom we most dislike or dismiss, precisely because their perspective is likely to be so different. Radical openness to even the most disparate ideas can turn out to be your saving grace.

We also hear a great deal these days about creating win-win rather than win-lose situations in business. To do that consistently, however, requires a mind-set very different from the one that constructs the zero-sum games we usually play. The more you view the world in black-and-white terms, the more likely you are to assume that for one extreme to prevail, the other must suffer a loss. It is only between the two polarities that we can construct mutually beneficial solutions, yet to think in those terms comes naturally only to people at higher stages of growth and maturity.

The capacity to dwell in that middle place can also lead us to a kind of equanimity—balance—in our personal and professional lives. We become much more comfortable in juggling the inherent tensions between competing interests without feeling compelled to bunk exclusively with one or the other. So it's no longer just short-term versus long-term, thinking versus feeling, or shareholder value versus employee security—it's how to creatively maximize *both* by balancing their equally valid interests. This does not mean that we cannot strongly favor one or the other when the situation requires it, but the *capacity* to take the middle way keeps us from being victimized by our own extremism.

On a more personal level, psychospiritual growth can produce an equanimity that goes a long way toward resolving the traditional work-life split. Before they have achieved a Postconventional level of maturity, most people feel acutely the conflict between their personal and working lives, and they generally resolve it only by investing themselves completely in one or the other. But at the Postconventional level, Strategists gain the capacity, in effect, to transcend the conflict by replacing the need for achievement with the desire to serve a higher good. The conflicting pulls of work and family may still be there, but the yardstick of success in either sphere has now changed. Strategists serve an ultimate purpose born of their expanded worldview and now seek to serve this higher good through work, family, and community life. They have found the middle way.

Introspection and Self-Awareness

Of all the characteristics essential for leadership of modern organizations, I believe the most important is self-awareness. A host of ills (and evils) follow those who lack a fundamental knowledge of their strengths and weaknesses, along with the self-mastery to handle them both. And it is only through assiduous attention to the inner life that such self-knowledge can grow. Nothing external to you can accomplish this work, except to the extent that the externals foster or accelerate the inner work.

THE PERSONAL FRUITS 151

Of this, the most influential voices of our age speak in unison. If you peer into the life of practically any person you deeply admire, any man or woman who has made a positive difference in the world, you will find that inner work precedes outer work—inner mastery comes before outer mastery. Gandhi's statement, "Be the change you wish to see in the world," has become a mantra for many because it captures this lasting truth.

The wellspring of self-knowledge is introspection: serious self-reflection on our own motives, prejudices, actions, gifts, and graces. But again the question we have often asked in this book: Where does that capacity "come from"? Is it something we learn or "just do"? Is it available to all or only to some of us? Practically all of us, of course, are capable of making the time and effort to reflect on ourselves and our lives. But according to adult developmental theory, we only come to have an expanded third-person perspective that allows us objectively to explore our true natures through introspection when we have reached stage 4 (the Achiever frame).[12] Until that point in the developmental continuum, our point of view is so self- or other oriented that it is very difficult for us to view ourselves objectively. It's like asking a young child to admit breaking the lamp and then to explain dispassionately his motivations for doing so—you are unlikely to get an objective answer. Perhaps this helps explain why so many people spend years learning meditation and other reflective practices and yet remain the same self-absorbed, delusional, unaware people they always were.

For those ready to receive the gifts (as well as the pain!) that introspection can bring, there comes a knowledge of one of life's great truths: *the problems you encounter in your world are problems that are within you—change yourself and the world around you* has *to change.* Not only are you the one variable that you have the most chance to influence, but changes in your thoughts and behavior unerringly affect a broad swath of interactions, relationships, and problems. Their very fabric is changed because your role in the dynamic that created them is now different. One of the most prolific minds of the twentieth century put it this way: "If things go wrong in the world, this is because something is wrong with the individual, because something is wrong with me. Therefore, if I am sensible, I shall put myself right first. For this I need—because outside authority no longer means anything to me—a knowledge of the innermost foundations of my being. . . . The true leaders of mankind are always those who are capable of self-reflection."[13]

Beyond a certain point, there can probably be no personal growth, no individuation, without the capacity for self-reflection. It is only through the work of introspection that we acquire a clear sense of our identity and its complexities. We discover our inner resources and are able to draw down on them when the need presents itself. We are less rent by internal contradictions and less likely to be immobilized by them. Over time we become more authentic, more whole, more self-responsible, and more autonomous. The benefits of all of this to our organizational life are manifold, but two bear special mention.

The first has to do with the psychological phenomenon of projection, possibly the most disruptive force in organizational life. It is an axiom of psychology that everything that is unconscious within us is projected outward onto the world. That is, all the despicable traits we are least able to see in ourselves we will find ways to see in other people—whether they have them or not. (The converse is also true: there may be brave and beautiful things about us that we are afraid to acknowledge, preferring instead to see them in the people around us.) So the common manifestation of projection in a business setting is that boss or coworker whom we absolutely cannot stand to be around because he or she is too judgmental, too anal, too flighty, too . . . whatever. It's like one of those trick mirrors at the fair where we think we are looking at another person but in fact are looking at ourselves. For the person seriously engaged in self-reflection, this becomes increasingly less possible to do. As we become aware of our own weak places, we come to see how our exaggerated reactions to others are dead giveaways that the process of projection is at work in us. Any person who has seen the dynamic at work in himself or herself and has been able successfully to withdraw the projections can testify to the truth of the proposition that changing oneself does indeed work a change in the world.

For people in leadership positions, awareness of projection can be important in another way. Those in positions of authority almost always find themselves the objects of the projections of others, be they positive or negative. The self-awareness that comes through introspection is extremely important for the leader's grounding in reality. Overidentification with the positive projections of others, of course, can give leaders a sense of false pride that sets them up very nicely for a subsequent fall. But to internalize and believe the negative projections can paralyze leaders or create such an atmosphere of distrust that nothing gets done. In either case the task of leaders is to possess within themselves such clarity about their strengths and weaknesses that they are able to distance themselves from both positive and negative projections. The psychological process is called disidentification, but its deeper basis is spiritual. It is an awareness—a knowledge—of who one is in relation to Ultimate Reality, as well as just who one is to oneself and others. It is finding the fullest sense of one's identity in God.

Another way in which introspection and self-awareness mature us as leaders is illustrated by the life of Gandhi. As Erik Erikson points out in his psychological biography of him,[14] Gandhi worked very hard to integrate feminine attributes into his thoroughly masculine being. Trained in lawyerly rationality and steeped in his society's paternalism, Gandhi took up a variety of traditionally female activities (spinning cloth is one famous example) in a conscious attempt to develop his feminine side. The lesson here for us is that we all have aspects of our personalities that are weak, neglected, and undeveloped. To become more mature, more whole, is at least in part a process of strengthening and integrating those aspects of ourselves into an ever larger and multifaceted personality. But to do that requires, ab initio, the capacity to see clearly those soft spots within ourselves. For you and me the task might not be quite as ambitious as Gandhi's attempt to integrate his contrasexual side. But all of us have a healthy supply of unhealthy places within us, and much of what we mean by individuation or personal growth consists in uncovering, admitting, strengthening, and integrating them.

The world's great spiritual traditions have always invited us to reflection and introspection. It is there that we meet ourselves, warts and all, and there that we encounter the divine. And for those who have allowed God to blast open their narrow worlds, it is where we come to discover the unique place of our life and work in God's order. In the words of two of history's mystics, one from the Christian tradition and one from Islam (Issac the Syrian and Abdulla al-Ansari, respectively):

Enter eagerly into the treasure house that is within you, and so you will see the things that are in heaven; for there is but one single entry to them both. The ladder that leads to the kingdom is hidden within your soul. Flee from sin, dive into yourself, and in your soul you will discover the stairs by which to ascend.[15]

Know that the Prophet built an external kaaba of clay and water, and an inner kaaba in life and heart. The outer kaaba was built by Abraham, the holy; the inner is sanctified by the glory of God himself. On the path of God two places of worship mark the stages. The material temple and the temple of the heart. Make your best endeavor to worship at the temple of the heart.[16]

Faith: An Expectant Hope

Faith is a hallmark of the spiritual life. More than mere belief in a particular religion or creed, faith is a kind of abiding trust; a complete confidence; a total committedness that says, in effect, "No matter what happens, I am casting my lot here." It is enormously personal, which might cause you to question what this particular fruit of the spirit has to do with our organizational life. Yet have you ever seen an entrepreneur so committed to a vision of the future that her optimism was positively contagious? Or a CEO whose fervent hope in a failing enterprise kept him upbeat long after you would have thrown in the towel? Or a woman prepared to leave a secure but stifling position for the promising uncertainty of a new direction? If you look around, you will see evidence every day of the effects of people's faith. It keeps us focused on our purpose, gives us energy and resolve, and gives us a framework in which to see the larger reasons for our efforts. I believe it is true that *every* person has an underlying structure of faith; the critical question is, Faith in *what?* Our logical reasoning abilities? Mommy and Daddy? Cocaine? God?

James Fowler, the author of *Stages of Faith,* felt that there was clearly a tacit structure of faith underlying each of the stages of adult development. The difference lies in the person, ideal, or entity on whom that faith rests. At the higher levels of adult development—and the higher reaches of spiritual maturity—our ultimate faith is not so much in ourselves or others or our human organizations, societies, or nation-states. We "cast our lot" with a larger reality that has transcended all of those more limited interests and in which we believe their true hope lies. So it's not that the entrepreneur, the CEO, or the woman making a career change can't have confidence in their own intellect, experience, and pluck. But the kind of faith that is the fruit of a genuine spirituality knows that such things are, if you will, only the boat by which we travel and the oars by which we move. They are not the river; and unless we are in *its* flow and moving in *its* direction, our feverish human efforts are quite unlikely to get us there.

This kind of faith is a curious thing. We don't "acquire" it in either of the normal ways. That is, we don't become convinced by reason and logic to have faith in Ultimate Reality, although the application of our rational powers can strengthen our faith. Nor do we gain faith blindly through our emotions, although the feelings that accompany our belief can open the door to a deeper faith. For those who come to possess this fruit of the spirit, faith flows from a personal knowingness that comes only through a devoted inner life. No one can give us that knowledge in the way we usually "learn" things. The best someone can do is to point us in directions where we might reliably find such knowledge. We may then discover that is was within us all the while.

To be possessed of faith is to have a particular view of the world and the flow of time. Life is not neutral or static—all things are in process, with life's balance favoring growth and development toward larger goals. The laws of thermodynamics may hold their immutable sway over the physical realm and biological life itself, yet the flow of human history and of each individual participant seems ever against the grain of decay and dissolution. It is as if time itself has some purpose, some ultimate goal toward which it struggles, however inscrutable that goal might be to us human observers. With that understanding as a backdrop, a person of faith sees in all events and in all people their capacity to participate in the larger movements of life. All is potential, all is capable of growth and development. Every employee can be more productive and fulfilled, every entrepreneurial idea has a chance to blossom into something of value, every business has an opportunity to make a meaningful and lasting mark—as long as each can find its place in this larger upward movement of history. And there is the understanding that

Time may take its own sweet time about that. To faith, the concept of time is future oriented, long-term, and consistently optimistic. This concept resonates with Reinhold Niebuhr's statement that "[n]othing that is worth doing can be achieved in our lifetime; therefore we must be saved by hope."[17] For an organizational leader who has faith, an expectant hope for the future is joined with infinite patience in the present.

Although faith can provide us with purpose, resolve, strength, optimism, and hope, we have so far made it seem as if it's the individual, through his or her faith, who brings all these qualities to bear in our working lives. The truth is that it's not that one-way. Faith is its own self-fulfilling prophecy. To be totally committed to yourself and your own powers (such as they are) is to get exactly that—nothing less but certainly nothing more. To be completely invested in a group or movement or organization is to get in the bargain all of the human frailties and screwed-upness that eventually surface in any human amalgam. But faith in God—real faith in God—gives you God. Just take the time to ask someone with a devoted inner life about that. Does a saving insight seem sometimes to come "out of nowhere"? Does just the right person or event or book seem to come into the person's path when she needs it most? Is there a strong sense that something beyond the person's powers is prospering her work in synchronistic little ways—or even blocking it at times in others? She may work as if everything truly depends on her, but I bet she'll tell you that it doesn't.

Since fall 1989 I have had a certain passage from Goethe hanging on the wall of my office. It was during that time that I finally gave way to the insistent inner urging to leave my safe corporate position and follow a different path. I enrolled in the Shalem Institute's spiritual guidance program and began the process of trying to turn my adjunct position at Wake Forest University into a full-time teaching job. Like many other things in life (including, incidentally, this book), if I'd known it was going to be so hard I might never have tried it. It was over a year before my vocational situation was resolved, during which time I had to endure all the anxiety, financial concerns, and self-doubt of anyone who's ever been between jobs. But I never lost sight of my faith nor sight of my goal to live a more creative and fulfilling life.

Yet my faith hardly prepared me for what was to happen during those months. Chance meetings became supportive friendships; casual conversations turned into sustaining consulting relationships; unexpected expenses were met by equally unexpected windfalls (as, for example, when an insurance check for a tree felled in Hurricane Hugo, less the cost of cleanup, was precisely to the penny what was needed to pay for that year's Christmas). Small wonder Goethe's words are still with me:

> Concerning all acts of initiative and creation there is one elementary truth, the ignorance of which kills countless ideas and splendid plans: That the moment one definitely commits oneself, then Providence moves, too. All sorts of things occur to help one that would otherwise never have occurred. A whole stream of events issues from the decision, raising in one's favor all manner of unforeseen incidents and meetings and material assistance, which no man could have dreamt would have come his way. Whatever you can do, or dream you can, begin it. Boldness has genius, power and magic in it.

Sense of Self/No-Self

One of the great paradoxes endemic to the spiritual life is that it encourages both a strong sense of self and an abiding selflessness. Both sides of the dichotomy must be lived to the full. Through introspection and self-awareness we come to know and value our uniqueness, our distinctive gifts, our developing strengths—our preciousness. Yet the wisdom literature of our traditions tells us in one voice, though many languages, that our hard-won identities must be set aside if we are to grow toward God. Our religions differ greatly in terms of how we are to accomplish this, as well as in the images they have for what its accomplishment looks like. But they agree that our sense of self gives way to a sense of no-self as an essential prerequisite to our rendering true service to mankind and fealty to God.

Developmental theory helps us understand how this happens. In the earlier stages of adult development and throughout Kohlberg's Conventional level, our focus is on building a strong, stable, and discrete identity that can stand over against society's ever present peer pressure and mass consciousness. The old saying that you must have something before you can give it away is quite applicable here. But as one progresses to the higher stages of adult development, the need for an image of self founded on a single well-constructed identity begins to decrease. To use Robert Kegan's terminology, one begins to move from an *institutional* self-image, which insists on a coherent and internally consistent identity that is impervious to change, to an *interindividual* frame of reference. From this new perspective a person is able to see that he or she *has* an identity among a universe of others, but is no longer so invested in it that he or she can't experience radical change. In fact, the self becomes the willing vehicle through which transformative change takes place. Interviews with individuals who have tested at these higher stages show an increasing disdain for the self-absorption and self-importance of earlier stages,[18] even as they understand the original necessity for building a strong self-image.

Blaise Pascal said that man was nothing in relation to the infinite, but everything in relation to nothing. This statement makes perfect sense to those inclined to the spiritual life. It is truly astounding what humankind has been able to accomplish in only the last half-century. We can take justifiable pride, not only in our individual capabilities but also in the accomplishments and future promise of our human organizations. Yet the equivalent of cosmic laughter must ring out whenever we entertain our grandiose thoughts of human perfectibility, immortality, or our countless other schemes to achieve god status. (Cloning, anyone?) Most of us, in fact, adhere to a sort of functional atheism. Whether or not we give verbal assent to the existence of an "infinite," we live every day of our lives in total denial of the first part of Pascal's statement. We are possessed of a self but mortified by the notion of no-self. In such a state we have little chance of finding our way to an authentic meeting with God—an authentic spirituality. In the words of Morton Kelsey, a Jungian analyst and Episcopal priest:

> We are children. There is no question about Abba's receiving us. All we have to do is acknowledge our childishness and come. This is the reason why the broken and simple, the poor in spirit, the anxiety-ridden, the mourning, the meek, the unsatisfied and unful-

filled, the hungry and thirsty, the persecuted and ridiculed find it
so easy to turn to God. . . . Those who are doing quite well on their
own and think that they have life securely within their grasp don't
like to admit their ultimate helplessness and come as children before Abba. They don't feel the need of it. It also may be beneath
their dignity.[19]

Organizational leaders who have achieved a sense of self/no-
self are fairly easy to spot. They are very positive in their self-image
and accepting of themselves, but at the same time they can exhibit
qualities of modesty and humility that may seem strangely incon-
sistent to those who have not achieved that level of maturity. They
have what Warren Bennis and Burt Nanus call positive self-regard,
a crucial quality of transformational leadership that is "not a crow-
ing self-importance or egoistic self-centeredness. . . . But they do
know their worth. They trust themselves without letting their ego
or image get in the way."[20] They have minimal defenses and can be
open to even the most negative feedback from others, confident
that they can separate the wheat of what is true and helpful from
the chaff of others' negative projections. Such people know, as Lao
Tzu said twenty-six centuries ago, that "he who feels punctured
must once have been a bubble,"[21] and have long since abandoned
their over-inflated self-images. They are comfortable with exercising control in their ever growing sphere of influence, but harbor
no illusion about the fact that ultimate control lies beyond their
grasp. They have "abandoned the exhausting illusion of self-
sufficiency and become the grateful recipients of the gifts that life
provides."[22]

Someone once said that the man Jesus of Nazareth did not
have an identity—that he was constantly receiving his identity from
God. I like that notion, despite its measure of hyperbole. Much of
our life's energy, for a great many years, goes into the crafting,
preening, and polishing of our identities. But our self-images can
only get us so far in life and only so far along the continuum of
adult growth and maturity. Unless we are able to crack open our
identities to the influence of Ultimate Reality—indeed, unless we
are able to relinquish the crafting process itself—we will remain
forever nothing more than the fragile casings we have created for
ourselves. We'll always be bubbles waiting to be punctured.

Learning: The Acceptance of Failure

Everyone agrees these days that a "learning orientation" is critical to career success. Without lifelong learning skills, you will inevitably find yourself trying to cope with tomorrow's problems using yesterday's outmoded assumptions. Yet there is a special kind of learning that seems to be accessible to only some of us—a learning that walks hand in hand with the acceptance of failure. Start by thinking about it this way: we learn how to ski by oozing down the beginner slope; we learn how to shoot a basketball by standing right beneath the hoop. Years later we might be able to say we know how to "do" both of those things, even if our degree of expertise never changed a whit. But to be able to slalom down the expert slopes or to rain "threes" from beyond the arc, we will have to have fallen more times than we can possibly remember and missed more shots than we will ever make. You just can't succeed without failing—a lot!

But those examples become more difficult to follow when we try to apply them to the "game of life." We don't like failure. It hurts our self-esteem and threatens our identity. It can strike us at the very core of who we believe ourselves to be. People often take their own lives after some perceived failure, or else so withdraw their energy from life that they commit a sort of emotional suicide. Much safer, for most of us, simply to stay on life's beginner slopes.

It is a distinguishing mark of true emotional and spiritual maturity that a person accepts failure and loss as part of the fabric of life. And I don't mean just a stoic, existential acceptance through which one sees failure as one's "cross to bear," but rather the knowledge that, at least some of the time, a lack of success is the necessary cost of having reached for success in the first place. Defeat is the occasional price of victory. Failure is simply the other side of life's singular coin, and you will have to accept it if you wish to pocket that coin. To do so requires a maturity possessed only by some. It requires the ability to look beyond our constructed identity to the larger forces at work in our life and in the world. It requires a transcendent purpose for our life and work that can weather the setbacks that inevitably come from our efforts to stretch and grow. It takes freedom from groupthink and our own exhausting efforts at self-sufficiency, and contentment that the locus of ultimate control lies in a trustworthy God. And perhaps more than anything else it takes a *faith*—a passionate knowledge—that what lies on the far side of *any* failure is a renewed opportunity for even greater success. In the words of Robert K. Greenleaf: "Loss, by itself, is not tragic. What is tragic is the failure to grasp the opportunity which loss presents."[23]

Grasping that opportunity is the essence of the deep learning that can follow in the wake of loss or failure for those who have achieved a certain level of psychological and spiritual maturity. Their setbacks serve as an opportunity for serious reflection on their weaknesses and foibles; and while such introspection gives them new tools, an optimistic faith allows them to set out again on the path that is before them. This goes beyond skill-based learning (which is all that learning is to many people); this is *learning how to live.*

When one reaches this level of maturity, even life's apparently random disappointments and tragedies do not lose their opportunity to be meaningful. In my experience, most people at this level believe, with St. Augustine, that "God permits evil only in so far as he is capable of transforming it into a good." In the modern vernacular, God never closes a door without opening a window. There is in every tragedy a hidden opportunity for something new and better to emerge, if one can step back and take a broad enough perspective. This is the abiding optimism that bears such people up even in the face of great personal loss and enables them to be a compassionate and graceful presence to others whom tragedy has struck.

There is one other way that the acceptance of failure can result in deep learning, though it often takes the discernment of a rich inner life to see. When we have aligned our life and work with God's purposes and committed ourselves in the way of which Goethe speaks (as cited earlier), it is true that we are prospered in very real and material ways by an unseen reality. But it is also true that, having made that commitment, we may find our efforts blocked if we have somehow taken a wrong turn or succumbed to the wrong motivations. I have often wondered if this wasn't what King David meant when he said in Psalm 139, "You hem me in, behind and before, and lay your hand upon me." Sometimes our "failure" is simply the tugging of our reins to move us back to our authentic path, back to where our deepest intention is to be. It's like my friend Robert Johnson has been heard to say: "I take two steps backward for every one step forward; but it's all right, because I find that I was headed in the wrong direction to begin with!"

Creativity: Openness to Intuition and Inspiration

The ancient Romans believed that their leaders, philosophers, and poets were followed around by small, tutelary spirits called genies, who whispered into their ears all truly original thoughts. This is the origin of our word *genius*. The true roots of creativity remain a subject of study and speculation, but all would agree that creativity involves, at least in part, an openness to the deeper reaches of the human psyche. The more one nurtures and cultivates this inner connection, the greater one's chance of "catching" the creative spirit as it passes. Thomas A. Edison, undoubtedly one of the great creative geniuses of our age (and a very religious man), often told friends that, rather than feeling responsible for his many inventions, he thought of himself as a mere conduit for forces greater than himself—the ideas merely "came through" him.

For some time now, our overly rational, left-brain views of business have been slowly giving way to a more balanced approach that values intuition and other nonrational (as opposed to irrational) ways of perceiving the world. In the words of the CEO of innovative Silicon Graphics: "You have to do all your homework, but then you have to go with your intuition without letting your mind get in the way."[24] This is particularly important for organizations in the throes of chaotic change, where new and sometimes radical solutions are the only alternative to organizational decay and death. Says creativity specialist Roger Harrison: "Never in my years as a consultant have I seen an organization changed in any fundamental way through rational planning. The leaders I have seen influence their organization's characters and destinies have always operated out of intuition."[25]

A lot of what passes for "creativity training" in business these days is nothing more than providing a safe environment for people to come up with sensationally stupid ideas. It does nothing to tap the true sources of creativity. So how do we really do that? First and foremost, by giving ourselves the time and opportunity to be touched by the creative spirit—to be *in-spired*. Most of us do this very poorly, if at all, despite the continuing reminders that the world gives us: the solution that "appears" only after we've exhausted our efforts and taken a break; the thoughts that seem to come "out of nowhere" when we're engrossed in a particularly beautiful sunset; the new perspective that comes after we've "slept on it" overnight. Instead, we approach many of our thorniest problems, particularly those associated with work, with a driven kind of I'll-get-to-the-bottom-of-this-if-it-kills-me mentality (and eventually it *may!*).

The recent experience of a friend of mine, a litigation partner in a large Dallas law firm, is a good example of the creative spirit at work. Ron was the lead attorney in a large and messy lawsuit against a West Coast company owned by a flamboyant and self-assured entrepreneur. Ron had been taking the depositions of the company's officers for over a week, working sixteen-hour days, sleeping little, taking no time away from the task at hand, and generally wearing himself down to a nub. The day had now arrived to question the top man. Ron was concerned that, despite the enormous time and resources spent so far, he and his team were no closer to clearly establishing his client's rightful claim in the case. The first day's testimony by the owner revealed little; that night Ron took to his bed for a fitful five hours of sleep with a mixture of exhaustion and depression. But then, somewhere deep in the night, out of the midst of some foggy dream, he heard an authoritative voice boom at him: *"What is the question you have failed to ask?"* Ron sat bolt upright in bed, still half asleep, saying to himself, "What? What does that mean? What question could I possibly not have asked?" And then, in the way so typical of communications from our unconscious, it was as if the idea had stolen into his head and was now suddenly before him: "Ask about his criminal record."

It would be awkward, Ron thought, and perhaps a little embarrassing, to ask such a question. After all, there was no real issue of criminal wrongdoing in the lawsuit and no reason to think that the CEO-owner was anything other than the stalwart community leader he portrayed himself to be. But when the opportunity presented itself the next day, Ron asked the owner if he had ever been charged with any offence other than minor traffic violations. The man paused, then said he didn't understand the question. "Well, let me be very specific then," Ron said, sensing he had hit a nerve.

"Have you ever been charged or convicted in any state or federal court of any criminal felony?" Now flushed and clearly agitated, the owner asked for a recess to confer with his attorneys. When they returned, they laid an offer of settlement on the table that resulted in a resolution of the multimillion-dollar suit that was very favorable to Ron's client and fair to all concerned. It seems that our successful entrepreneur had been in a different line of work several years ago—trafficking in narcotics—and was reluctant for that to be front-page news again. Something as "irrational" as a dream had done for Ron and his client what no amount of logical thinking and furious activity could achieve.

Our dreams can serve as a vehicle for the creative spirit precisely because we are unconscious when we dream. We spend our conscious waking hours in the "productive" pursuit of solutions, outcomes, goals, and deadlines, disdaining as unproductive the kind of quiet downtime essential to creativity. Those with a mature inner life have the advantage: they realize that you must sometimes go slow in order to go fast; that it takes patience to hear the sound of your own intuition in the midst of our noisy culture; that it is in the discipline of daily periods of quiet openness that you find your connection to the wellspring of creativity that is inside of you—which, many believe, is nothing less than the ceaselessly creative energy of God. It is no wonder that a recent study of contemplative practices in organizational life found that the use of periods of silence was perceived to have a more important effect on creativity at work than any other practice.[26]

Bernard Murchland's thoughts on the phenomenon of creativity bear out its connection with the inner life.[27] To him, the observable aspects of creativity include far more than just an original approach and mastery of technique. There is, first, a kind of *restlessness,* an incessant urge that pulls such men and women toward the fulfillment of their highest potential. Second, there is an *eccentricity,* not in the way we usually use that word but in the literal sense of being off center—having the ability, as Emerson said, to establish an original relationship with the universe. Third, creativity involves *receptivity* to unconscious sources of insight, and appreciation for the "unproductive" time that is necessary to connect with one's intuitive springs. Murchland also observes that the truly creative exhibit a passionate *commitment* to what they do, an *enthusi-*

asm that is life affirming, and a sense of *freedom* from all that would restrain the creative urge. But perhaps most surprisingly, Murchland feels that true creativity requires a capacity for *suffering:* an infinite patience and a tolerance for the frustration, ambiguity, and failure that is inherent in all creative work. "Each effort they make," says Murchland, "is a raid on chaos, a defiance of human limits, a gesture towards infinity."[28]

Although creativity and spirituality are obviously not synonymous, a genuine creativity may well flow from the kind of devoted inner life that spirituality entails. *Receptivity* to the "still small voice" within is the essence of the spiritual life, and there is a *restless* push toward growth and development that Carl Rogers said was the very mainspring of creativity. There is a tendency of those who value the spiritual life to be *off center* from society's point of view, but only because they have exercised their *freedom* to choose a new center. They are *committed* and *enthusiastic* about their work, because they are powered by its transcendent meanings and the sense of purpose that produces. And, as we will explore more fully in Chapter Eight, there is a capacity for *patience*—translated as "longsuffering" in the King James version of the Bible—which is a fruit of the spirit in our day as much as it was in St. Paul's. It is through our inner search for God, our "gesture towards infinity," that we find not only God but God's creative spirit as well.

Humor

Yes, everyone has a sense of humor (except for my fourth-grade teacher, but that's a different story). But there are wide differences between us in the kinds of humor we employ and enjoy. Imagine for a moment the person (more often a man, it seems) who gets his jollies telling one racist, sexist, or cruel joke after another. "Did you hear the one about the . . . [insert ethnic group here]?" "What's the difference between a blonde and a . . . [insert derogatory noun here]?" It's a kind of zero-sum humor that derives its pleasure from denigrating others. Don Rickles, for example, has made quite a name for himself with an acerbic form of satire that seems to divide the world into two classes: himself and those he calls "hockey pucks." Now, I'm not saying that such humor isn't funny or that I haven't laughed at it; but I would also ask you to observe that this kind of humor is primarily at the expense of others, sometimes in the most cruel and demeaning of ways. It wears very thin very quickly, even when you aren't the brunt of the joke.

Contrast the style of someone like Johnny Carson (or, for those of you old enough to remember, Steve Allen). There is a subtlety, a wittiness, an ability to take the smallest nuance and translate it into the opportunity for laughter. There is a sense of irony and a keen taste for life's contradictions. But perhaps most important, there is an ability to laugh at oneself and invite others to see the humor inherent in their humanness.

I lead you on this little tour of late-night comedy in order to make this point: there is a type of humor characteristic of the lower stages of adult development that reflects the same zero-sum mentality inherent in other aspects of early-stage development. With growth and maturity, even our sense of humor changes in some identifiable and important ways. Prefabricated jokes can still be "funny"—remember that the wider circles still include the concentric circles within—but they no longer typify our sense of humor. Said Abraham Maslow of this distinction: "one can judge the level at which people live by the kind of humor they laugh at. The person living at the lowest need levels is apt to find hostile and cruel humor very amusing. . . . The Abraham Lincoln type of humor— the philosophical, educational type of humor—brings a smile rather than a belly laugh; it has little to do with hostility or conquest. This higher type of humor cannot be understood at all by the person living at the lower need levels."[29]

This is more important to organizational leadership than you might immediately think. Max De Pree, former CEO of Herman Miller and author of several books on business leadership, lists a mature sense of humor as one of his twelve key characteristics of successful servant leaders.[30] To me, he is right for at least three reasons. First, it is enormously important to be able to laugh at yourself, not only for its therapeutic value but also because of what it says about you as a person. You may have a very strong identity, but your ability to laugh at yourself says that you are not so wedded to it that you cannot step back and see your own weaknesses. It says that you are not overly defensive, and this message can silently encourage others to give you feedback and share their ideas, even if they think you might disagree. It indicates in you a degree of humility, that rare quality of spirit that can be very charismatic and can actually increase your personal power with others. The capacity for self-effacement is an aspect of self-mastery.

Second, the kind of humor we are talking about has an existential quality that allows mature leaders to see even the most difficult situations as they are and yet find within themselves the justification for a wry smile or two. Instead of unrelenting contradiction they see irony; instead of inexplicable reversals of fortune they see the satire of fate. Humor can be a source of strength and an affirmation that the slings and arrows of life will not finally defeat us.

Third, from a very practical point of view, business leaders had better rise to a higher form of humor, or they will find themselves in big trouble. Practically every workplace in the United States is substantially more diverse than it was a mere ten years ago in terms of gender, ethnicity, and religion. At the same time, our skins seem to be significantly thinner. Whatever the excesses of "political correctness," it is still undeniable that the kind of humor endemic to the lower levels of adult development is simply no longer tolerable in the work environment. And if you think that carrying it on in the men's room, behind the warehouse, or otherwise "in private" is still acceptable, a quick look at the recent multimillion-dollar racial harassment lawsuit against prominent executives of Texaco (who have since been fired) should disabuse you of that notion.

One of my recent coaching clients (let's call him Ted) is still learning this lesson. His preferred method of criticizing the performance of his subordinates is to use sarcasm and personal insults, earning him the near hatred of many of his employees and the concern of his superiors about his future with the company. Both reactions shocked and puzzled him. "I would never intentionally hurt anybody," he says. "It's just my way of making a joke." But it is a form of humor not particularly funny to its recipients nor effective as a management tool. It is simply a way in which this particular manager, who tested predominantly within the Opportunist stage of development, avoids legitimate workplace conflict and vents his barely hidden disdain for others. At this writing, Ted is still on a form of probation with his employer, his future quite uncertain.

James Thurber once said that while the wit makes fun of other persons and the satirist makes fun of the world, the true humorist makes fun of himself. Those with an intentional spiritual life come quite naturally by this more mature form of humor. Their sense of self/no-self gives them the capacity for a perfectly healthy form of self-deprecation that is both genuinely funny and quite endearing to others. This capacity, in fact, is one of the distinguishing marks of an authentic spiritual maturity. What's more, it is the rootedness in Ultimate Reality that gives such people the ability to find irony and satire in the midst of chaos and crisis. The big picture is never the momentary storm or the current calamity, although those must be wrestled with and subdued in the course of our daily lives. The larger reality is ever and always God. We become able to see the problems *du jour* as just that—and maybe even laugh at them—not because they are inconsequential but because our lives are anchored in something that is *more* consequential and ultimately in control.

Energy

A Western reporter once asked Gandhi, "You have been working fifteen hours a day for fifty years. Don't you think you should take a vacation?" Flashing his typical toothless grin, Gandhi replied, "I am always on vacation."[31] So it is with practically every great spiritual leader through history. They are reported to have had an uncommon level of energy and zest for their tasks despite advancing age and any number of physical maladies. It's not the dissipative kind of energy that comes from obsession or worry or workaholism, which eventually simply drains us dry; it rather seems to come from some inner store, a seeming connection to an abundant source to which they may continually return for refreshment. What's more, they seem adept at avoiding those people and situations that would sap their energy in unproductive or unhealthy ways.

When I ask people in workshops to list the traits of the truly effective leaders they have known, they rarely include energy or physical vitality. Yet when you ask them about it specifically, it's as if they take for granted that their leaders will just naturally need more disposable energy than most. These leaders are, after all, the ones we expect to consistently handle the most physically and mentally demanding organizational tasks without failing, flagging, or complaining. So how do organizational leaders tap into the kind of energy that is refreshing and self-renewing, rather than dissipate their personal energy until they are spent and empty?

I don't want to make this seem easier than it is. Growth into your full stature as a person and a leader is anything but easy. But we might gain some insight by looking at two words we often use synonymously with high energy: *inspiration* and *enthusiasm*. I imagine that practically all of us have had the occasion to do "inspired" work. It usually happens when we know that we are doing something important and are aware that we have the ability to do it well. Time seems irrelevant, and normal distractions lose their power over us. Our energy very naturally flows toward and into the work, yet we can stay at the task for unusual lengths of time without feeling a loss of physical stamina. For as long as we are "in the groove," something seems constantly to be replenishing us. It is much the same when we feel "enthused" about a project or task. Apart from the physiological release of stimulants into our bodies, we experience mentally a combination of focused attention and excitement that helps us bring our full selves and our complete attention to the task at hand. To do inspired work or to work with great enthusiasm is to taste the kind of energy that those at the highest levels of spiritual maturity are accustomed to receiving and spending in their daily lives. It is not surprising, then, that both of these words have such rich spiritual derivations—to be "in-spired," of course, means to be imbued with spirit; to be "en-thused" (from the original Greek) is to have God within you. Our linguistic ancestors saw this energy as coming quite literally from a connection to the spirit of God.

William James was the first to study religion extensively from the psychological perspective. He found that one of the primary characteristics of a deeply spiritual life was a "zest which adds itself like a gift to life, and takes the form either of lyrical enchantment or of an appeal to earnestness and heroism."[32] Those high-sounding words may not translate very well into our own time. Yet it is certainly true that among the unexpected gifts of psychospiritual maturity are an enthusiasm about life and work; a spontaneous strength; a deep reserve of intellectual, emotional, and physical energy; and an openness to inspiration. The results can sometimes indeed be heroic.

Vision

We recently marked the thirtieth anniversary of the assassination of Dr. Martin Luther King Jr. Despite the fact that most of the population of the United States was not alive when King died, it is a rare soul who has not heard the resonant tones of his "I Have a Dream" speech. Even if you can't recall exactly what he said, I bet you can call up in memory the passion, fervor, and conviction with which he spoke. His dream, his *vision* of America is indelibly imprinted in our cultural psyche. But I believe that the power of King's vision was not dependent on his eloquence, or even on the righteousness of his ideas. I believe that his vision insinuated itself into individual hearts and collective history for the same reason as would any other really great vision of a future-in-waiting: because King came to a place in his life and work where he could see things from the perspective of the ultimate values in life. In short, *he could see things as God saw them.*

I mean this quite literally. The reason for the greatness of any vision is not its grandiosity or its ambition or its prescience; it is great because the person who has it has come to a place in her life where she can "en-vision" a future way of being that is aligned with God's purposes in the world. And by that standard a great vision need not be of some huge cultural change. We can have truly great visions of ourselves, our work, our families, or our companies that spring from this same way of seeing the world.

My friend John had a truly great vision for his own professional life, which I watched develop during the fifteen years I have known him. It began, as great visions usually do, with a nagging dissatisfaction with things as they were. Despite his partnership position with a large and well-respected law firm, John was becoming increasingly disaffected with the kind of work he was doing, the values of the people with whom he was doing it, and the pressures that the almighty "billable hour" was creating in his life. When the opportunity came to become in-house counsel for a growing retail company that had been one of his primary clients, he jumped at the chance, seeing an opening to leave behind the pressures and peccadillos of private law practice. Unfortunately, John soon became a living example of one of Kohlberg's axioms: his level of psychological, spiritual, and moral maturity was sufficiently beyond that of his superiors in the company that they not only misunderstood his approach to many business problems but felt threatened by him as well. They began looking for, and finally found, a business reason to fire him.

There followed for John a two-year period of tremendous introspection and personal growth. He wrote extensively, spent time in a spiritual retreat center, and earned a certification as a pastoral counselor. He also honed his own personal vision of what his life could be—of how his unique gifts and talents could be used in the world in a way that could both respond to God's pull on his life and give him the sense of personal satisfaction he craved. Not surprisingly, the call eventually came. Another law firm in a nearby city had a need for a person with just John's skills and was willing to cooperate with him in structuring his work and his compensation in ways that would avoid the pitfalls of his earlier experiences. John is now happier than I have ever seen him, doing good work with topflight business clients, alongside people whose values he shares.

There are a lot of other great visionaries out there. They are people who can see the potentialities hidden in any situation of reality-as-it-is and envision a future-in-waiting for themselves and their organizations that partakes of their greatest strengths, operates on their highest values, and creates a new reality that is uniquely theirs to claim. Such visions, like John's, are uniquely *personal*. Not that organizational vision statements don't have their important place, but the kind of en-visioning of which I am speaking begins as a purely personal process and grows out of a person's authentic center. It is his way of answering the central questions in his life: What is it that really matters? What do I really care about? What do I most *want* from life?

Developing such a vision employs many of the fruits of a spiritual life we have already discussed. John, for example, required a period of deep *introspection*—providentially given to him by his spell of unemployment—for him to clarify his vision of the future. He also had to have *faith*—a forward-looking optimism that presumes that even the worst of temporary setbacks (even losing your job!) may actually be the doorway to a new and better life. Vision also makes use of our capacity for *big-picture thinking*, because vision is less a matter of climbing the ladder of success than determining if the ladder is scaling the right wall. It is, as we have said before, a matter of asking the right question.

I'm afraid that many of us don't really have a compelling vision for our lives and our businesses because we lack these fruits of a truly devoted spiritual life. Our "visions" are really more like goals: to be financially secure, to satisfy our customers, to beat out the competition. There's nothing necessarily wrong with these goals, mind you; they just don't have any compelling energy affixed to them. They don't attract people. It's like my friend John trying to get me juiced over a "vision" of his making $300,000 a year, or Dr. King using that momentous occasion on the Washington Mall to deliver a polemic on fixed racial employment quotas.

That's the thing about truly great visions. They are not about measurable goals, or effectiveness, or "winning." Those who have only such goals (and there are many among us) will often "succeed" only because they have set their sights so low. They take pride in winning at checkers when they could be gifted at chess. True visionaries are sometimes not successful in the traditional sense, but they are invariably *fruitful*. Their passion, energy, and commitment are contagious, drawing others to them and to the causes and values they represent. They scatter abroad the seeds of hope on which the future is built.

True Integrity and Its Necessary Companion, Courage

Integrity is oft in the news these days, more often from its perceived absence than from some example of its presence. We all have our notions of what it means, but I am particularly attracted to the fact that it derives from the Latin word for "whole" or "entire." To me, to have integrity is to be undivided, without fragmentation, unified, unique. It is congruence in thought and action, word and deed, beliefs and the way one lives one's life. Yet that kind of inviolability is not all that most of us mean when we use the word *integrity*. If it were, then surely historical figures like Genghis Khan and Adolph Hitler would have possessed integrity, as they seem to have been unwaveringly true to their destructive and power-hungry natures. No, our notions of integrity seem to imply a certain *goodness* as well, an adherence to ultimate values that are prized and given credence by practically all of us. And that's where the spiritual life becomes an important part of human integrity, because it is through a devoted inner life that we can come to discover, internalize, and consistently live out those ultimate values.

To have this kind of integrity is to establish a sort of standpoint in the world—sometimes even a standpoint over *against* the world. Such integrity announces that we have come to apprehend our unique place in society and our chosen roles and duties with respect to others. But for those following an intentional spiritual path, it also means that our standpoint is firmly placed upon God's values and purposes in the world, as we are coming to understand them in our own lives. For the spiritually minded, the ultimate test of integrity is not whether our actions fit with our images of ourselves or the expectations of others but whether they are congruent with God's will in our lives as best we are led to understand it. We may not have a separate word for it, but that is a different kind of integrity altogether. Call it True Integrity.

If True Integrity is a standpoint, then courage is what keeps us firmly in place there. We all know how fierce the pressures can be that seek to remove us from our stand: the opinions of others, the "way things are," the "way things have always been," not to mention our own needs, fears, and neuroses. It takes great personal courage, exhibited daily and even hourly, to keep your feet planted in your own unique standpoint. But those who have embarked on their own spiritual journey have at least one significant advantage. They are likely to have begun their journey in the first place not because they thought it was a "good idea" or because they thought they "should" but as a response to a *felt incongruence* between their lives as lived and their lives as en-visioned by them. The incongruity was the burr in the saddle, if you will, that spurred them on toward authentic spiritual growth. To feel the kind of incongruity that comes from giving way to internal or external pressures is just not tolerable for people who have truly committed themselves to aligning their life with Ultimate Reality. They know from experience that they cannot long endure that kind of fragmentation without great personal and spiritual cost—and pain. For them, integrity has its own rewards.

As Mark Twain observed, courage is the mastery of fear, not the absence of fear. The juvenile motto "No Fear," which I see displayed on so many twenty-something chests and bumpers, is just the current version of the ancient mix of invincibility and foolishness that has always been the province of youth. It has little to do with true courage. Instead, barring the kind of tragedy or illness that brings it to us sooner, it is usually in midlife that we first discover the limits of our courage. The crisis can happen in any number of ways, but the script will go something like this: there is something about ourselves or our lives that begins not to work for us. We begin to realize that this "something" does more harm than good, and we begin the sometimes lengthy process of preparing ourselves for radical change. It may be an addiction, a neurotic attraction (or repulsion), a relationship, an original career choice—all we know is that some aspect of reality-as-it-is is weighing us down, and the future-in-waiting requires that we lighten our load.

I have experienced this in my own life and have worked with many others who have as well, and I can tell you that *this* is a place where great courage is desperately needed. There is often a sense in such a moment that to give up on what one knows—what has become habitual and familiar even if unhealthy and increasingly painful—is to somehow let go of one's hard-won identity, one's anchor in the world. What is required here is the courage to weigh anchor and move forward, in faith that the pain of the transition always has a shorter life than you think it will, and with the knowledge that your anchor must ultimately rest in that which is larger than yourself and greater than your fear. This brand of courage, so essential for our growth into the full measure of our maturity, is one of the most reliable fruits of the spiritual life. The justification for our fears diminishes, after all, in the same measure that we allow God control of our lives.

Questions and Exercises for Further Reflection

1. When you picture the "flexible flyer," what characters from TV, stage, or screen come to mind? ("Hawkeye" Pierce from M*A*S*H is one of my favorite examples.) What kind of "control" do such people exercise? What seems to be the source of their strength?

2. Where in your life now do you need a sense of perspective—an ability to see the whole forest instead of a bewildering maze of trees? Can you separate—mentally and emotionally—from the tan-

gle of earthly problems for long enough to achieve a big-picture view? Ponder the image of the sea hawk, flying high over the ocean's currents. With seemingly endless patience she glides, constantly attuned to the movements of the teeming schools of life beneath her. If she had merely sat on the surface of the water, relying on her skills and quickness to try to snare passing fish, she would eventually perish. As it is, patience and perspective make for a swift and certain catch. The Chinese proverb asks, "Can you remain still, while the water is turbid and cloudy, until in time it is perfectly clear again?" Do you have the patience required to achieve that kind of perspective?

3. There is a story of two sisters who argued over an orange. Each wanted it for a recipe she was intending to make. Neither would give in to the other, for to do so would mean the loss of the delicious dessert each had in mind. They finally decided to cut the orange in half, resulting in much smaller versions of their delicacies. Only then did they discover that, while one sister needed the pulp for her dish, the other needed only the peel. The next time you are faced with a decision that seems clearly to be a win-lose, zero-sum choice, remind yourself of the story of the sisters. What are the true interests of the parties? What at bottom does the "other side" really want? Have you asked the right questions to determine that?

4. In what do you have ultimate faith, complete confidence, unmitigated trust? Do you have that kind of confidence in a personal god, by whatever name called? If your answer is yes, reflect on the ways in which you actually act on that faith in your working life. In what ways are you holding back, preferring to trust in your own resources rather than taking a chance on an unseen god? If you find yourself holding back more than you would like, take the time to seek out a person who does not seem to live his life with much "functional atheism," and have a candid conversation. Read him the quotation from Goethe in this chapter, and ask him to tell you what he thinks of it.

5. Visualize for a moment your "identity." Think of it as an outer shell around you that you see when you look in the mirror and that you proudly display to others, composed of the type of

work you do, your educational and training background, your material possessions, your roles in family and community, and your most important skills. Consider what would happen if the elements that make up your identity were somehow suddenly taken away: you lost your job and credentials, bankruptcy took your possessions, tragedy or divorce deprived you of your family, and illness robbed you of your skills. What would your identity now be? How would you describe yourself to other people? Where would your identity now "come from"? Would the loss of your identity feel like the loss of a possession, or like the destruction of your life itself? Why?

6. Lee Iacocca was fired from his position as president of Ford Motor Company in 1978. In recalling the experience, he has said that this was at the same time the most humiliating event of his life and the indispensable prerequisite for the tremendous success that followed him in his subsequent years at Chrysler. Where in your life has some perceived failure ended up by opening the door to some unexpected success? What do you think of those people (few, but loud) who claim never to have failed at anything?

7. In 279 B.C., King Pyrrhus of Epirus defeated the Romans in a pitched battle. "One more such victory," he lamented, "and we are undone." Have you sometimes enjoyed successes (so-named Pyrrhic victories) that led you down a wrong path?

8. Novelist Flannery O'Connor said that she spent from nine to noon in her office every day, whether she was working or not, so that "if an idea should float past, I'll be there to catch it." Giving yourself time to be open to your own sources of creativity is no less important to you and your career. Where do you set aside that kind of time (albeit in smaller increments)? If your day currently does not allow for the "genies" to visit, the following habit of mind is suggested. Find, against all the pressures to the contrary, twenty inviolate minutes in the midst of each working day when you are simply unavailable to all but yourself. Some people are able to close a door and switch the phone to "send all calls"; some must retreat to a nearby park or church. One man I know drives three minutes to a parking lot overlooking a lake for the last half of his

lunch hour. Wherever you go, begin with a short prayer, poem, or saying that is meaningful to you as a way of clearing your head. Then, without an agenda or desire to "solve" anything, allow the cares and duties of the day to come in and mill around. Be patient with yourself—at first you'll use the time making mental "to do" lists. But with persistence, the time will become more of an opportunity to get perspective on the day. With practice, you will find that you develop the ability to lightly focus on the most important issues or problems, seeing them from different angles. It is in this relaxed solitude, when you are gently attentive to the cares of the day, that the unconscious sources of creativity can act.

9. Think of the last time you found yourself working (or playing) with tireless enthusiasm. What skills were you using? Why did the task seem important to you at the time? If you were called on to explain where the energy for that endeavor "came from," what would you say? Can you think of ways in which that experience might be replicated in other aspects of your working life?

10. Do you have a vision for your life, or merely goals? One way to know is to read the following passage from Emmet Fox's wonderful little book, *Your Heart's Desire:*

> Already in your past life, from time to time, God himself has whispered into your heart just that very wonderful thing, whatever it is, that he is wishing you to be, and to do, and to have. And that wonderful thing is nothing less than what is called Your Heart's Desire. Nothing less than that. The most secret, sacred wish that lies deep down at the bottom of your heart, the wonderful thing that you hardly dare to look at, or to think about—the thing that you would rather die than have anyone else know of, because it seems so far beyond anything that you are, or have at the present time, that you fear that you would be cruelly ridiculed if the mere thought of it were known—that is just the very thing that God is wishing you to do or be for him. And the birth of that marvelous wish in your soul—the dawning of that sacred dream—was the Voice of God himself telling you to arise and come up higher because he had need of you.[33]

Now, ask yourself this question: Is the vision that I have for my life and my work at all consonant with that inner voice that has told me of my Heart's Desire? What would it mean to act as if I more fully believed what that voice has told me?

11. Is there a sense of incongruity, a nagging feeling of something missing, in your life right now that keeps you from feeling a sense of True Integrity? Are you able to articulate what that "something" is? Do you have the courage to try to find the words for it by talking it over with a wise and trusted friend; a minister, priest, or rabbi; or a psychologist with a spiritual base?

Chapter Eight

The Interpersonal Fruits

Keep away from people who try to belittle your ambitions.
Small people always do that, but the really great make you
feel that you, too, can become great.
MARK TWAIN

"We should remember," Stephen Covey wrote, "that effective interdependence can only be built on a foundation of true independence. Private Victory precedes Public Victory. Algebra comes before calculus."[1] I agree. The developmental model of organizational leadership that we examined in Chapter Six helps us understand that it is the inner-personal attributes that are central to the mature, effective brand of leadership so needed in today's environment. These particular fruits of a devoted inner life form the solid foundation on which interpersonal and organizational skills may be developed and honed. But without the inner-personal traits, our capacity as organizational leaders is limited indeed.

For example, I spend a lot of time working with businesses on issues relating to understanding and dealing with a diverse workforce. These days, practically every major company will tell you that this is a critical managerial skill. I can teach managers to become more aware of the differences between people and their varying cultures, values, and perceptions. We can also learn how to deal with those differences in the ways we interact with others. In other words, a diversity consultant can help you master the organizational skills and interpersonal techniques necessary for managing diversity in the workplace. But what are infinitely more important for this critical managerial competency are the *inner-personal* qualities that we discussed in Chapter Seven. If you have a deep acceptance of yourself and others, a sense of self/no-self, a sense of humor that is constructive and not demeaning—in short, if you have the qualities inherent in a mature inner life—you are already more than halfway toward knowing how to manage diversity issues. Those innate qualities provide a firm foundation to which a diversity consultant might add supplemental knowledge, understanding, or technique. Your private mastery makes public leadership infinitely more effective.

In this chapter we will explore the "relational" fruits of a working spirituality, which build on the "attributional" fruits of Chapter Seven. Remember, however, that these important leadership traits are best understood not as skills to be learned nor as qualities to be acquired like so many certifications or degrees. Think of them instead as the manifestations in your public life of the process of growth and maturity that is going on within you. True mastery of interpersonal relations is accessible only to those who have transcended purely personal concerns and matured into a broader frame of reference.

Empathy: Seeking to Understand

Francis Bernadone, known to Christians as St. Francis of Assisi, asks in his famous prayer, "O divine master, grant that I may not so much seek . . . to be understood as to understand." It is good to ask for help with this, for it against our normal tendencies. The human desire to be understood by those around us—and once understood, valued—is one of the most powerful forces motivating our behavior. We do not often see the importance of seeking *first* to understand.

Yet research clearly shows that the most critical difference between successful and unsuccessful organizational leaders is in their ability to listen to, hear, and genuinely understand the perspective of others.[2] Certainly among the business managers who come to me (or are sent kicking and screaming) with the goal of "fixing" some particularly problematic behavior, by far the most common cause of their trouble is an inability or unwillingness to effectively understand those with whom they work most closely.

Not surprisingly, there are some developmental reasons for this that go beyond mere "listening skills." Research has shown that as individuals move toward the later stages of adult development, they become better able to *empathize*—that is, they perfect the ability to participate in another person's feelings or ideas.[3] Empathy is not the same as sympathy, which implies a measure of agreement with the other person. It is instead the ability to take others' perspective, to "walk in their shoes" or "get inside their head" and see things as they see them, even if one personally disagrees with their position or has feelings about the issue that are radically different. Being a "good listener" is important; but if by that we mean only that we have learned certain skills and techniques that make the other person *feel* heard, we have still largely missed the point. To empathize is to both hear *and* understand, and to grasp both the thoughts the other person is trying to convey and the feelings he or she has about them.

Empathy is a critical business skill. One of my clients, Stan, is having to learn this the hard way. As the CFO of a growing company and an expert on Total Quality Management (TQM) processes, Stan does a terrific job of talking the talk of teamwork and empowerment. He is an excellent communicator and has the proven ability to get his people excited about the future of the company and their role in its success. When you interview his coworkers, however, both peers and subordinates say the same thing: Stan's actions don't match his words, even though he seems truly to believe the words themselves. He is consistently critical of the ideas of others, fails in many cases even to understand them accurately, and uses sarcasm and belittlement to deflect them away. He seems wholly insensitive to the effect that his derisive comments have on those around him, particularly his subordinates. So despite his wide breadth of knowledge, substantial intellectual prowess, and decades of experience in the financial arena, he is in danger of crashing his career. In the old management paradigm, Stan's skill and knowledge alone may have ensured his success; today, his complete lack of empathy could lead to his failure.

There are learnable skills and behavioral modifications that can help Stan remain in his position. But his true hope lies in his ability to grow and mature. At age fifty-two, his level of adult development tested out at barely above the Opportunist stage (Kohlberg's stage 2). His frame of reference remains limited largely to his ego and its own needs and interests. To include the interests of others, even in terms of a bargained-for exchange, is still something of a stretch for him. To be able truly to take the perspective of others, to understand them and their interests in depth, will take the will to grow and a devoted effort over time. Fortunately, when it comes to the human spirit, all things are possible.

Vulnerability

If you wish to exert an influence, you must be open to being influenced. That is a law of our human interactions, as true in dealing with coworkers and political constituents as it is in the relationship with your own children. To truly influence others—as distinct from the use of raw power, coercion, or bribe—requires an openness to the influence of the other.

Vulnerability is one word for that kind of openness. But it's a dirty word to most of us, isn't it? It implies a certain weakness, a susceptibility to something harmful or negative; indeed, we associate it with victimization. Our meaning here, of course, is quite the contrary. Mature vulnerability assumes the existence of a strong and well-developed ego that makes victimization by others unlikely. It is the notion of self/no-self applied to our dealings with others: we have a strong sense of our identity, yet we must be able when appropriate to set it aside in service of the larger goal of truly relating to others. This simultaneous sense of both self and selflessness, so enigmatic to others, is the natural possession of those with a mature spiritual life.

Vulnerability in this sense is really just the opposite of defensiveness. It implies that we have learned over time to relax the walls around our egos (so carefully constructed in our earlier years) so that true interaction with others can take place. We can hear them even when they are questioning and critical of us, confident that we have the self-knowledge to separate out what is true and useful from that which is not. We can be open to others' feelings and emotional needs without being trapped by them. But equally important, in vulnerability we have the capacity to share with others our own pain, fears, and needs, letting others experience our humanness in its richness and its poverty. Such is the very foundation on which we build intimacy in our family lives, credibility in our working lives, and authenticity in our personal lives.

Far from implying weakness, this kind of vulnerability requires considerable personal strength. And it may be a strength that the leaders of our organizations can no longer do without. Consider, for example, the increasing emphasis placed on feedback in many modern companies. In most institutional 360-degree processes, managers use negative feedback to fashion their "action plan" for the coming year, and how successful they are in implementing that plan becomes at least one important measure of their managerial effectiveness. Executives are expected to welcome the feedback, learn from it, and proactively respond to it. Yet this comes much more easily for some than for others. Research has shown that openness to negative feedback increases with developmental level.[4] Stage 4 Achievers are considerably more accepting of criticism than those at lower levels, but even they have difficulty with their defensiveness when the feedback threatens their well-ordered view of themselves and the world. It is only at the Postconventional level, populated by the most psychologically and spiritually mature among us, that people become radically open—vulnerable—to the opinions and perceptions of those around them.

The work done by Kerry Bunker and others at the Center for Creative Leadership gives yet another glimpse of the value of vulnerability for organizational leadership.[5] In his work with both governmental and for-profit organizations, Bunker has found that most leaders, particularly in times of radical change, will adopt "elaborate masks" to obscure the frustration, fear, and insecurity they are undoubtedly feeling, believing that this will imbue them with the credibility they need to lead their organizations. In truth, quite the opposite occurs. The leader's failure to acknowledge his emotions in an environment of change and loss can actually harm his credibility by presenting an image that is seen as lacking in candor and authenticity; at the same time, such behavior increases the leader's sense of aloneness and isolation. Moreover, the failure to acknowledge and validate the raw emotions—indeed, the anguish—that accompanies our endless reorganizations, downsizings, and mergers can lead to a buildup of anger and cynicism that can thwart any efforts at corporate healing. To allow others to see your human fears and concerns, as well as your openness to theirs, can be very freeing to all concerned as well as healing to the organization. As Bunker observes, "Personal vulnerability emerges as a core competency that lies at the heart of helping leaders understand and respond to the needs of others. Expressing vulnerability becomes a leadership tool when it opens the door to connecting with others at the basic level of humanness."[6]

Those whose vulnerability has come as the fruit of a spiritual life have an added bonus, if you will. We have seen that empathy gives us a heightened ability to understand others. But through vulnerability we have opened an additional door to understanding *ourselves* and God's movements in our lives as well. I have found in my own life that God acts most consistently on me in the opinions and perceptions of others, even if I may initially want to reject them. Wrong turns may be exposed, right ways illuminated, and fallacies debunked when you truly listen to someone else tell you of their thoughts and feelings about you and your actions. It's as if God, unable to reach us directly in our overly busy lives, uses his creatures to carry the message. This may not happen every day, but it does happen—and often through the most unlikely of messengers! Thomas Moore writes of this mystery in his beautiful little book, *Meditations on the Monk Who Dwells in Daily Life:* "Only in an ego-mad world do we think that destiny is revealed in our own will and thought. You know something that I don't know about where I want to be. If I just listen to myself, I will be trapped in a circle. If you don't speak to me about what you see and suspect, then I won't know the direction in which I want to go. . . . The monk sees the will of God in his superior. I can see the deep will that guides me in the thoughts and reflections of my neighbor."[7]

Tolerance

The movements for racial and gender equality in this country have taught us a great deal about what true tolerance really is. When I was growing up in the Old South of the 1950s, tolerance of other racial and ethnic groups was, for many, simply a matter of doing them no physical harm. Thus to politely isolate (that is, segregate) others from the cultural mainstream was really thought to be a form of tolerance. The Civil Rights movement redefined racial tolerance; yet the focus was all too often on the assimilation of minority groups into a system still built on the values and assumptions of the majority—insisting, in short, that everyone else conform.

In today's environment, people with significant differences from the cultural norm are asserting that it is not enough to simply be "tolerated." (After all, doesn't that sound pretty dismal if you are the one who is merely tolerated?) Today, true tolerance implies that we accept and value the manifold differences between us, even if we don't embrace or sometimes even understand them. True tolerance means we suspend judgment about our differences in favor of relating to others at the level of their essential humanness. There is an assumption of equality and a presumption of adaptability that admits of the possibility of actually being changed through one's relationship with the other. If, as we pointed out at the outset of this chapter, the ability to manage diversity is such a critical business skill, then true tolerance is its essential prerequisite.

There is probably no interpersonal trait for which the level of psychospiritual maturity makes such a noticeable difference. The earliest stage of the Conventional frame of reference (stage 3), for example, is characterized by a nearly complete rejection of those who are perceived as different from the norm. One's self-image at this stage is dependent not only on the opinions of a chosen in-group of peers but also on the ability to differentiate oneself from perceived out-groups. It's as if one has to define *I* in terms of what is *not-I*. The result can be seen not only in the ridicule and cruelty of the typical teenage clique but also in the intolerance and hatred of many equally immature adults.

In contrast, those at the highest observed levels of adult development become paragons of the type of tolerance of which we are speaking. They come to see themselves, as one researcher has put it, as "just one 'other' in a network of interconnected beings or part of an infinite whole. . . . [T]hey can cherish the essence in seemingly the most undifferentiated beings and feel at one with them. They respect the humanity in others and, therefore, do not need them to be different than they are."[8] Between these two extremes lies the continuum on which most of us find ourselves struggling, learning, and growing.

In addition to its profound implications for diversity in the workplace, true tolerance is important to the development of another essential managerial skill: managing conflict. We all know that conflict in the workplace is inevitable. But we are coming to realize that, as in the political arena, it can also be quite constructive. There is, in fact, no progress without conflict. There are certainly personality factors that make some of us more conflict-averse than others, but there is also increasing evidence that our tolerance for conflict—and thus our ability to manage it constructively—is closely related to our level of adult development.[9] In fact, Torbert's research has convinced him that we can be consistently creative at conflict resolution only when we have moved beyond the Conventional level altogether to the Strategist stage of development.[10] Apparently, there is something about moving beyond both self-absorption and group orientation that allows us more easily to divest ourselves of the need to be "right" in favor of the need to be creatively effective.

I am convinced that true tolerance is typically so well evolved in those at the higher levels of adult development because of an aspect of the inner life that they share. We simply cannot go very far on the inward journey without encountering all the aspects of ourselves that we wish were not there—our weak, neglected, neurotic, immature, and shameful parts that we are generally very successful at hiding from our conscious egos. These aspects are what Jung referred to as our Shadow: all the facets of ourselves that in the process of ego building we deemed undesirable and banished to the dungeons of our psyche. The creation of the Shadow in the first place is an important part of our individuation process, for it helps us define clearly who we are in relation to the world and others. But to become truly mature, to rise to the higher levels of human development, we must confront those long-forgotten parts of ourselves. They did not, after all, disappear; and one of the axioms of depth psychology is that life's "second half" cannot be successfully negotiated unless and until the contents of the Shadow are understood, befriended, and (at least to some extent) transformed.

To fail to confront your Shadow is to ensure a lack of tolerance in your interactions with others. The reason has to do with the universal psychological mechanism of projection, which we discussed in Chapter Seven. Everything of which we are unconscious, the maxim goes, is projected outward onto the conscious world. If we are unaware of our Shadow, it is certain that we will see the weaknesses, soft spots, and quirks that it contains, not in ourselves but in the people with whom we interact. And who will be the targets for our projections? People who are sufficiently *different* from us that they offer convenient "hooks" on which to hang them. I dare say that the greater part of the prejudice, hatred, and intolerance in our world flows directly from our inability as individuals to confront our shadow qualities. The faults we see lie not so much in those whom we think we see them in, but in ourselves.

A strong inner life is the antidote to negative projection and the birthplace of true tolerance. Not surprisingly, research by Allen Bergin and others confirms the correlation between an intrinsic religious orientation and the concept of tolerance as measured by the California Psychological Inventory.[11] Apparently, as Jesus so colorfully put it, you can't spend much time worrying about the speck in your neighbor's eye when your inner life has made you fully aware of the plank that is in your own. And you can no longer allow yourself the psychological trick of taping your own warts onto the faces of others. As we mature and grow, we slowly learn the wrongness, the danger, and indeed the sinfulness of presuming that "different" somehow means "inferior."

Empowerment

Empowerment was something of a rallying cry for the 1990s—the cornerstone of TQM and a major facet of nearly every management fad to roll through business in the decade. So why is it that so many of the managers I encounter misunderstand it altogether? To many it's a simple matter of delegation—really, abdication—of significant tasks or areas of responsibility to others, with the idea that they will sink or swim on their own. More common is the manager who will delegate and then in the name of mentoring become so immersed in the details that one wonders why they bothered to involve others in the first place. Still others see empowerment as soliciting the ideas and input of subordinates but then go about making decisions in the same autocratic, secretive way they always have. The truth is that empowerment of others, in the truest sense of the word, is not an easy thing for most managers to do. It goes completely against their tendencies and all that has made them successful so far. Not to mention that it is messy, time consuming, and downright dangerous. Why bother?

My friend Samantha Janeway learned something about empowerment during her years as president of a manufacturing company with operations in the United States and Mexico. Through
an innovative process she herself helped develop, the company sys-
tematically packed down responsibility for idea generation, cost
cutting, and customer satisfaction to every level of the organization—literally *every* level. Probably for the first time, secretaries and
line workers now experienced the power to make decisions and
offer suggestions that would affect significant aspects of the company's business.

On the one hand, it was an absolute nightmare. Complaints re-
garding everything from working conditions to supervisors' attitudes increased dramatically because people now felt freer to
gripe. Morale actually went *down* after an initial euphoria wore off,
perhaps because workers were now being asked to operate outside
their normal zones of comfort, perhaps because their expectations
had increased. Most significant for Samantha, she was suffering the
anxiety of being in totally uncharted waters, places they never tell
you about in M.B.A. school. Yet the observable results were impressive. In a little over a year, some *two thousand* new and credible
ideas had been generated to increase quality, reduce costs, and
provide better service—everything from marketing strategies to
reusing scrap paper in the fax machine. More than four hundred
of those ideas were implemented, adding an identifiable $2 million
to the company's bottom line. Empowerment, for this one forward-
thinking executive willing to take a risk, had proven crazy, unpredictable, maddening—and highly profitable.

When Samantha retired two years later, the board replaced her
with an "old school" CEO with whom, in all honesty, they felt more
comfortable. In relatively short order, the processes she had instituted were dismantled, and management was restructured along
more traditional lines (and staffed with more traditional personalities). Now, several years after the company's grand experiment,
it is suffering through some pretty hard times. Customer service
has fallen off, and several large clients have left for the competition. Market share and profitability continue to decline.

It takes at least a Samantha Janeway to initiate a radical empowerment process in an organization, more still to sustain it over

time. Most of us content ourselves instead with watered-down versions, as if merely delegating were enough. Adult developmental theory helps us understand why we do this.

Wilfred Drath of the Center for Creative Leadership has explored this issue in his monograph *Why Managers Have Trouble Empowering*.[12] We know that the great majority of adults never mature beyond Kohlberg's stage 4 (which Torbert terms the Achiever), which makes this the de facto developmental level of most mid- and upper-level managers. Drath argues convincingly that the strengths and weaknesses inherent in this frame of reference make true empowerment of others seem like a real stretch. In the first place, people at this stage tend to look at working relationships very objectively and instrumentally. They form relationships with coworkers that are somewhat detached, based on mutual respect and mutual expectations. Intimacy and self-disclosure may be important in their family lives but are seen as inappropriate at work. Drath argues that true empowerment might not be possible without some degree of interpersonal closeness and the deep knowledge of the other person that the word *intimacy* implies. In any event, relationships that are totally objective and valued for their utility are unlikely to give rise to the level of trust and commitment that empowerment entails.

The second aspect of the Achiever stage relevant to empowerment is one we have discussed before: people at this level are likely to have a well-developed sense of identity through which they see the world, but they may have difficulty seeing beyond that identity. Valuing and accepting the ideas and opinions of others would not necessarily come naturally to such people. Moreover, genuine empowerment might actually require that they set aside for the moment certain aspects of that hard-won identity—such as the need for control, the need for recognition, and the desire to be "right." For empowerment ever to mean more than "empowering you to do what I want you to do," Drath concludes that it will be necessary for managers to grow beyond the Achiever frame of reference: "To develop further, the manager must learn to take her or his identity as an object so that the very structure of self can be open to examination, the demands of the identity can be contemplated and evaluated by the self, and the person can find deeper relatedness and intimacy with others without risking a loss of self in the process."[13] In other words, the manager must grow into the Post-conventional, Strategist stage of development.

Empirical support for Drath's thesis can be found in the research done by Fisher and Torbert. In their study of how M.B.A. students and alumni handled a variety of in-basket problems, they found that subjects at Kohlberg's level 5 (analogous to the Strategist stage) more consistently looked for collaborative rather than unilateral solutions.[14] They sought out the opinions and concerns of others before making and implementing decisions, rather than taking action alone or dumping the matter off to someone else. In other words, they genuinely empowered others.

Empowerment is the natural extension of the spiritual life into the world of work. People with a strong spiritual core—like Samantha Janeway—seem to have an abiding belief in the potential of others regardless of their rank or status and seem committed to helping bring that potential out into the open as part of their service to the world. They've had sufficient practice at giving up control in their lives that they don't mind walking out on that limb again in the context of their work environment. In fact, they have an abiding trust that the right answer or outcome will emerge in spite of their loosening of the rein—perhaps even because of it! As M. Scott Peck says of such a person, "His primary motives are to serve God, his organization, his superiors and his subordinates, and the primary means of his service are those of empowerment. Whenever constructive, he seeks to give away his power rather than retain it."[15] This does not mean that you won't make decisions or take actions that require your individual initiative or the exercise of your personal authority. Unilateral, even autocratic action has its time and place. But with a deepened spirituality comes the *capacity,* the state of mind, necessary to truly empower others. When the locus of your concern moves from ambition, control, and office politics to the interests of God in the world, it's amazing what can happen.

Communicating Purpose Through Metaphor and Symbol

Organizational leaders may have rich and compelling visions for themselves, their work, and their companies; yet if they are unable to communicate their vision to others effectively, the vision and its promise remains only an inner-personal fruit. To truly affect the life of the organization, the personal vision must engender enthusiasm in others, induce their commitment, and translate into their own individual matrices of meaning and purpose. We occasionally see leaders in organizations who have this talent, this power. They are able to appeal not just to our reason and logic but to our deeply felt emotions as well. When their vision touches on our ultimate values and our longing for the things of God, they even have the power to appeal to us at the level of our spirituality.

I believe that such leaders have something in common. It's not charisma or glibness or a way with words. In fact, not just any words will do. It is the capacity to use *symbol and metaphor* to convey layers of meaning beyond that accessible to mere rationality and its word-forms. "The heart has its reasons which reason knows not of," goes Pascal's famous line, and it is the ability to tap this deeper realm that gives to leaders the ability to connect their vision with organizational reality and the lives of others.

Jung believed that our most evocative human symbols were actually expressions of the *archetypes*—that is, these symbols gave visible forms to the underlying structures that are the foundations of our human psyche, which we hold in common with other peoples regardless of time, race, or culture. This helps to explain why the cross, to pick but one familiar example, not only is the central symbol of Christian culture but also can be found in one form or another in the sacred art and architecture of many peoples who never heard of Jesus of Nazareth. The symbol, Jung observed, has a very powerful psychological effect. It attracts our energy, perhaps because something inside us identifies it with a deep structure of our humanity. Symbols even act as transformers of energy, as anyone who has ever been deeply moved by one of the rituals or sacraments of her religion can attest.

With this in mind, you might think of metaphors as word-symbols. Love is *not* a rose, of course, but poets have long used the symbol of the delicate flower with prickly thorns to describe the human experience of love in ways that literal descriptions can't touch. The more elusive your concept, and the more deeply you wish to have it understood, the more important your skillful employment of the word-symbol. The great spiritual teachers have always known this. When Jesus said that the Kingdom of Heaven was like a treasure hidden in a field, and Shantideva (a sixth-century Buddhist saint) said that illumination was like a blind man finding a pearl in a dustbin, they didn't mean these things concretely and literally. Instead, the images engendered by the words become the conveyor of meaning for concepts that might otherwise be difficult to explain—perhaps even impossible. Moreover, such images meet each individual hearer where he or she is, so to speak, allowing each person to connect to the image in a way that is personally meaningful.

Metaphors can be very powerful in our daily lives. If business is a "jungle" to you, then certain behaviors will likely ensue from your finding personal meaning in that kind of image. If business (or life) is a "game," then one would expect it to be "played" in ways that would not be wholly consistent with the kind of spirituality of life and work that we explored earlier. If you listen carefully to your bosses (or to yourself if you are one), you may hear their attempt to organize a framework of meaning for your particular workplace. They may do it well or poorly, concretely or poetically; they may choose familiar word-symbols like *family* and *team*, or ones that are spoon-fed to them by the latest management fad. And, if you listen, you can hear the metaphors change over time.

This is where leadership born of a deep inner life can excel. In the first place, those possessed of a mature spirituality seem better able than others to access the realm of metaphor and symbol, and use it more freely and frequently. As James Fowler observes, this is likely due to the fact that such people have "been apprehended in some measure by the depth of the reality to which the symbols refer and which they mediate."[16] In touch with the living reality of which the world's great religions speak, they grow increasingly at home in the realm of the symbolic and archetypal, able to use its language to convey their vision and the deep sense of meaning they see in the world.

Such people have the power to change our prevailing metaphors—and thus our whole way of thinking—about work. You may be one of them. We saw in Chapter One the evolution of our cultural attitudes about work and business to the sorry state in which they now languish. But we also saw in Chapter Two that, at least for some, the inherited view is now changing. Metaphors of work as self-development, as vocation, and as servanthood are heard in more and more places and seem to gain greater acceptance with each passing year. Strong voices from the world of business, such as Robert Greenleaf, Peter Block, Max De Pree, and James Autry, are using new metaphors for work and life that are connecting with the personal visions of increasing numbers of people. As more organizational leaders manifest this particular fruit of the spirit, we can expect our metaphors for work to come more fully to reflect the rich potentialities of this important part of our life. This is why the current interest in spirituality and work is important, even if the level of our discourse sometimes never makes it above the trivial. For our metaphors to begin to admit of the possibility of a spirituality of business and organizational life is no small step in the evolution and history of our concepts about work. If, perhaps, you thought that the Simone Weil quotation with which I began this book was just so much idealism, now would be a good time to read it again. Over time, we change the world by changing our metaphors about the world. And the good news is that the most spiritually mature among us are the most adept at doing just that.

Power and Powerlessness

Power is an inevitable fact of life. We live daily within the structure of the power relationships that are inherent in our society and its laws, our families, our voluntary associations with others, and our workplaces. Even the richest man in the United States, Bill Gates, answers to the board of his public company and, most recently, to the U.S. Justice Department and its antitrust attorneys. Power in and of itself is neither good nor evil, it just *is*. Yet we know that some kinds of power tear down, while others hold together; some inspire fear, while others inspire trust; some seem appropriate and legitimate, while others make us worry for the very soul of the person in possession of it.

Power and its exercise may be inevitable, but there are two distinctions that make all the difference: the *type* of power employed and the *purposes* for which it is used. At one end of the scale is *coercive* power: I can impress my will upon you or a situation because I have the physical or psychological power to do so and regardless of whether your desire may be different from mine. It is power at its rawest and least differentiated, only slightly distinguishable from that displayed in the animal world. *Positional* power asks that you submit to my will because you *ought* to. The rules, written or unwritten, of this particular society, family, group, or company say that you should obey me because I am a policeman, father, boss, Grand Pooh Bah, and so on. This type of power is often linked to coercive power but doesn't have to be—it appeals to our sense of order and propriety, but often with the unspoken assumption that coercion could follow for those who fail to abide by the rules. *Persuasive* power says, in effect, that you will obey because I will convince you that you *want* to. I will appeal to something inside you— whether patriotism, idealism, self-interest, or another of the myriad human motivators—to make your will consistent with my own. This can be linked to *personal* or *charismatic* power, which so attracts you to the force of my personality that you are easily persuaded to my point of view.

At the other end of the spectrum from coercion is *consultative* power, through which I seek the input and perspective of others without seeking (at least initially) to mold them to my point of view. I may borrow elements from each of the other power styles where appropriate, even exercising my prerogative to use positional or coercive power to make and implement a decision when the situation calls for it. The preferred use of consultative power, however, is to build consensus around the issue to be determined. Even when that is impossible, those who are affected by the decision feel heard and understood, and go away with the sense that they were participants in a process in which power was legitimately used. They "obey," if you will, not because they have to or ought to or because I make them want to—they do so because they *choose* to.

At this point in our explorations, it probably won't surprise you that with an increase in the level of adult development, there is an increased capacity for more refined exercises of power. Those at the Diplomat stage, for example, have been shown to be much more likely to use coercive power, while those managers two levels higher were much more adept at consultative techniques.[17] The more psychologically and spiritually mature we are, the more "power tools" we have at our disposal. In dealing with the Saddam Husseins of the world, it may well be that only coercive power will do. But the difference between the "Butcher of Baghdad" and the spiritually mature leader is that while the former is capable *only* of the most primitive uses of power, the latter has an entire arsenal from which to choose. Whether on the stage of world politics, in the corporate conference room, or at the family dinner table, a person's capacity to choose the type of power to be employed may make all the difference in determining if that power has been appropriately and legitimately used.

Of even greater importance is the *purpose* for which the power is used. A great many people in business employ power primarily to further their own ambitions and interests. They see other people and situations as chessmen on a board, to be maneuvered with sufficient skill that they "win" the game—or at least keep from "losing." Experience tells me that those who consistently use power in this way are of one of two types. They may use power for their own benefit in order to compensate for some deep feeling of insecurity or inferiority that generally goes way back in their personal history, or else they are locked in an early developmental frame of reference. In the first case, they act out of compulsion; in the second, they are simply acting consistently with a stage of maturity at which people have a hard time seeing beyond self-interest or understanding why someone would even want to. Unfortunately, our culture has so long honored the unfettered pursuit of self-interest that we have largely ignored the damage that the ambitious use of power does to both the user and the used.

Power can also be used in furtherance of the interests of a group, organization, or society. This is often referred to as *socialized* as opposed to personalized power, and it has within it great potential for good. Owing to the dual nature of power, however, there is also great danger here. One must have some reliable internal compass that monitors the aims and methods of the group, lest one find oneself using socialized power for monstrous ends (as have some of the more radical elements of the antiabortion movement, for example). Of equal importance is the eternal truth of Lord Acton's famous observation: "Power tends to corrupt and absolute power corrupts absolutely." People who have been imbued with socialized power, whether as manager of a corporate working group or president of the United States, would do well to examine every day the extent to which the exercise of that power has prospered the most laudable goals of the organization and the well-being of its members, and the extent to which it has chipped away at their own human-ity. All exercise of power is either creative or destructive, never neu-tral. In some measure, power always builds up or tears down, and it is only in vigilance, honesty, and self-awareness that we can remain attuned to the difference.

The safest way to navigate the perils of power is to use it, to the best of our human abilities, in the service of a power higher than either our own interests *or* those of our human groups and orga-nizations. People who are devoted to an explicit spiritual path in their lives tend to view the exercise of power as either a visible form of service to God and humankind or as something they hold in stewardship for a Higher Power, to be used in ways consonant with its purposes in the world. Sometimes, such people even report that they experience themselves as *conduits* for a power they see as ulti-mately residing only in God, instruments for its effective use in the world. Obviously, there is great danger here as well, as we have learned from ayatollahs, bad-hair preachers, and countless mis-creants of history who have used "God's will" to justify the feeding of their own egos and ideologies. Yet if we look carefully enough we will see an even greater number of people—more humble, more selfless, less noisy—who see the exercise of the power they are given as both a difficult spiritual challenge and an opportunity for service and stewardship. The compass with which they navigate the perils is their own devoted inner life, in which prayer, quiet in-trospection, and the disciplines that align them with God's pur-poses provide a constant check on their own motivations and blind spots. As you progress along that inner path, it becomes increas-ingly more difficult to deceive yourself about the interests your use of power serves, and increasingly more rewarding to serve those of God.

But there is more to the spiritual use of power, something that touches on one of the real mysteries of our existence. It is best cap-tured by Jesus' enigmatic statement to the apostle Paul, "[P]ower is made perfect in weakness" (2 Corinthians 12:9 [NRSV]), and by the events reported in Luke leading up to the beginning of Jesus' ministry (Luke 4:1–13). Recall that when Jesus went into the wilderness following his baptism, we are told that he was tempted by Satan in three different ways: he was given the power to turn stones into bread for his famished body; he was given the chance to rule all the kingdoms of the world if he would but worship Satan; and he was challenged to throw himself down from a great height and be rescued by the angels in order to prove who he was. In our language, Jesus was being confronted with the temptations of three different types of power, the exercise of any of which would have served his own personal purposes. He was offered coercive power, the ability to impress his will on his environment to serve his own needs; he was offered positional power over all other people; and he was entreated to the personal and charismatic power of sensationally proving his identity as the Son of God, what Henry Nouwen calls the temptation to spiritual flashiness.

Now, notice something here. Practically none of us would begrudge Jesus the power to provide for his own bodily needs. He was, after all, extremely hungry. And considering who he was, we probably would not have quarreled with him showing Satan a thing or two by accepting the third challenge. And, if the truth be known, many of us would have accepted the classic devil's bargain of the second temptation. But Jesus knew something most of us never could guess. By emptying himself of all power—by becoming personally powerless—he acceded to a kind of spiritual power that put all else in the shade. By all accounts, he emerged from the desert and began his ministry with a power and an energy that the world had seldom known, challenging the limits of human love and transcending the limits of human life. In eschewing both personal and socialized power, the spiritual power with which he lived his remaining years of ministry was somehow "made perfect" and was offered back through a life of service and stewardship. Real power, it seems, lies just the other side of powerlessness.

Love: By Whatever Name Called

Only in the last few years has the use of the word *love*, so central to religion and the spiritual life, gained some small degree of legitimacy in business. In most places it will still draw strange looks and the usual sexual jokes or else get you branded as one of those touchy-feely types whom we relegate to the confines of our HR departments. Yet "[g]ood management is largely a matter of love," says retired publishing executive James Autry. "Or if you're uncomfortable with that word, call it caring, because proper management involves caring for people, not manipulating them."[18] We do develop "safe" language to talk about this fundamental human quality in the context of organizational life, though I would argue that we are only giving it a thin disguise. When we deeply care about others, their life, happiness, and future; when we wish for them the same personal growth and material success that we would want for ourselves and contribute to that in any way we can; when we deeply respect their humanness, treasure their uniqueness, and believe in their potential—we are in fact expressing one of the purest forms of love that we can hope to achieve. And that is precisely what strong, mature, and committed leaders do in business and elsewhere.

C. S. Lewis gave to this kind of love a special designation in order to distinguish it from the many other ways in which we use the word. He called it gift-love, a typical example of which would be the kind of love that moves a man or woman to work, plan, and save for the future well-being of his family when he may never live to share or see it.[19] Gift-love is also, it seems to me, a possible explanation for the manager who spends countless hours mentoring promising subordinates who might one day outshine him; or the supervisor of the downsized department who devotes time she doesn't really have to placing her people with the competition; or the owner of the factory ravaged by fire who keeps his workers on salary and health benefits during reconstruction even though the law doesn't require it. Such love, which we might also call altruism, can be seen in our business lives with greater frequency than perhaps we in our cool, detached, rational self-images would like to admit.

Distinct from gift-love is what Lewis calls need-love, so endemic to most of our human interactions and relationships. Need-love is "that which sends a lonely or frightened child to its mother's arms,"[20] and recurs countless times in our lives as we seek to get our very human constellation of needs met through the people and things we unabashedly use for that purpose. We're probably no less susceptible to loneliness or fear than we were as small children; we just find grown-up substitutes for our mother's arms.

Gift-love longs to serve, even to suffer, without thought of reward or recompense. It cares for, respects, provides, and serves, not out of any sense of duty or obligation but because its very nature is to do so. This is, to put it directly, the divine love of the Divine itself, where "there is no hunger that needs to be filled, only plenteousness that desires to give."[21] And let's be clear about this: when managers or leaders, no less than spouses or parents, lay themselves out in the selfless service of others, or give of their time and expertise, or share selflessly their resources without expectation of reward or sense of obligation but solely in the hope that the recipient can be helped to grow to his or her full stature as a person, then this is nothing less than participation in the divine love of God, regardless of the forum in which it happens or the names by which it may be called. Love lives in business and organizational life as vitally as it does in any other important human endeavor.

As Lewis observed, we are quite unable in our humanness to sustain gift-love for very long at a time or to keep it from an admixture with the wide array of our many needs. Our motives are rarely pure and unsullied—even for the best among us. Yet if the spiritual giants through the ages are to be believed, that is no reason to despair. Those with a committed spiritual life have always been encouraged to see their faltering and imperfect attempts at gift-love not as failures but as graced moments of kinship with God's love and purposes in the world. The relationships and situations in which they inevitably fall short are but the opportunities for continued spiritual growth, the anvil on which their maturity is forged. It is not even particularly necessary (fortunately) that they *feel* loving toward those who are the objects of their gift-love. With the pressures and demands of daily corporate life, it is quite unrealistic to expect us to constantly stir up emotions within us that we would normally identify with human love. But in our actions toward those we manage and work with, the steady and reliable way in which we respect others, contribute to their happiness and growth, and give of ourselves for their good, we do indeed *love* them in a way that best partakes of the nature of God and fulfills our own nature as beings made in God's image.

It is here that spirituality best breaks free of the prejudices and misconceptions that so often surround it. Spirituality is not about retreat from life but rather the fullness of life. As Howard Thurman put it, we come into the divine presence "not by leaving behind what are usually called earthly things, or by loving them less, but by living more intensely in them, and loving more what is really lovable in them."[22] For those living a deep spirituality, the highest aspects of our human experience must be infused into the most mundane and commonplace to have any real effect. Love, "the greatest of these," mustn't be celebrated only in our families and friendships: we must give it room to grow on the shop floor, the conference room, and the sales meeting. In fact, because our families and friends must bear so much of our need-love, it may just be that our organizational lives are the best place for gift-love to flourish. If, as has been observed, altruism is the truest mark and paramount condition of effective leadership,[23] the workplace is *the* place where that is best learned.

Suffering, Service, and Sacrifice

In the film *Shadowlands,* director Richard Attenborough traces the poignant and all too short relationship between C. S. Lewis and young Joy Gresham, who is dying of cancer. During a brief period of remission, she and Lewis take a trip into the English countryside, where they enjoy all the companionship, intensity, and frivolity that are the province of newlyweds. When in a moment of seriousness she tries to remind him that the happiness will not last and that she will soon die, he protests that they should not think of that now and spoil the time they have together. She then says something to him that hits the accomplished author and scholar with the force of a revelation and becomes the centerpiece of the movie: "The pain then is part of the happiness now. That's the deal."

Love and suffering are inseparable companions, though in our addiction to need-love we so wish to believe it untrue. You simply cannot be radically open to gift-love without being radically vulnerable to suffering. They are two aspects of the same experience, two sides of the same coin—that's the deal.

I learned the truth of this a few years back (though I continually have to relearn it), lying on a bench at a Carmelite seminary in Silver Spring, Maryland. I was ending a period of study at the Shalem Institute and had just said good-bye to a small group of classmates who had been my intellectual and spiritual companions for those precious weeks. I had never felt closer to a group of people in my life, and as they all winged their way back to their homes scattered across the hemisphere, my heart was breaking from the thought that I would never see most of them again. Then the thought hit me: I had rarely felt such pain because I had rarely given myself permission to feel such love. In my all too human effort to steel myself against the hurts and disappointments of relationships, I had failed in equal measure to make myself radically open to love's depths. It took only a brief glance from where I lay to one of the ever present crucifixes to remind me that, as the life of Jesus taught us, great love is joined with great sacrifice as surely as the horizontal and the vertical are joined in the cross.

We will be forgiven if this isn't news we really want to hear. Everything in our culture tells us that suffering is unwaveringly bad—to be avoided or relieved where possible. It is an obvious truth that there is much *unnecessary* suffering in the world. It is equally true that many religious people, particularly Christians, have the notion that suffering for its own sake is somehow virtuous (though my own observation is that such a belief tends to produce people who are less virtuous than they are dour, rigid, and judgmental). But there is also suffering that is the appropriate and inevitable result of gift-love and cannot be avoided without costing us the chance to love others in that way.

When Max De Pree, retired CEO of Herman Miller, says "Leaders don't inflict pain; they bear pain,"[24] this is what he meant. A manager who is possessed of the kind of psychological and spiritual maturity we have described in this book will be capable of acting out of gift-love in the service of those who look to him or her for leadership, but will also have the capacity to bear with their failures, absorb their occasional negativity, and patiently nurture their growth and development. To do such things, to lay oneself out and open for others in the way that servant leaders do, is to accept the necessary sacrifice and suffering that ensues. These leaders will occasionally take risks with people who will disappoint them, or will empower those who are not yet mature enough to handle the responsibility, or will spend time and energy in the nurturance of someone so locked in an immature frame of reference that he or she does not even wish to grow beyond it. They may even find themselves betrayed in some particularly ruthless act of office politics by someone whom they have sought to mentor.

But, you see, gift-love is never based on reciprocity. It does not wait to see what you are willing to give to it before committing to give to you. In the context of organizational life, gift-love is embodied in managers or leaders who consistently spend and are spent in ways that grow the organization, advance its highest purposes, and contribute to the continuing growth and development of all its people. They have counted the cost of such a lifestyle of service, its openness and vulnerability, and found it far preferable to a life of self-protection, closedness, and self-interest.

To sacrifice one's own personal ego-needs in the service of larger purposes is inevitably to suffer. And yet this comes more easily—almost naturally—to people whose pursuit of a spiritual life has already led them to the kind of opening, acknowledging, and aligning with a Higher Power that results in the dethroning of their ego. The research done by Fisher and Torbert seems to confirm this in their finding that individuals at the very highest stages of adult development have often experienced a complete disintegration of their ego-identity—a sort of psychological "near-death experience,"[25] which enables them to subjugate their own needs and interests in favor of the highest human values and the demands of Ultimate Reality. In his role as a leader or manager, such a person could much more readily come to see himself as a resource for others and an instrument for God's purposes in the world rather than as just "the boss." He would come to see himself as a true servant leader, rather than as the kind of person George Bernard Shaw describes: "a feverish selfish little clod of ailments and grievances complaining that the world will not devote itself to making you happy."

I believe that in service to others lies one of the great mysteries of the spiritual life. It is the reason why Baron von Hugel advised his famous directee Evelyn Underhill to devote several days each week in service to the poor when she was having trouble with her spirituality. It is also the reason why the most mature and impressively powerful leaders among us, including those we encounter in organizational life, spend significant amounts of their time and energy in selfless service to others. When we are able to disengage from our own selfish little gaggle of needs, when we can truly spend and be spent in the service of others, the little space we thus empty out in the center of our psyche becomes a space that can now be filled by the spirit of God. I don't pretend to know how it works—only that it does. And to the extent that it does, it is possible for us to say along with the apostle Paul that, in some measure, it is no longer we who live but the power of God that lives within us. If a life of spirituality can be said to have an end goal, this is it.

A closing, cautionary note. "We get into trouble in the spirit," warns Thomas Moore, "when we make spiritual practice the project of creating a certain kind of self."[26] Our look at the fruits of a spiritual life has been intended to shed light on the connection between spirituality and some of the vital aspects of work, management, and leadership as they are coming to be understood today. It is distinctly *not* intended as a self-help recipe for becoming more personally effective. To attempt to "use" human spirituality in that way is to create a conundrum from which you cannot possibly escape: that which requires you to move completely beyond your self-interest is being used to further your self-interest. You are seeking the fruit without the tree—an understandable impulse in our consumerist society but a literal impossibility. You are asking the wrong question.

What's more, although most of us would plant an apple tree, let's say, solely for the fruit it will eventually bear, this is not at all the way the spiritually mature view the inner life. To them, it is the planting and the cultivating that are all-important. The fruits are graced additions, to be sure, but it is the *relationship with God* that is of utmost importance. To paraphrase an old spiritual adage, if you seek only the fruits, you'll not get the fruits; but seek God and you will get God, with the fruits thrown in to boot.

Questions and Exercises for Further Reflection

1. In the next conversation you have with someone that involves disagreement or conflict, try the following: do not make a decision about the matter at that time but tell the other person you would like to think about the issue for a day or so. During that time, sit down and list all the things you believe that person felt about the issue—her emotions, not her logical arguments. When you get back together, relate to the other person your perceptions about her feelings and ask if they are accurate. To the extent that they are, you will know you have done a passable job of empathically listening. To the extent they are not, you will know that you have continued to let your own interpretations and projections get in the way of true understanding.

2. Visualize two experienced fencers, dressed from head to toe in their protective gear, swords drawn. Neither can be hurt by the other's thrusts because their outfits are too impregnable, but human

touch is denied to them as well. Or think of those fake sumo wrestling costumes that you see from time to time at carnivals or sporting events, with several feet of rubber padding between you and your "opponent." It is unlikely that you could be hurt no matter how hard your adversary rushed you, but while so protected it is also impossible to get truly close. What does that say to you? What is the price of self-protection at home or in the workplace? Is it always worth it?

3. If the place where you work does not have a formal feedback program, establish your own. Find someone whom you trust to be completely honest with you and periodically engage him in conversations about how you are doing. Watch carefully for your own reactions and overreactions to what he has to say. Do you find yourself looking around for some protective gear to slip on? Do you find yourself rationalizing or explaining away some of the things you hear? Practice the habits of mature vulnerability: listen carefully to what the other person is saying; thank him for his feedback; ruminate over what you hear, especially that which feels negative or unflattering; and reflect on it until you feel you can see objectively and honestly what the other person was trying to convey. Then act in observable ways on that which seems to have been on target.

4. Think of the diversity that exists in your workplace. No, I'm not just talking about its racial or gender composition. How are the people there different from you in terms of their education, family background, learning styles, intelligence level, age, or interests? How well do you "tolerate" them? Do you keep your distance? Try to ignore the fact that the differences exist? Expect them simply to conform? Do you ever indicate an interest in their lives and what "makes them tick"? Do you feel that their differences add something, or is their presence there just a necessary fact of life? What could you learn from them, if you were so disposed?

5. Where did you first learn that in order to be "professional," relationships at work had to be detached, objective, and instrumental? Do you still believe that, or at least act as if you do? Have the litigation-happy 1990s (sexual harassment suits and the like)

made relationships in the workplace more stilted, or has the increased time and energy we spend at our jobs made for a greater sense of companionship and camaraderie? What do you think of Wilfred Drath's assertion that a certain degree of intimacy is necessary to generate the trust required for true empowerment of others?

6. Listen carefully in your own workplace for the prevailing metaphors. What do they say to you about how life and work in your organization are viewed? What behaviors do they encourage? Are the metaphors original or borrowed from somewhere else? If they are not unique to your particular situation, they have little chance of being effective. Winston Churchill, an absolute master of the inspiring metaphor, is said to have written every word of every speech he made to the English people during World War II. Would the course of history have been different if the war-weary Britons had been subjected to worn-out metaphors rather than Churchill's stirring and original rhetoric? Might a different metaphor create a different future for your company?

7. Look again at the descriptions of the various kinds of power: coercive, positional, persuasive, personal, and consultative. Which do you use most commonly with your spouse? With your children? At work? Now reflect on the last time you used the wrong type of power for a particular situation or used it for the wrong purposes. Did your behavior look to all the world like a regression to an earlier stage of adult development from the one you like to think you occupy? Were you able at the time (or are you able now) to see from your broader frame of reference that your use of power was inappropriate?

8. What are the acceptable words for love in your workplace? How would you describe the most caring, giving, altruistic boss or coworker you ever had (assuming, of course, that you've been fortunate enough to have one)? What do you think people mean when they say they love their jobs or their work? What kind of love is that?

9. At least once a month (more frequently if the opportunity presents itself), practice doing something kind for someone else,

being certain that there is no opportunity for recognition and no hope for reward. Make an anonymous gift to a person (not an organized charity) who has a specific need. (And, no, you cannot take a charitable deduction for this.) Write a note of commendation or thanks to the employer of someone who simply does his or her job well and cordially. Better still, find surreptitious little ways to do that sort of thing in your own workplace, being extremely careful to cover your tracks. Practice gift-love until it becomes almost natural to you. And remember, your personal feelings toward the recipient are of little ultimate consequence.

Part Four

Inspired Living and Leading

Answering the Call of a New Age

Chapter Nine

Toward the Future: Shifting Sands and Paradigms

> *I feel that all mankind is entering a new age, and that the*
> *world is beginning to obey new laws and logic, to which*
> *we have yet to adjust ourselves.*
> MIKHAIL GORBACHEV

Hegel observed in *The Philosophy of History* that the great civilizations of the world each decayed and fell largely as a result of a sort of morbid overreliance on their own first principles. The shining values upon which they were founded became the contorted harbingers of their downfall. Our own Western culture and its values were founded on the intellectual and scientific movement of the seventeenth and eighteenth centuries that we call the Enlightenment. Before that watershed time in our collective history, it might well be said that our view of the world was largely unitive and meaningful. The world was "alive and imbued with purpose; all creatures part of a Great Chain of Being, with man between the angels and the lower animals; events explained by divine purpose or by their function in a meaningful world."[1] In accord with the basic Ptolemaic theory, the earth was the center of the universe with the heavens revolving in predictable order around it. All was well.

But to the Enlightenment mind, reality was remarkably dualistic.[2] The story really begins with Galileo Galilei (1564–1642). Eventually tried as a heretic by the Catholic church, Galileo redrew our

209

map of the universe by dividing it into two parts: *primary,* including matter, mass, and motion; and *secondary,* consisting of the metaphysical, supernatural, and moral. By the latter part of the seventeenth century, Sir Isaac Newton would develop his principles of mass and gravity by describing the world as a lifeless machine that operated in accordance with inexorable, mechanistic laws. Newton was by all accounts a devoutly religious man, yet he steadfastly refused to permit any mention of religion to enter into his debates with scientific colleagues. Even the words *machine* and *mechanistic* themselves point to the split that was being created in our collective psyche: both derive from the same root as the word *machination:* "of the Devil." It was left only to the philosophies of Voltaire and Descartes to fully instill in the Western mind this dichotomy of fact and value, subject and object, material and spiritual.

Layered atop this dualistic worldview was the Enlightenment's insistence on personal autonomy and freedom at all costs. The writings of John Locke and Jean Jacques Rousseau fueled the revolutionary fervor of the age but also the cult of human personality, which endured long after the time that Western political systems restabilized. Locke, in particular, had a profound effect on the formative years and founding fathers of the United States.

When we look back on the Enlightenment and its two offspring, the Age of Reason and the Age of Science, we can see rather clearly the first principles of which Hegel spoke. And thank goodness for them! The Enlightenment isolated faith from reason and material from spiritual, yet in doing so it freed our culture from the stranglehold of medieval superstition and ignorance while unleashing all the wondrous advances of the scientific revolution. Moreover, the Enlightenment saved us from the oppressive collectivism of that time and gave us in the values of individuality and freedom the very bases of our democratic society.

But look, if you will, at what those shining values have wrought. We are living, at the beginning of this new millennium, on the ragged extremity of our inherited view of ourselves, our institutions, and our world. The Enlightenment, which wrested the values of individualism, reason, and empiricism from the established order of the day, has undergone a sort of enantiodromia (to use Jung's word), in which its very virtues have become its greatest dangers. As Alexis de Tocqueville foresaw a century ago in his *Democ-*

racy in America, the pursuit of unencumbered autonomy without moral reflection on the deeper levels of meaning results in an ever greater self-centeredness, self-interest, and license. Crime of all collar-colors, our ever increasing litigiousness, and our insistence on rights and entitlements are but a few examples of the tyranny of the collective being replaced by the tyranny of the individual.

And what of reason and empiricism? Despite our continuing societal belief in science and "progress," there is a nagging sense that we have ridden that horse about as far as it will go in pursuit of a better life. As the very foundation of Newtonian physics is challenged by the understanding that we *cannot* totally understand quantum mechanics, and Heisenberg's uncertainty principle makes it clear that we may *never* do so, our boastful confidence in humankind's ability to solve all of nature's ills through technology lies mired in a morass of incurable viruses, uncontrollable natural disasters, and the looming collapse of our fragile ecosphere. Science can produce for us a new super-high-density television on which to watch the mess we've made of things, but we're losing hope that it can solve the mess for us.

Our survival, or at the very least our happiness, depends on a cultural reorientation no less radical or pervasive than that of the seventeenth and eighteenth centuries, but distinctly away from it. Like the Enlightenment, such a shift will likely take place incrementally and over a significant period of time. But as our grandchildren look back on the world as it was in the year 2000, they are likely to see radical differences in our fundamental assumptions, our institutions, and our way of being in the world.

The depth and pervasiveness of such a change in the way we see reality is what is rightly called a paradigm shift. I know, I know. That expression has been trivialized by its overuse in recent years (e.g., "the new paradigm in office furniture"), but it is the best way we have to describe the process by which *the fundamental assumptions and values that are shared by practically everyone in a culture are questioned and changed.* There have been only a very few such transformative changes in the entire history of Western civilization. The emergence of Christianity in the fourth century as the dominant institution of Western culture was one; the Enlightenment was another; and there are clear indications that we are on the doorstep of a third.

In every corner of our society there are intimations of this kind of tectonic change, as if the immovable object of who we have been has at last run up against the irresistible force of who we will yet be. And all of the movements of our day, whether in politics, business, religion, or our personal lives, tend either to recognize and embrace some aspect of that future way of being or else to run willy-nilly toward the perceived safety of a past that may no longer exist. To try to give form and definition to the changes taking place around us is a little like watching a vase fall from a mantel—you know it's going to break, but there is no way to know exactly the direction the pieces will go. What we do know is that the outlines of the new paradigm are beginning to be seen all around, in such things as our increasing awareness of the interconnectedness and underlying unity of all things, the valuing of subjective experience and inner wisdom, the search for community and cooperation alongside individualism and competition, a realization of the place of mystery in medicine and science, and the search for deeper values to control and balance our commercial lives. Most of all, we see this change in the growing search for *meaning* in the midst of chaos and complexity—the growing need for a sense of connectedness and purpose in the events of our outer lives and the deeply rooted desire for our lives to have a harmonious connection to an ultimate source of meaning and value, by whatever name called.

Put in secular language, this search is what the depth psychologists call the drive toward wholeness—the most powerful of all human motivations. There is inside us an incessant (even where unconscious) desire to address the dissonance felt within ourselves and our human systems. I believe that at its best this central human need is providing the energy for the cultural change we are seeking here to describe—a paradigm shift of first-class proportions. As that need increasingly flows up against the obstacle of our failing institutions and our ailing worldview, it will seek a new gradient for its natural flow.

These changes are like tectonic shifts in the earth's plates, real and colossal but hidden to many, perceptible only to those with the instruments of measurement: intellect, inquiry, a sense of history, and perhaps a belief in the teleological quality of human existence. There is not likely to be a John Locke of our time. The world has become too highly specialized and compartmentalized for any one person to define for all the shape of our evolving culture the way Locke did for the Enlightenment. Instead there will likely be a thousand different voices, each from a different perspective, yet each with its own inflection describing the changes in that person's corner of our culture and pointing the way toward a shared future. Such people are the lamplighters in our search for the parameters of the new paradigm, and they are appearing all around us. *From some corner of practically every discipline, field, and endeavor there are signs of a search for a unitive view that heals the split between who we feel we should be as persons and who we feel obliged to be as agents of an aging culture.*

The corner of the world with which we will concern ourselves here is that of our business and organizational life. For many years business has been thought of by those interested in the moral and cultural life of the society as either a necessary evil or, at best, a neutral force. And not without justification. As Alvin Toffler recounts in his futurist book *The Third Wave,* the prevailing "factory" model of business organization, which served the old paradigm so well, put its greatest stock in such values as punctuality, obedience, and rote, repetitive work.[3] Soon all sorts of institutions—schools, hospitals, government bureaucracies, even churches—took on the same values and work characteristics as the factory, along with its division of labor, hierarchial structure, and mechanistic procedures.

But the signs of the new cultural paradigm are evident in business as well, as the ascendancy of new values challenges our most basic assumptions about work and leadership. What's more, this most pervasive and powerful institution is proving itself to be a force *for* change, not just a victim of change. Despite all the justifiable criticisms of the excesses of business—themselves a function of the "ragged edge" of the Enlightenment mentality—we can see today that some of the lamplighters of the paradigm shift are in fact the people of and in business. The changes being forged there, from the empowerment movement to the emphasis on innovation to employee development efforts, both evidence the changing cultural paradigm and accelerate it. And so it *must* be. As history has shown,[4] movements aimed at overthrowing and replacing the prevailing cultural norms (including the hippies of our own age) generally fail to realize their utopian visions because they seek to actualize those visions before they are fully forged and formed on the hard anvil of reality. But the business of business *is* change, discarding the obsolete for the more effective and disregarding convention when it no longer works. We can have every expectation that business will not only mirror those changes in the surrounding society that it deems beneficial but also create and disseminate changes that further its own unique ends. Business is the ultimate "reality check."

In this chapter we will explore some of the changes endemic to the new paradigm that are sweeping through business—some of which have even had their genesis there. What we will see is that a spirituality of business is not only totally consonant with those changes; it is actually more consistent with the directions of the new paradigm than are the outmoded values and assumptions of business as it has been practiced in the past. But more than that, we will see that many of the fruits of a spiritual life that we explored in the preceding chapters are indispensable qualities for life and leadership in the post-Enlightenment world that is emerging around us.

Meaning Over Manipulation, Purpose Over Technique

"The vision thing." Those words have been part of our common parlance ever since George Bush stumbled over them like a Chevy Chase pratfall in the late 1980s. Those were turbulent years, with layoffs and downsizings, mergers and acquisitions becoming common experiences in even the most established and conservative companies. And vision became just the "thing" we began to look to for our salvation.

There was a very familiar pattern among the businesses of that day, replicated thousands of times. Sales or return on assets would begin to drop. The management team (if not already replaced by a "new" management team) would begin to look around frantically for answers. The most common solutions: set ambitious sales goals or quarterly profit targets, then drill into the troops the sense of urgency about meeting them. The manipulations could be positive (cash incentives, special recognition) or more often negative (dire predictions about the viability of the company, threatened job losses). For many of these companies, living quarter to quarter and under the constant threat of catastrophe became a way of life.

But if you asked the employees of such a company about the vision of the enterprise, or their own, you would rarely hear anything beyond a recitation of those short-term goals, or "Staying in business," or "Keeping my job." It's rather like a dog chasing its tail: there is clarity about the goal, but chasing it isn't sustainable forever, and reaching it is little more fulfilling than a mouthful of fur.

Enter the organizational transformation (OT) movement. Growing out of the ideas of influential theorists such as Douglas McGregor and Peter Vaill, OT placed great emphasis on "establishing a vision of what is desired and working to create that vision from the perspective of a clearly articulated set of humanistic values."[5] Words like *purpose, mission, energy,* and *flow* joined "the vision thing" as central concepts for a new way of looking at organizational change. And as these ideas began to take hold in business, organizational leadership became less and less a matter of skill sets and technique as "the capacity to influence and *organize meaning* for the members of the organization"[6] as well as the ability to personify the vision in all aspects of one's professional life.[7] The company's vision itself became seen as a vehicle for connecting with employees' own innate sense of meaning and purpose and aligning it with the organization's aims. Rather than seeking to motivate employees solely through promises of rewards and security, the appeal to vision attempted to inspire them to transcend their own immediate (immanent) self-interest for the sake of the transformative vision of the organization and its larger mission in the community and society. The appeal was clearly to a more *transcendent* set of values and priorities.

In business today, you never leave home without your vision statement. True, some of them are trite and lifeless, having been imported from some consultant's boilerplate or the musings of the CEO. But the ones that are done well are uniquely tailored to the organization's particular strengths, and they stretch the imagination of those involved in the enterprise toward goals that are downright inspiring. The idea has now permeated business and nonprofit organizations alike: that productivity and ultimately corporate success come from the intrinsic motivation of employees and that motivation comes most reliably and sustainably from the alignment of the employees' personal values with stated corporate ends. And management research is emerging to support this conclusion. At the level of the organization, there is ample proof that a sense of mission or long-term vision is a cultural trait that is positively correlated to corporate effectiveness, and particularly to profitability.[8] On the individual level, numerous studies have shown that the power of money and perks to motivate workers is declining in the new business paradigm; motivation comes more from the work itself, what it means to the individual, and how it is related to an overall framework of meaning created by the organization. The idea that human beings will respond like Pavlov's dogs to job-related rewards and punishment is simply unsupported by scores of studies on the subject.[9]

The OT movement, which began as a forecast of the paradigm shift to come in business, is now a mainstream part of our commercial lives. Its emphasis on meaning over the traditional motivators of money and perks, and purpose over mere technique, gave many businesses a framework by which to escape the endless tail-chasing of their past and presaged the current emphasis on vision and mission. OT is one of the several major movements that have taken place in business in the past three decades, bringing sweeping changes and challenges to our traditional business models. And as our explorations in this chapter will suggest, many of these movements—OT clearly among them—*seem to anticipate and set the stage for a spirituality of business and leadership.*

Admittedly, spirituality has little to say to the so-called managerial competency movement, as spirituality does not focus on technical skills and competencies, and it eschews painless solutions, cookbook approaches, and one-minute anythings. But if you look at the language of empowerment, servant leadership, OT, and (to some extent) TQM, you will find a substantial confluence of both thought and terminology with the arguments and premises I have put forth in the preceding chapters. Problems of language and legitimacy (along with occasional hard-boiled skepticism) may prevent writers in these areas from being as explicit as I have been; but if one examines the concepts employed in the management literature alongside the fruits of a spiritual life, the parallels are obvious. Many authors, in fact, simply use "safer" language to describe the same process. Perhaps Peter Vaill was right all along when he asserted more than ten years ago that "to a large extent executive development for leadership of modern organizations *IS* spiritual development."[10]

A number of authors have pointed out the linkage that one can easily make between concepts in the OT literature and human spirituality. Gordon Dehler and Ann Welsh, for example, looked at the role played by emotion in the transformational change process and then looked at how notions of emotion and feeling might just be less threatening ways of talking about spirituality. Pointing out that transformational leadership seeks to create fundamental, nonincremental change in organizations by aligning the individual's core values with those of the company's leadership, Dehler and Welsh conclude that such an alignment occurs primarily at the level of the subordinates' spiritual realm. "From the perspective of OT," they conclude, "alignment occurs when the vision is used by management to infuse work with spirituality and meaning through transformational leadership and intrinsic motivation—thereby resulting in employee behaviors that lead to enhanced organizational performance, and thus reinforce and re-energize the fundamental vision."[11] Or as it was put by Bennis and Nanus in one of the classic works in OT literature: "By focusing attention on a vision, the leader operates on the *emotional and spiritual resources* of the organization, on its values, commitment, and aspirations."[12]

If one looks to OT theory for the kinds of leadership traits necessary to transform organizations, there is a remarkable parallel to the fruits of a spiritual life as we recounted them in Chapters Seven and Eight. Noel Tichy, for example, put together what he considered to be an inclusive list of such characteristics in his book *The Transformational Leader.*[13] To Tichy, such leaders must have *courage* and *integrity*—the ability to stand against the status quo as well as the ability to articulate a set of core values and exhibit behavior that is totally congruent. They have *faith and hope* in people and ultimately work toward the *empowerment* of others. They are lifelong *learners,* able to talk about mistakes but able to view them less as failures than as learning experiences. They have *flexibility* as well as the ability to deal with *complexity and ambiguity,* and have the *perspective* to reframe problems in a complex, changing world. They have *vision* and are able to translate those dreams and images (through *metaphor and symbol*) so others can share them. But, perhaps most important, they achieve *self-awareness* through *introspective self-reflection,* "the basic condition necessary for their own self-renewal that makes them able to play a self-renewal leadership role."[14] In other words: inner work, outer fruit.

Individualism and Relatedness: A Balance Returns

The Enlightenment mentality combined with the frontier spirit in the United States to give those in this country an almost sacred view of individuality. Long before President Herbert Hoover labeled us "the society of rugged individualism," our heroes were solitary figures of great personal courage and strength: pioneers and Indian-fighters, cowboys and gunslingers, patriots and rumrunners. With the coming of the Industrial Revolution and the rise of business corporations, we have simply transferred hero status onto the "rugged individuals" of commercial life: the business tycoon, the wildly successful entrepreneur, the corporate raider. The archetypes of our national identity have left the battlefield and the prairie and gone into business.

But part of what we mourn these days in the decline of our institutions and our loss of a sense of community is a natural outgrowth of our overemphasis on individualism. In the non-Westernized countryside of India, in sharp contrast, one feels completely enveloped in the roles and expectations of culture, community, and caste to such an extent that there is barely any sense of individualism apart from the context of the group. The upside, my friend Robert Johnson found, is that there is scarcely any concept in the Indian mind of what it means to be lonely. For those of us immersed in this society, it is almost impossible to think in those terms, much as we would find many other aspects of rural Indian life incomprehensible. Our problem is that, as a culture, we have never been able satisfactorily to resolve the natural tension that exists between our reverence for individualism and our reveling in the sense of community. And we have steered hard to the first.

In the emerging new paradigm, a yearning for a sense of community can been seen in the ascendancy of such values as interdependence and a realization of the interconnectedness of all things. Traditionally considered to be more "feminine" values, such concepts are becoming considerably more mainstream in a society that purports to seek gender equality and has slowly come to acknowledge the existence of the masculine and feminine in each of us. They are also coming to be more valued because they are *true*. This yearning for community was a chord within us that began to be struck in the 1980s by books such as Scott Peck's *A Different Drum*, and has continued to sound with the blossoming of community-building movements of all sizes and shapes.

Those of you in business will easily recognize this shift in your daily lives. What's the emphasis on teams in your organization as opposed to ten years ago? How important are cross-functional efforts, cross-training, and cross-pollenization as opposed to individual efforts? If someone says that you're "siloed," isn't that almost as bad as being called incompetent? *Teamwork, team building, organizational citizenship, prosocial organizational behavior*—these are the buzzwords and bywords of business these days. And even the old dogs are learning new tricks. Several months ago I was enjoying a conversation with one of the senior executives of the fifth largest U.S. commercial bank. He scores something of a double whammy when it comes to this particular new trick: not only are business executives supposed to be an egotistical lot (second only to politicians and car salesmen in one survey), but he was a lawyer as well, a member of perhaps the most individualistic of professions by training and temperament. Yet when he spoke of the need for increasing teamwork among his staff of attorneys, he couldn't have sounded more like a post-Enlightenment leader: "They know their job is to work together, because as smart as they are individually, there's not one of them as smart as *all* of them. In this day and age we can't afford any Lone Rangers. If they insist on acting that way, then maybe this isn't the place for them, because the team concept is very important to our success."

The management literature of today that best reconciles individualism and community has its roots in the life and work of a quiet, scholarly businessman by the name of Robert K. Greenleaf. A management researcher with AT&T, Greenleaf was also a devout Quaker, and he struggled within the context of his own life to blend the tenets of his belief with his work. For Greenleaf, it was a mythic novel by Herman Hesse that galvanized his thoughts and formed the basis of his cornerstone book, *Servant Leadership*, written in

1977. Hesse's unlikely hero is a young boy named Leo, who accompanies a group of travelers on a journey to the East, performing the most menial tasks as their lowly servant yet sustaining them with his extraordinary spirit and grace. When Leo unexpectedly leaves the troop, the journey falls into confusion and disarray. It is only many years later that one of the travelers discovers that Leo is actually the head of the great order that had sponsored the journey—the servant who was in fact a great and noble leader.

The idea of the servant as leader has deep roots in our Judeo-Christian culture, and Greenleaf's work has had a natural appeal to men and women seeking to reconcile the inevitable tension of relationship and individualism, personhood and group affiliation. The solution, in short, is this: that self-actualization is ultimately for larger purposes; that leadership is ultimately for the good of those people and institutions led; and "he [or she] who would be the greatest among you shall be your servant" (Matthew 23:11).

Ten years after Greenleaf's death, his work is now more popular than ever, as our shifting paradigm begins to restore the balance of individualism and relatedness. New editions and anthologies of his writings are selling more copies than the original works. Organizations such as the Greenleaf Center for Servant-Leadership and the Institute for Servant Leadership sponsor well-attended conferences and workshops around the country and spread the philosophical basis for the movement through their publications and membership activities. Moreover, Greenleaf's concepts have significantly influenced the writings of popular business authors, such as Peter Block, Max De Pree, and many others. You will also find the principles of servant leadership cited often in the literature of employee empowerment, to which we turn our attention in the next section of this chapter.

Needless to say, the fruits of a spiritual life are the veritable stock-in-trade of the servant leader. For Greenleaf the "very essence of leadership" came from "more than usual openness" to *inspiration* and *intuition*.[15] True *empathy*—the ability to listen and seek fully to understand others—is also required.[16] The servant leader must have *faith*, which to Greenleaf was the necessary prerequisite "for one to maintain *serenity in the face of uncertainty*"[17] (my emphasis). Conceptualizing, which is the "prime leadership talent" to Greenleaf, has much in common with our notions of *perspective* and *big-*

picture thinking.[18] Other tools necessary for the leadership journey include *self-awareness, integrity* of word and action, and, of course, *service.* But perhaps the greatest insight for the emerging leaders of our generation was Greenleaf's frank assessment of the role of *suffering,* loss, and the acceptance of failure as the way to a true *learning orientation:* "[Servant leaders] will suffer," he said, "but they will not be hurt because each loss grants them the opportunity to be greater than before.[19]

Despite its clear religious roots, the concept of servant leadership has succeeded in becoming a mainstream part of the new business paradigm. What a wonderful vindication for the life and work of the visionary Greenleaf, who wrote more than twenty years ago, "I am mindful of the long road ahead before these trends, which I see so clearly, become a major society-shaping force. We are not there yet. But I see encouraging movement on the horizon."[20]

Democratization Over Command and Control

For those of us who grew up during the Cold War, the events of the last decade of the millennium staggered the imagination. NATO now includes a number of nations that, a short time back, housed nuclear missiles aimed at our cities. Fledgling market economies are struggling to grow in some of the most unlikely soils on the planet. The quotation from Mikhail Gorbachev that opens this chapter proved its truth, as the sprawling empire he once ruled simply ceased to exist. Taking the broad view, more has happened in the past ten years to advance the cause of social democracy than in any comparable period in the world's history. And it was accomplished not by force of arms but by shift of paradigm.

In our own culture, we can most clearly see the rising tide of democratization in our workplaces. Whatever our level in our organizations, we have expectations that far surpass those we would have had a decade or two ago: for information about important corporate developments, for meaningful feedback about our own performance, for a voice in decisions that affect us, for our ideas and even our criticisms to be heard. A Berlin Wall of sorts has been crumbling for years in our own companies.

As with the other major movements in business that we have explored, *empowerment* has passed from management theory to successful practice because it responds to the realities of the new business paradigm. Managers have embraced it (or have at least tried) because it *works*—because it stands the challenges of the current reality in a way that the techniques of the old paradigm cannot. The following is one representative quotation from a managing director of century-old, ultraconservative Royal Dutch/Shell:

> In the past, the leader was the guy with the answers. Today, if you're going to have a successful company, you have to recognize that no leader can possibly have all the answers. The leader may have a vision. But the actual solutions about how best to meet the challenges of the moment have to be made by the people closest to the action. . . . The leader has to find a way to empower these front-line people, to challenge them, to provide them with the resources they need, and then to hold them accountable. As they struggle with the details of this challenge, the leader becomes their coach, teacher, and facilitator. Change how you define leadership, and you change how you run a company.[21]

But as we discussed in Chapter Eight, many managers and management scholars mistakenly assume that empowerment is simply a matter of delegating or, at most, sharing authority. A deeper analysis, such as the one done by Rabindra Kanungo and Manuel Mendonca,[22] discloses that true empowerment requires a strong belief in the self-determination and self-efficacy of those empowered. And to enable subordinates in such a way, Kanungo and Mendonca conclude, requires that the leader have an altruistic or selfless quality that seeks the employee's development and growth, even where the leader's own interests are not directly and personally served.

In keeping with what we learned in the previous chapter about genuine empowerment, a certain quantum of *faith* is required in the essential goodness and potentiality of other people. To access that faith within ourselves demands the fruits of *vulnerability* and *self/no-self*, as one's personal ego-needs intentionally take a back seat to the developmental needs of others. As any successful manager in the new business paradigm will tell you, empowerment is risky business, if only because you are wagering the possibility of failure—over which you have limited your control—against a pay-off that is much greater down the line. Call that selfless altruism or love or just good business horse sense, but it all boils down to the same thing.

Excellence: Effectiveness Over Efficiency

The Total Quality movement swept through business in the 1980s, born of Japan's growing share of the world's technology and automobile markets and the fear that we were on our way to becoming a second-rate economic power capable of producing only shoddy, overpriced products. Until that time the emphasis of postwar organizational management was on efficiency—designing systems and incentives that would minimize the time required for preset tasks and increase production in quantifiable ways. My father, a retired insurance executive, still remembers the hated little men with stopwatches who swarmed around the office, timing everything from keystrokes to bathroom breaks. Mind you, no attention at all was paid to the *quality* of the final product, only the *quantity* of it that was produced.

The quality movement, as it came to be known, both reflected and advanced one aspect of our changing paradigm: the emphasis on effectiveness over mere efficiency, of quality over mere quantity, of excellence over mere adequacy. At the level of the organization, the system had to change in ways that would, in the words of quality guru W. Edwards Deming, "eliminate numerical quotas" and "remove barriers to pride of workmanship."[23] At the level of the individual, where effectiveness, quality, and excellence originate, the quality movement laid great stress on the person's attitude toward his or her work. To quote another of the prominent theorists of the day, quality at the individual level could only be achieved "through an acute reappraisal of his or her moral values."[24] The organization then becomes a "locus of shared values and moral involvement"[25] where the ultimate goal is to align the company's mission with the employee's strongest motivators. The upshot of all this has become a familiar management mantra by now: workers who believe in what they are doing, are committed to the organization's goals, and are empowered to use their innate talents and abilities to achieve them will quite naturally produce goods and services of excellent quality.

Although these concepts have had some important effects on business and are indeed part of our changing paradigm, they are not new at all to those with a deeply religious orientation. The Christian religious critic Dorothy Sayers wrote eloquently on the subject of excellence more than fifty years ago. "God is not served by technical incompetence," she said, and only work well done could dare to call itself God's work. The great failing of the church, she observed, was in failing to teach that *all* work was God's work and should be done with the same care and quality as if rendering that work to Ultimate Reality itself.[26] The fullest use of one's endowed talents to create products and services of usefulness, quality, and beauty is at the very heart of the Judeo-Christian message about work. Retired businessman James Autry puts it in a more modern context: "I believe that work can become a spiritual discipline [only] when people do what they set themselves to do with an abiding sense of excellence, not only in the results they achieve, but in the very effort itself."[27]

While the central concepts of the quality movement are not new, their popularity has nicely set the secular stage for the emergence of spirituality in the workplace. Someone with a spiritual orientation might see the precepts of TQM this way: if through a "reappraisal of . . . moral values" you come to see work as an essential aspect of your spiritual life, you have a motivation toward excellence that no mere management fad could invoke. If your organization can empower you and "remove barriers" to the use of your God-given talents and abilities, your excellence in pursuit of the organization's aims becomes possible. And if the "shared values and moral involvement" succeed in aligning your deepest sources of meaning with the company's mission, then you have a powerful and sustainable alliance between the appropriate commercial needs of the enterprise and the spiritual yearnings of the people who work there. If you will, a match made in heaven rather than Japan.

So why hasn't this happened? Why haven't we built upon the promising platform created by the Total Quality movement? Why, in fact, do many observers feel that the failures of Total Quality have been greater (though less publicized) than its successes?[28] Two decades of research tell us that the failures of TQM result largely from our human foibles in implementation, rather than from some defect in its central principles. The data seem to show that the introduction of TQM actually *increases* the degree of the organization's control over workers, although in theory it is supposed to decrease.[29] Empowerment, it seems, only thrives to the extent that it doesn't threaten the existing entrenched power relationships (as evidenced by Samantha Janeway's story in Chapter Eight). Furthermore, the inherent logic of excellence and its emphasis on continuous improvement can create a workplace atmosphere of increasing tension and can lead employees to burn out.[30] But perhaps most important—and typically human—is the tendency for TQM efforts to produce committees, quality departments, endless meetings, experts, and consulting gurus that create their own weighty bureaucracy and drag down the core precepts to the level of mundane jargon.

And the reasons for these very human failings? Our discussion of adult development in Chapter Six gives us the answer. Since the 1950s we have seen a number of efforts, including TQM, OT, and others, to move organizations beyond the Systematic Productivity stage of development to a plane where they can constantly recreate themselves to respond to ever changing external demands. The problem, as Fisher and Torbert point out, is that only executives who have moved to the Strategist stage or beyond can fully appreciate the value and logic of that kind of organizational change.[31] Because the vast majority of today's executives never progress beyond the Achiever stage, the leadership of our organizations remains locked in a frame of reference that (as we saw in Chapter Six) lacks the ability to *re*frame itself in response to the demands of the shifting business paradigm. It always feels itself just a little behind the curve. So while movements like Total Quality and OT set the stage and opened the door for a respiritualization of work, *it is only in the kind of growth and development that spirituality fosters that we have any hope of realizing the full benefits promised by these significant advances in management theory.* Only if a meaningful number of our management leaders achieve the Strategist frame of reference can we escape the current impasse. And spirituality, as we have shown, holds the key.

Spirituality Is About . . . (d) All of the Above

All around us, if we have eyes to see, are the signs of our changing cultural paradigm. And when we examine those signs closely, it is astounding how many of them are related to the growing need for meaningfulness and connection to deeper truth that we have called spirituality. Some seem to grow directly out of that soil; others seem simply consonant and complementary. Still others—like OT, the empowerment movement, TQM, and servant leadership—seem positively to *anticipate* and set the stage for a spirituality of business and leadership that is starting to find its place in the hearts and lives of working people. Far from the pietistic and privatistic concept some imagine, spirituality turns out to be concerned about the whole of life in all its richness and variety, *particularly* as it is coming to be lived in the new paradigm.

Take, for example, the observable shift toward greater forms of collaboration and cooperation. Our worldview is changing from one that sees all things as separate and competing for self-gratification, a sort of cosmic winner-take-all game show, to one in which the parts of the whole are interconnected and interdependent, striving first for the preservation of the whole and only secondarily for the advancement of self. In science, we see this shift in the decline of reductionism as the way of explaining all natural phenomena; in the turning of our metaphors from the world as a machine to the world as an organism; in the change of our view of the universe from one chaotic and purposeless to one with self-organizing systems and meaningful patterns; in the change from insistence on immutable laws to evolution in the laws themselves.[32] In organizations we see it in the increasing recognition that with the growing complexity and interdependence of society it is nearly impossible to accomplish anything of lasting importance while acting alone. In government, the past three decades have taught that well-intentioned policies dictated by official Washington will only scratch the surface of pressing social needs without the buy-in and collaboration of local and state governments and, indeed, their constituencies as well. And in business, usually a bit further in front of the curve than our other institutions, this shift has not only brought us matrixed "org" charts, cross-functioning, and teams but also major collaborative ventures between some of the most unlikely business partners. Who would have thought a mere decade ago that Microsoft would be teaming with Apple to bring us a new compatible product line, or GM with Mitsubishi, or American Airlines with USAir? As chronicled in such books as Robert Hargrove's *Mastering the Art of Creative Collaboration*,[33] business is learning that the lessons of teamwork and a win-win mentality work equally well at the level of industry-wide strategy and that beating the stuffing out of your competitor is not the only way to get desired results.

My colleagues at the Center for Creative Leadership have seen this change in the evolution of the "competitive" exercises done with mid- and upper-level executives as part of their Leadership Development Program. For more than twenty years now, the program's first day has included a hypothetical problem in which each participant is asked to create a fictitious candidate for an important position and then to try to "sell" that candidate to a group of peers, each of whom is similarly motivated to sell his or her own creation. The remarkable thing, say the observers behind the one-way glass, is that while participants consistently used to pull out all stops to see that their candidate won, they often now defer to the choices of others when clearly superior to their own, and actively look for ways to build consensus around the "best" candidate, whoever its sponsor may have been. In short, the end goal of choosing a candidate that best serves the interests of the group and its aims is paramount to individual success. Sure, we still have people who want to "win" the exercise, but if they're too obvious about it at the expense of the team process, they are certain to hear about it from the others.

If you think again of the fruits of a spiritual life, it is easy to see how they make collaborative work and win-win solutions seem quite natural. With the maturity of the higher levels of psychological and spiritual growth comes an expanded *perspective* and a sense of *self/no-self* that allows one to see beyond the immanent interests of ego and personal needs to the broader circles of community and higher values of ultimate meaning. Combine these traits with a strong motivation for *service* and you have a portrait of a collaborative, consensus-building leader for the new priorities and challenges of business.

———

In the fast-paced, rough-and-tumble world of the new business paradigm, "managerial leadership is not learned, managerial leadership is learning."[34] No longer is the ability to do a particular job or task a guarantee that you will be permitted to do it, for money, into the indefinite future. Workers these days, and managers in particular, are expected to learn new skills and abilities constantly, or they will find themselves among the ranks of the unemployed—and unemployable. As James MacGregor Burns foresaw more than twenty years ago, the most marked characteristic of the leaders of our day would be "their capacity to *learn* from others and from the environment—the capacity *to be taught*."[35] And as we saw in Chapter Seven, the *capacity to learn* life's lessons with grace, even the humbling mouth-full-of-dust ones, is a hallmark of the spiritual life.

But these days, learning goes farther than that. Just as no college course could prepare you for all the challenges you would face as an adult, no seminar, workshop, or how-to book can prepare you today for success in business or organizational life. Things are simply too complex, and they change too rapidly. In the last decade, we have seen a rise in what has been called intuitive leadership, a reliance on our innate human faculties for knowing something "in our gut"—not at the expense of our logic and our five reliable senses but simply as another way of perceiving the world around us. Intuition is an alternative way of knowing and one that can be enormously helpful in a world that does not always lend itself to studied analytical conclusions. Indeed, while one is waiting for the hard data to come in, golden opportunities may disappear forever. Playing one's hunches is no longer just the province of entrepreneurs and other gamblers; I now see this quality overtly acknowledged in some of the most successful business executives I encounter. This gives legitimacy to a capacity of our mind that has always been available to us but is now acknowledged as a "strategic tool" in traditional business.

The larger society, of course, has also embraced alternative ways of knowing and the legitimacy of subjective experience, as evidenced by the abundance of books on everything from intuition and creativity to "channeling" experiences with other-worldly figures. But as we discussed in Chapter Seven, our capacity for *creativity, intuition,* and *inspiration* comes most reliably from our connection to the source of the creative spirit within us. As it did for Ron, the attorney who listened to the source of wisdom within and won a major victory for his client, spirituality can teach us the centuries-old ways to align ourselves with the ceaselessly creative energy of God and give it life in even the most mundane or "secular" aspects of our day. To paraphrase philosopher Nicolas Berdyaev, we are moving at this shift-point of history from an ethic of obedience to an ethic of creativity; from structure, hierarchy, and rule to energy, imagination, and originality. And that is the spiritual life's veritable stock in trade.

——o——

Our ways of knowing about the world around us are changing in other respects as well. The Age of Reason and the Scientific Revolution taught us that the way to understand a phenomenon was to break it down into its smallest indivisible parts and then to analyze those parts. In other words, if you reduced complexity and multiplicity down to its singular building blocks, you had a better chance of understanding the phenomenon as a whole. This approach works great if what you're trying to understand is a chemical compound, but it does not always do justice to the dynamics of our humanity. So, for example, Freud used a reductionistic kind of analysis to determine that our dreams are "nothing but" wish fulfillment and the discharge of repressed energies. Similarly, many economists have studied our behavior around the production and consumption of goods and services and determined that we are "nothing but" monetarily motivated creatures—thus partaking of that particularly noxious fallacy known as economism.

But that view is changing these days, and with it, business. The increasing emphasis on organizational development, employee empowerment, and enlightened human resource initiatives stands in testament to the fact that business has all but abandoned the idea that people are nothing but economic animals. We've also radically changed our approach to business problem solving: from sole reliance on a reductionistic focus on minute details to systems thinking, from counting individual trees to studying the entire forest. As one senior forecasting analyst for a top-ten U.S. bank said to me: "The old school used to look at forecasting profits in a pretty mechanistic way. Each individual area crunched their numbers, and then some senior officer made a decision based on the 'hard data.' Today it's more of an intuitive exercise, based on how you believe the numbers interrelate to each other and to uncertain future events you can only vaguely anticipate."

Systems thinking, as the opposite of reductionism, takes a special quality of mind. The process our forecaster is describing certainly takes an openness to *intuition.* But perhaps even more than that, what is required is a higher *perspective,* a *big-picture* way of looking at the issues that sees in panorama and is able to analyze the interconnections between discrete and apparently separate problems. As we saw in Chapter Seven, that ability is less of a developable skill than it is a way of seeing and being in the world, and it comes most naturally to those who have achieved a high level of psychological and spiritual growth. Not surprising, then, that our forecaster is a man who has a deeply committed religious life and has tested at the Strategist stage of adult development.

———

It matters little where we live or what our jobs: there is for most of us a palpable sense that the pace of our lives has accelerated, that more is required of us in less time, that an ever greater complexity pervades all aspects of our day. We spend little time rocking on the front porch of our minds and ever more toiling in its kitchen. Our personal sense of chaotic and unrelenting change but mirrors what is going on in the culture at large. Our secular, rationalistic humanism, an inheritance from the Enlightenment, gave us the comforting belief that we lived in an orderly and essentially predictable universe, where human progress would eventually tame the world and its unruly problems. Why, most of you can surely remember the euphoric predictions of decades past that by the dawn of the new millennium, technology would be so advanced we would all work no more than an average of fifteen hours a week. What *would* we do with all that spare time?

Now, chaos theory teaches us that complex phenomena, such as the world in which we live, are inherently unpredictable and don't appear to "progress" toward anything in particular, except ever more change, disturbance, flux, and flow. Chaos theory is a "shaking of the foundations of the modern world," says Irving Kristol of the American Enterprise Institute, that puts us "at a unique moment in Western culture, the collapse of secular, rationalist humanism."[36] It's the difference between the utopia we once thought science could create and the Jurassic Park we now fear that it will. "In truth," says biologist and author David Ehrenfeld, "we are not inventing our future. We are just engineering changes whose outcomes we cannot predict and which often turn out to be terrible."[37]

What does it take to manage and lead in this kind of environment? What kind of qualities and traits would you have to have? To me, part of the answer can be found by looking at the very popular movie and TV series of years ago, M*A*S*H. The hero, of course, is "Hawkeye" Pierce.[38] Here's a doctor trying to save human lives in the middle of a country where everyone else is intent on ending them. He's under constant pressure to perform, but in the most impossible of circumstances: explosions all around, a complete lack of resources, constantly on the move, and surrounded by idiots. Just like your job, only funnier, right?

Looking back at the fruits of a spiritual life from Chapters Seven and Eight, what do you see in Hawkeye? For that matter, what characteristics do you wish you had that would help you better weather your own M*A*S*H? *Humor,* of course, is Hawkeye's stock in trade—the kind of ironic humor that affirms our humanity in the midst of even the most inhumane conditions. He also seems to me the very image of the *flexible flyer,* the one who can live at once symphonically and chaotically, approaching work with a kind of lightness and playfulness that belies the seriousness of his tasks and the stressful conditions under which he performs them. But Hawkeye also speaks to us of a kind of *integrity,* born of the *courage* to be uniquely himself. It's not an integrity that's defined by adherence to someone else's rules (such was never Hawkeye's strength) but one born of the ability to stick in his own unique standpoint, despite his own fears, the opinions of others, and the swirling chaos of the world around him.

The world will not return to the placidity and predictability we at least *believed* it had in the past—and this may not be all bad. In the new paradigm of life, as in business, to be staid, stable, and stationary is to be in some stage of decay. We grow as human beings through our flexible adaptation to the changes and challenges life puts before us. As uncomfortable as change sometimes is, we are at our best when we are navigating it, learning from it, and growing toward it—when we are "in process." And the more alive we are, the more in process we will be.

The Next Great Movement in Business?

The most important quality an organizational leader can possess in the new paradigm is personal maturity. As Maynard and Mehrtens point out in their futurist book *The Fourth Wave,* maturity will be the prime quality of the CEO of the future, permitting him or her the *self-awareness* to avoid unconscious programming, self-deception, the urge for power, and other temptations that ensnare less developed personalities.[39] The achievement of this kind of maturity is at the very heart of spirituality. It is not the reason for the spiritual quest, for that is found in the individual search for meaning and drive for wholeness. But the result of the process of psychological and spiritual growth is just the kind of maturity that Maynard and Mehrtens describe. The fruits of the spirit are in fact the badges of such maturity.

Personal growth and maturity, and the behavioral changes they produce, are not simply helpful adjuncts to business leadership; they are its essence. To live and prosper in the new business paradigm, where our venerated old methods and even our view of the world have been turned upside down, requires qualities that cannot be learned from a book, skills that cannot be taught. These qualities and skills develop instead in a slow and steady process of maturation and growth—a human process that is fundamentally the same whether one sees it through the eyes of science or religion. We have known it and studied it and written of it literally for centuries, but we are only coming now to apply it to the world of work and organizational life.

That is why I believe that, by whatever name called, embracing a more spiritual view of business, its people, and its purposes will be the next great movement in business. It holds the promise of tying together the fundamental principles of the other great "movements" of postwar business theory, yet transcending them. It points us toward a reliable way of developing within ourselves the traits and qualities needed for life in the new century. It provides the hope for leading our organizations out of decay and stagnation into an exciting and effective—even if frightening—future.

But most of all, spirituality will take deeper root in business because it responds to our most basic human need for a sense of coherence and purpose in what we do in our lives, healing at last the split between life and work created by the old cultural paradigm. Spirituality is an ancient idea, though ever new, to paraphrase St. Augustine. And for our business and organizational lives, one whose time has truly come.

Questions and Exercises for Further Reflection

1. Consider yourself for a moment to be a futurist, one who divines and forecasts what things will be like in the time to come. What evidence do you see in your workplace of the paradigm shift we have described? There are many ways, other than the principal ones we have identified, in which these changes are making themselves known around us. We simply do not always see them as the precursors of a paradigm shift. What other harbingers of a fundamental change in worldview can you identify? Is it your tendency to accept and embrace them, or do you find yourself wishing for the "old days"?

Chapter Ten

Personal Spiritual Growth

*We have placed too much hope in politics and social
reforms, only to find out that we were being deprived of
our most precious possession: our spiritual life. It is
trampled by the party mob in the East, by the commercial
one in the West. [History] will demand from us a
spiritual blaze; we shall have to rise to a new height of
vision, to a new level of life, where our physical nature
will not be cursed, as in the Middle Ages, but even more
importantly, our spiritual being will not be trampled
upon, as in the Modern Era.*
ALEKSANDR SOLZHENITSYN

Some time back, one of the big downtown churches in the city
where I live decided to try something new. The staff organized
what they called a Festival of Faith for a springtime Sunday afternoon, a smorgasbord of seminars and discussion groups that would
explore topics related to religious life but that was not part of the
normal church curriculum. Now, you must understand that such
a thing was quite a stretch for this congregation of more than five
thousand people (and in fact has never been repeated). This is one
of those pillar-of-the-community churches with a spectacularly or-
nate sanctuary; where worship services are very traditional, the
"first families" of the community always occupy the same pews, and
decorum requires that only the finest of clothing be worn for the
weekly encounter with the Almighty. "Outreach" programs give an
outlet to the congregation's social concerns, with individual responsibilities neatly divided between those who contribute money

and those who give of their time in order to spend the money. Everyone does well and does good.

One of the festival's discussion groups, led by the senior minister himself, bore the intriguing title "Spiritual Growth." I watched as the handful of interested participants filed into the small Sunday school classroom with notebook and pen in hand, each with that passive demeanor (well known to any teacher) that says: "You talk, we'll listen, but don't expect us to say anything." The minister, a wonderful preacher and a deeply religious man, talked of the value of such practices as journaling, meditating, and reflective reading but seemed strangely uncomfortable in doing so. The members of the small audience either took incessant notes or sat with quizzical interest, but otherwise had little to offer.

The tedium was finally interrupted by a woman who was one of the stalwarts of the church and a committed contributor to its social programs. "All of the things we are discussing are done alone," she observed. "I don't know, but this seems to me awfully selfish or self-absorbed. Didn't Jesus say that he was there when *two or more* were gathered in his name?" As well as the minister tried to handle the question, he did not seem particularly convincing—either to the questioner or to himself. The conversation was soon back on the familiar topics of communal worship, social action, and "good works."

The fact of the matter is that we simply do not honor individual forms of worship in this culture in the way that we honor corporate forms. We do not honor, or really even *trust,* religious experiences we may have as individuals in the way we do experiences within the context of a larger "community of faith." The ancient axiom of Catholicism, *non salus extra ecclesiam*—there is no salvation outside the church—still rings true in our cultural psyche. The greatest proof of this is in the simple fact that we don't find *time* for our individual religious life in the same way we zealously guard our time for church or synagogue. If we even bother to give time to such personal spiritual pursuits as religious reading, it's at the margins of the day after all that is *really* important has been done, and even then we can't help but see it as an unproductive or wasteful use of precious minutes. Or else it just seems dangerously self-centered, as it did to our woman in the church discussion group.

Yet this is precisely where the process of growth outlined in the preceding chapters takes root and flourishes. It is simply not possible to proceed very far along the path of spiritual growth without honoring the need for individual time, without valuing subjective personal experience, and without cultivating and exploring your own inner life. The wisdom of the ages, if one but culls out the most self-serving of the messages of organized religions, is that the spiritual life *begins with the inward journey* and *moves outward* from that. If it does not begin there, it is simply a matter of outward forms—a parody of the religious life in which church is merely a forum for social connection and advancement, and "outreach" a way of assuaging one's conscience. Faith without works may be dead, as St. Paul argued, but works without a deeply rooted, faithful inner life is shallow, superficial, and ephemeral. More important for our purposes, it does nothing to advance one along the way toward true spiritual growth and the development of the kind of maturity we have described as essential to life and work in our new cultural paradigm.

In this chapter we will explore the essential attitudes, practices, and disciplines that open the door to deep inner work and spiritual growth. We'll affirm what our church discussion group seemed to miss: that spiritual growth is not merely for an elite few chosen for a contemplative life, an "interesting" religious lifestyle adopted by those in monasteries, convents, and the like. The spiritual life is the manifestation of our powerful innate religious urge—the urge not only to worship and praise in unison with others but also to explore and cultivate a deeply personal relationship with the ground of being. It is the desire to experience God in a real and immediate way and to grow toward wholeness and the fullness of our uniquely crafted lives and destinies.

What we will examine are the guideposts of the inner life, the building blocks of spiritual growth. No claim is made to comprehensiveness, for a single chapter of a single book cannot capture the myriad ways in which people profitably seek—and are sought by—God. The attitudes, practices, and disciplines suggested here grow out of my years of work with business and professional people who lead very active lives and find these to be both effective in nurturing deep inner change and relevant to their daily life in the workplace. They thus give to these practices the precious gift of time and energy (though not without some struggle), because in their lives of busy-ness and busi-ness these practices foster a greater connectedness to God and to their deepest selves. These practices are also, not coincidentally, those that can lead over time to the kind of growth and development we described in Chapter Six and to the fruits of the spirit that grow directly therefrom.

We'll continue with our imagery of the fruits of an inner life, because the metaphor of organic growth is so applicable here. Those who have trod this path before you will tell you that there is nothing linear and straight-line about it. The question "Are we there yet?" was appropriate for childhood trips in the back seat of the family car, but not for this sojourn. Our psychological and spiritual growth is instead like that of a plant: slow, incremental, dependent not only on its own resources but on daily contact with the source of energy on which all life depends. It encounters obstacles along the way, but with patience and resilience grows around them. It envelops that which it cannot move. And like all vital things it is subject to the ebb and flow of cycle and season. There are times of rapid expansion and dormancy, vitality and decay. There are days so brilliant they dazzle the senses, nights so long they seem never to end.

So whether you seek to walk this path more consistently in your life and work, or to boldly set forth upon it, let's look at ways in which you might cultivate your own soul and harvest the fruits of the spirit—right in the midst of a thoroughly active and productive life.

Tilling the Soil: Solitude, Silence, Sabbath, and Meditation

> We cannot give ourselves to spiritual things if we are always swept off our feet by a multitude of external activities. Business is not the supreme virtue, and sanctity is not measured by the amount of work we accomplish. Perfection is found in the purity of our love for God, and this pure love is a delicate plant that grows best where there is plenty of time for it to mature.
> THOMAS MERTON

To nurture our spiritual growth requires, as a simple first condition, that we give it space and time in which to flourish. In the midst of our busy, often hectic lives, we must prepare a fertile spot for it to take root and grow. And the first and indispensable step for this is the discipline of *Solitude*. I use the word *discipline* quite intentionally, because for most of us who are parents and workers, spouses and community members, it takes a concerted and assiduous effort to build solitude into our daily lives. But it is absolutely essential; a spiritual life is virtually impossible without it. To cultivate any relationship takes time, but to cultivate any sort of a relationship with God requires time alone. We can "multitask" in practically every other aspect of our lives, but we must be undivided in our attention here.

Christians have in the life of Jesus a consistent model for the importance of solitude. Not only did he begin his ministry with an extensive period of time alone, but the gospels record him "withdrawing" to a "lonely place" practically every time he had an important matter to ponder or event to digest.[1] Most of us can't afford forty days in the desert, of course, but what we can emulate is the *rhythm* of Jesus' life and work—the times of active engagement followed by the periods of pulling back, times of his high-visibility outer work followed by times when he would mysteriously disappear for his own inner work. His many words of advice about the active life are interspersed with admonitions to "go into your room, and when you have shut your door, pray to your Father who is in the secret place" (Matthew 6:6).

What we can watch for, emulate, treasure, and use are the countless opportunities for "little solitudes" inherent in every day. For me these opportunities include the fifteen minutes or so between the time I awaken and the time I stumble off toward the toothbrush. Or the time I spend brooding over a morning cup of coffee before beginning my day's work. For others it may be the time in commute, or when they steal out to a vacant park bench after lunch, or after the kids have gone to bed. I was delighted to find that Joseph Campbell found it doing laps in the pool and having a drink every day. I've even heard it suggested that smokers have a great advantage over the rest of us because their habit forces them into isolation several times a day to enjoy a cigarette. Would but that the rest of us were so addicted to moments of solitude that we had to develop a similar (but safer) habit! The point is not in the physical place you find or the activities that surround you or even the stretch of time you can devote to it. The point of solitude is the quality of your attentiveness and openness to the gifts of the spirit. It's as if God has something to give us, but our hands and hearts are all too often way too full to receive it.

Why is that? Let's be honest. Although it's true that our days are very busy and our nights full of multiple responsibilities and commitments, it is simply not true that we are incapable of finding times for solitude in our life. We need only ask the millions of people who have found it and made it a priority to do so. What are we so afraid of? Well, for one, the solitude itself. We can't seem to separate the notion of aloneness from loneliness, and we somehow feel that to be temporarily deprived of human contact will render us lonely. How many of you keep the television going when you're in the house by yourself, even though you're paying not one whit of attention to what's on, just so another human voice will filter into your ears? Or instinctively turn on the radio every time you crank up the car, not because you like the music or Rush Limbaugh but because you somehow fear the silence? Perhaps we are afraid of solitude because we don't really know what we'll hear if the chatter is turned off. Perhaps we are just afraid to know God, or ourselves, all that terribly well.

But there's another aspect to our avoidance of solitude that has to do with our very notions of time itself. In this culture, at least, we have no sense whatsoever of this interesting concept called the "present." I'm not sure we even know it exists except as an abstract concept. We know "past" because we tend to dwell upon it, and we know "future" because we dwell *in* it, but what is this thing called "present"? The way we look at time reminds me of the way my daughter preheats the kitchen oven. She'll turn the thermostat way past the desired temperature on the assumption that this will make the oven get hotter, quicker. I'm also reminded of travelers who crowd into the first car of the airport tram because it will get to the terminal a whole fraction of a second earlier than the rest. We are constantly living in the future, and everything we do is designed to get it here more quickly. It's as if we are constantly pulling the fabric of time toward ourselves, ill-content to let it flow toward us at its own pace (as it will, quite without our help, of course), and thus unable to appreciate, much less fully enjoy, the richness of the fabric that might at this moment be in our hands.

Blaise Pascal said that most of the misfortunes of humankind derived from our inability to be still in our own room. Try and prove him wrong by sitting very still and watching the reactions of your mind carefully. Do you find yourself almost immediately thinking of the things you *could* be doing, *should* be doing right now? Are you really there, or is your mind someplace in the past or future?

Not long ago I went back to the Jesuit novitiate in Wernersville, Pennsylvania, to celebrate the tenth anniversary of my life-changing retreat there. I sat on a bench at a corner of the beautiful, expansive grounds overlooking the Lebanon Valley below. I had intended to stay until the next day but had no particular schedule except to walk the manicured gardens and reacquaint myself with the rich memories of my time there. Sitting on that bench, surrounded by the timeless trappings of that spiritual community and the equally timeless beauty of God's creation, I had the feeling that the flow of the fabric of time had stopped dead still; that this moment, in all its fullness, was all there was; that it, and each and every other moment I might experience while sitting there, was completely full of the potentiality of life. In every moment was every thing. But then it happened: I started to think of my schedule back home. When should I leave? If I went back soon I could get home by 10 P.M. and get a fresh start tomorrow. There was, after all, this and this and this to do. Sacred time, or the sense in which all time has a sacred quality, ceased at that moment. I was now living in the future, a moment of pure solitude now nothing more than a marker in chronological time.

When we measure things by doing, we cannot help but think of what has been done and what remains to be done afterwards. But when one is simply *being*, every moment has the capacity to be rich and complete. This is why solitude is important. The practice of solitude has the capacity to root us in the present. It clears the decks of the past and the future and enables us to enjoy the sacrament of the present moment. It breaks up the hard ground of hurriedness and exposes within us our fertile inner soil. The seeds of our own self-knowledge and of the knowledge of God are constantly being broadcast around us. Solitude gives them space to take root and grow.

———◦———

Silence is the sound that solitude makes. For in solitude the goal is not so much to shut out the world and its sounds as to become more alert and aware of them; not so much to diminish the things around us as to lessen our own ego and its hulking self-absorption for long enough that the reality of the world around us might come in. Silence is not the absence of sound but rather the allowing of a symphony of sounds—the wind in the trees, the insistent cry of a single mockingbird, the distant rush of a stream, as well as our own deepest thoughts and emotions—to enter our awareness, a symphony that might otherwise be lost amid the noise and psychic clutter of our lives. And so a day filled with noises and voices *can* be a day of solitude and silence, provided only that the focus of our attention moves from our ego and its needs to God's creation, its creatures, and our own innermost self. We seek in silence and solitude to become detached *from ourselves,* in order to see all things from a fresh perspective—God's perspective.

At the Jesuit novitiate in Wernersville, almost all our time was spent in silence; that is, we were strongly encouraged not to speak except at special times. And yet the place was filled with sound. All these years later I still recall the sensory flood of daily life there, from the bells that marked the cycle of worship to the cheerful whistling amid the clatter of the kitchen, to the buzz of a heat-maddened summer fly intent on finding its way into my room. One even discovers, after a while, a completely different way of communicating. All the retreatants became rather quickly adept at smiling, nodding, or gesturing in such a way as to convey our thoughts and feelings quite clearly, and actually with a great deal more eloquence than our typical "Hi, how are you?" will ever have. So expressive was the "silence" that during the course of my stay I actually made several very good friends without ever having spoken a word!

Some of our most fruitful uses of solitary time come when we turn down the volume on our own cares and concerns and crank up the volume on the rest of the world. That may mean listening to the sounds of nature or of children playing, or to the conversation of an elderly couple, or to the concerns of a troubled colleague. Many also find in music a doorway to the inner life, agreeing with Beethoven's observation that music is a more direct way to God than words.

But whatever works for you, *begin it*. Whether through heightened attentiveness to the things around you or by following the Psalmist's advice to "Be still, and know that I am God" (Psalm

46:10), give life to your moments of solitude by anchoring them in silence. You may find yourself astounded how this habit of mind can calm and center you in your day. You begin to develop a certain ability to get outside the orbit of your own personal worries and begin to feel a sense of connection to things and people around you that you previously thought to be the province only of mystics and other weirdos. In time you might even find the desire and the courage to extend those moments of silent appreciation into the normal flow of your day: as does the middle manager with whom I work who spends a couple of minutes quietly focusing before important telephone calls; or the associate director of a charitable foundation who observes a period of silence before beginning every meeting as a way of inviting others to gather their thoughts and put aside other matters; or the executive who will call a "moratorium on words" whenever a meeting gets hopelessly stuck, in order for participants to pay attention to the wisdom that resides in the space between the words. In the silence live your intuition, your creativity, and your connection with your very soul. Decide that you'd like to bring them to work with you.

Judaic law is replete with prescriptions and proscriptions intended to instill a certain rhythm in life. God himself worked for six days and then rested, and men and women were intended to do the same on their *Sabbath*. The land itself was given to lie fallow every seventh year. In our culture, I'm afraid, the notion of the Sabbath has degenerated into merely a religious custom to be obeyed only because it is "the law," or else an archaic inconvenience whose sole good is in keeping us out of the malls on Sunday evening. What we miss is what the Sabbath was always intended to do: provide a time for refreshment and refocusing, solitude and silence, rejuvenation and recollection, in the midst of an active life.

And this the Sabbath has always done exceedingly well. To visit with an orthodox Jewish family on the Sabbath is to see what was intended by the ancient law. The ritual of the meal, the sense of family and tradition, the recollection of stories, the reading and discussion of scripture, all give a sense of timelessness in a world where time is a ruling deity. People almost literally refuel in that environment, garnering energy and a sense of purpose for the week ahead while resting and recouping in that protected space.

Contrast this with how we generally spend our Sabbath, regardless of the day of the week on which it falls. Do we rest and recreate, or do we recreate our brains out in a pace as feverish as any weekday? Do we enjoy the present moment with our kids, our pets, our households, or are we a swirl of chores, "to do" lists, social functions, and obligations? Is our Sabbath just another workday with a different species of work?

This is not how we were created. We are rhythmic creatures. We need periods of high activity followed by times of rejuvenation. We need to go slow in order to go fast. The notion of a Sabbath— one day a week during which the pace of life slows and the focus of life turns inward—can provide the rhythm that we have long lost in our society. Just as we cannot work more than about twenty-four hours straight without being overcome with the need for physical rest, we cannot work more than about six days straight without the need for emotional, psychological, and spiritual refueling. This is why Sabbaths are so important: not (just) because they are required by religious law or social convention but because they serve the invaluable purpose of giving us an inviolate place for refocusing, remembering what is important in our lives, re-creating ourselves, and recollecting the fragments we have scattered in our hurried lives.

And it shouldn't end there. Although everyone has a unique individual rhythm, it is important for most of us to take a longer personal retreat every month or two. Whether an afternoon, a day, or (depending on one's family situation) an entire weekend, this extended time should be largely devoted to the disciplines we talk about in this chapter and the path one's journey has taken since the last such retreat. I use that time to review my dreams and look for patterns of what God might be trying to say to me through them. One friend budgets an afternoon a month so that she can go to her favorite spot on the beach and write in her journal about the important events of her life. Another spends a day hiking in the woods and "just thinking." Whatever your personal preference, you are creating an intentional space in which silence and solitude can do their good work; but you are also creating a rhythm to which your body and spirit will soon become accustomed. You will be able to feel it viscerally when your personal retreat time is nearing.

Finally, consider instituting a "super-Sabbath" once a year, preferably at a predictable time that you can schedule well in advance. Yes, it is difficult to set aside and guard that time. Yes, you may have trouble convincing your spouse or significant other that this is not a scene from the romantic comedy *Same Time Next Year.* The truth of the matter is, however, that it *is* a clandestine rendezvous between you and the deeper parts of your being, between you and the person you wish to become—between you and your God. If a dissolute Calypso poet like Jimmy Buffett can profess in his song "Changes in Latitudes" that he takes off for a weekend now and again just to reflect on the past year, then surely you can, too.

———————

I confess it. I can't seem to *Meditate* in the normally accepted sense of the word. Not that I haven't tried, but I don't seem to have the patience or the focus that are associated with the "classic" meditative practices. But fortunately this discipline encompasses much more—and is much more accessible—than most of us think. I like what Metropolitan Bloom said when asked to define this contemplative practice:

> Sit and listen—in religious terms it may be called waiting on God—but it's simply plain listening or looking in order to hear and to understand. If we did that with regard to the Word of God, with regard to the prayers of the saints, with regard to the situations in which we are, to everything people say to us or what they are in life, with regard to our own selves—we would be in that condition which one can call contemplation, which consists in pondering, thinking deeply, in waiting until one has understood in order to act. Then action would be much more efficient, less hasty, and filled, probably, with some amount of the Divine Wisdom.[2]

Sit and listen in order to hear and understand—now *that* perhaps I can do! But for what purpose, and to what or whom are we listening? In a recent study by the High Tor Alliance, meditation was reported to be the most important and most frequently practiced of all the contemplative disciplines and was credited with helping practitioners do everything from achieving inner quiet, to being one's "best" self, to connecting to the Divine.[3] What this says is that people practice meditation for reasons ranging from the simple goal of becoming still, to plumbing their own depths, to the sacred task of achieving a degree of communion with God.

Essential to attaining any such goal, however, is meditation's central principle: that to whatever degree possible in the time and circumstances one has at hand, one is *emptied* of the moment's cares and concerns and the "ten thousand things" that constantly clog our attentiveness and becomes *receptive* to something other and deeper than one's own consciousness. That "something" may be our own unconscious functioning, which despite its often bewildering quality is usually one step ahead of our conscious capacity for knowing and several steps closer to the Divine. But the receptivity that comes with meditation can even open the door to—and we should not be afraid to use this word—*revelation*. Prayer or meditation is clearly one of the phenomena that can trigger the sense of communion with the transcendent, a spiritual reality beyond the conscious self yet paradoxically experienced as within the self, a reality that most of us simply call God. Whatever ontology we attribute to it, this is the "still small voice" within, audible only to those who can become emptied and still enough to hear it.

Questions of "how often" and "for how long" are common, but answerable only in general. Of the silent, solitary, Sabbath time that you create for yourself every day, at least twenty uninterrupted minutes should be devoted to meditation in some form. The time or times of day do not matter, so long as you are mentally alert. Trying to meditate in the dregs of the day or when you are about to fall asleep is simply a waste of time. I particularly like the way Scott Peck describes his meditative time—and his honesty.[4] He has the admitted luxury of claiming three forty-five-minute periods during the day: one in early morning, one in late afternoon, and one before bedtime. Yet by his own admission he only spends about 10 percent of that time in prayer or meditation. The rest of these daily respites are spent "just thinking." He simply figures that if he calls it something more lofty, people will feel less free to interrupt him while he's doing it.

Which leads to the question, What does one "do" during meditation? On what does one focus in order to empty and become receptive? The answers are of a surprisingly rich variety, even among the most accomplished contemplatives. Some of the more classic forms of meditation involve a mantra or other repetitive sound or becoming fully attentive to one's breathing. These are fine for those people for whom they work (though the first may expose you to ridicule from your teenage children), but I find that such practices tend to fill rather than empty me. Personally, I find that to direct my focus toward a single physical object that has meaning to me—the flame of a candle, perhaps—can in time have the required effect. Others direct their attention to the *thought* of a particular person or issue about which they are concerned. This can be a particularly fruitful use of meditative time in the workplace, as it is for a therapist friend who meditates on her patients or for the businessman who meditates on the day's critical issue. For each the goal is focused attention, sloughing off the dross of frenetic self-concern and finding the gold of deeper insight and communion.

If you are new to this, and particularly if you are a bit skeptical, let me suggest a profitable way to begin. Follow the suggestions put forth in point 3 of the Questions and Exercises for Further Reflection at the end of this chapter. Start slowly—about ten minutes a day for the first few days—and with a great deal of self-forgiveness. Within two weeks, when you have moved yourself up to twenty minutes a day, you will have made a substantial start in the habit of mind called meditation. What's more, you will become practiced in an important tool for increasing self-awareness that goes back hundreds of years in the Catholic church, called the Daily Examen. There is probably no more powerful way for inner work to translate into outer effect.

———

Like most of the people whose spiritual lives I am privileged to share, my friend John (whom we first met in Chapter Seven) finds that the disciplines of tilling the soil make his working life richer and more fulfilling. "It's like physical exercise," he's been heard to say. "Once it becomes a habit, you'd feel bad if you didn't take time for those things—it just becomes part of your life. But what it does for me really can't be measured. There's more of a sense of patience with everyone from my clients to my kids. There's more of a feeling of purpose that can really be energizing to this middle-aged body. And the more consistent I remain [with the disciplines], there's more of a sense that my actions are coming from the best place in me; that I'm more real somehow." Tilling the soil makes life richer and more fulfilling for John, but doubtless also for those who live and work around him every day.

The Planting: Prayer, Listening, Service, and Will

> Prayer is the fertile soil in which the insight into our
> true self in God takes root and grows. As our true
> awareness grows, as we see through the eyes of the Person
> we are, we see with a new vision. We see the Presence of
> God in all there is.
>
> JAMES FINLEY

Solitude, Silence, Sabbath, and *Meditation* help us become familiar and comfortable with the inner life. The Christian Orthodox saint John Chrysostrom said that if you find the door to your heart, you will discover that it is the door to the Kingdom of God. The disciplines we have discussed so far are all about finding that door to your heart. The disciplines we are about to explore are about opening that door and finding it possible to establish a personal and very real relationship with Ultimate Reality.

———◈———

The first and by far the most important of those disciplines is *Prayer.* By this I do not mean *only* the words you might hear on Sunday mornings or that might begin a meal around the family table, but prayer that is, in the words of Anthony Bloom, the Orthodox archbishop, "turned inwards, not toward a God of Heaven nor towards a God far off, but towards God who is closer to you than you are aware."[5] In other words, toward a Divinity that resides just the other side of that inner door to your heart.

There are three principal misconceptions about prayer that, I believe, stand in the way of reasonably intelligent people doing it very well. The first is the belief that it is we who do all the speaking, with our chances of being heard more or less inscrutable—as though we were shooting an arrow into the sky with no idea where it will land. But"[o]ne of the cardinal principles of prayer," says Thomas Hart, "is that God does speak and always speaks first."[6] In God's half of the "double search" we have spoken of before, God is continually inviting us to communion and communication in a way just as real as the words of this page are now speaking to you. What we say in prayer, then, is always simply a response to an invitation always given. Which leads us to the second mistake: all but the most egotistical among us must feel that it is the ultimate presumption and arrogance that we, *we* could actually be heard in our prayers and petitions by the creator of the universe. And yet that is precisely what centuries of great pray-ers have taught, including Jesus. He encouraged his followers to relate to God not just as Father but as *Abba,* which translates as "Daddy," with the same confidence and informality with which we might converse with our own parents. When we really allow ourselves to think about prayer in those terms, how incredible and profound is that? How thrilling?! As Thomas Merton said, prayer is to religion what cutting-edge research is to science: it is the exciting frontier of our humanness and the highest calling of our existence.

Yet the fallacy that most stands in the way of the fullest use of the human faculty of prayer is the notion that its primary purpose is to change God—to influence God in some way. Its primary purpose is to change *us.* "In prayer, real prayer, we begin to think God's thoughts after Him; to desire the things He desires, to love the things He loves. Progressively we are taught to see things from His point of view."[7] In prayer we *open* to the possibility of being directly influenced by God, we admit and *acknowledge* God's primacy, and we begin consciously to *align* ourselves with God's purposes in the world. I do believe that our prayers have an effect on God's activity, and there is in fact growing scientific proof that this is true (some from the medical research center in my home city). But the clearest effect of real prayer is in the way it quickens our spiritual and psychological growth, the way it fosters our development and maturity. The clearest mark of genuinely prayerful people is not their batting average with God but the observable fruits of a prayerful life.

Because prayer is primarily about changing ourselves, the actual words that we use are not of the greatest consequence. In so-called active or spontaneous prayer—prayers of thanksgiving, praise, petition, intercession—you are encouraged simply to use such words as are "completely true to what you are, words which you are not ashamed of, which express you adequately and are worthy of you, and then to offer them to God with all the intelligence of which you are capable."[8] Others find that to recite aloud meaningful passages from the Psalms or other sacred texts is just as conducive to the opening, acknowledging, and aligning that prayer entails. Contemplatives in the Western Christian tradition often recite the Lord's Prayer, slowly chewing on each phrase. Popular in the Eastern Orthodox tradition is the repetition of the Jesus Prayer, which says simply, "Lord Jesus Christ, Son of God, have mercy on me a sinner."

The more comfortable a person becomes with the great business of praying, the less necessary it will be to find one particular way, time, or place to do it. But better to put that the other way around: the more comfortable a person becomes with praying, the more *everything* becomes an opportunity for prayer. The great prayers tell us that when we have learned to give full attention to God at set times of prayer, our awareness of God seems to grow to such an extent that whether working or playing, alone or with others, we can continually turn and return to that presence. Theophan the Recluse, one of the ancient spiritual masters, put it very colorfully when he said that the awareness of God was like a toothache—regardless of what you were doing, it was with you all the time.

The beauty of a life lived in this way is that prayer takes no particular amount of our time, but can occupy our time at any moment. So we can reflect on a psalm or the Lord's Prayer during a morning shower, silently wish a blessing on our family as they depart for their day, cast a prayer inward for the troubled derelict we meet on the street, feel led to pray for wisdom and guidance for the afternoon staff meeting, and (one of my personal favorites) say a silent prayer over the bed of a sleeping child before ending our day. "Praying is living," said Henri Nouwen. At least it can be.

————◦◦◦————

As we have seen, the disciplines of tilling the soil create opportunities for being attentive to the movements of the divine spirit in our lives and the "still small voice" within. Prayer, too, can be a way of listening out for God, particularly when we reserve part of our prayer time for simple, quiet openness. This is often called contemplative, meditative, or centering prayer. But there are a great many other ways of *Listening* to God. For those who believe, as I do, that God's spirit is engaged in a real and active way in the daily affairs of men and women, one of the best ways to listen for God's footfalls is to become adept at reading God's movements in the common events of our lives.

Because such patterns are usually evident only in hindsight, you must become an expert at "reading your life backwards," sleuthing your own mystery for signs of God's grace and leadings. Spiritual direction (discussed later in this chapter) can be extremely helpful in this process, but such sleuthing is also an excellent use of your solitary and Sabbath time. The keys to reading your life backwards are simply to spend enough time in prayer and the other disciplines to begin to know how God works in your life, and to *believe* that a divine power has indeed been at work in a way that intends your good and your growth. Point 4 of the Questions and Exercises for Further Reflection at the end of this chapter will lead you through an exercise in doing this for yourself.

I could give you a number of examples from my own life; one of them concerns how I came to write this book. If I read my life backwards for the last ten years or so, I seem to have been pulled insistently (sometimes quite against my will) toward devoting the necessary time and energy to this effort. I had long been interested in the subject of work and spirituality but "had no time" to devote to anything beyond the occasional academic article. But then there were a series of "chance" meetings with people well outside my discipline who had important perspectives I had never thought about. A pot of money fell into my lap to do a symposium on this subject, leading me to meet and work with some of the important thinkers in this area. Most important, my career took some unexpected turns away from students and academic life and closer to consulting work with just the people whose stories appear in these pages. I finally concluded, with the help of an understanding spouse, that I could not *not* write this book. After years of watching God's "gee and haw" in my life, there was no doubt in my mind that this was the next unexpected twist in the process of following my own string and that any further delay would simply meet with some further frustration.

In addition to reading the events of our lives, we can also listen for God in our unconscious processes, though doing so takes a good bit of care and discernment. I say this because the unconscious contains personal and archetypal contents that can be dangerous and destructive. It is equally true, however, that consciousness is so bound up with our ego and its self-protection that it is often *only* through the unconscious that God can truly reach us. Thus such disciplines as meditation and contemplative prayer can put us at the doorstep of the unconscious (we called it earlier the door of the heart), but it is up to us and our human powers of discernment to be certain that what steps through that door is in fact "of God." Does it seem to seek our good and growth? Does it serve the purposes of love in the world? Is it consistent with the ways God moves in our lives? And in asking these questions we must be careful not to let our too-small images of God, or ourselves, interfere.

Again, a personal example. Some fifteen years ago I was riding down a superhighway in a new company car, dressed in my three-piece suit and headed off to fight some now-forgotten business battle. I was in a hazy blue funk that all the pleasant trappings of corporate life could not cure, biding the time and abiding the traffic as my mind wandered aimlessly across thoughts of court dates and schedules, posteriors to be kissed and bases to be touched. Suddenly, in the peculiar way that one "hears" an unconscious incursion, the thought was there full-blown in my head as if I had heard it with my ears: *"You do not have to live like this!"* At first I paid the words no attention—the usual fate of most messages from the unconscious. But these few simple words had hit me squarely between the eyes. They spoke precisely to what I was feeling but seemed unable or unwilling to admit. The more I let them sink in, the more power and truth those simple words seemed to have. I *wasn't* living life in a way that made me happy, I *wasn't* doing what I was best suited to do, I *wasn't* "following my bliss," and it *didn't* have to be that way. The key to discerning the trustworthiness of these words and to believing that they came from a divine source was in understanding how well they fit with what God would do, even if they didn't fit at all with what I consciously thought I wanted for myself. Within a year I had a plan for transitioning myself out of that career situation and on to the next challenge of my life.

Such incursions from the unconscious take place more often than we think, in the form of hunches, intuitions, forebodings, unexplained enthusiasms, or (as in my story) actual words. When in silence, meditation, or prayer we make ourselves receptive to them, they can be a source of insight—even wisdom—far beyond what we consider our conscious capacities to be. We should simply remember that although God can and does reach us through our unconscious, God is *not* our unconscious, and we must take care to test what we hear against what we know.

When such incursions take place in sleep we call them dreams. Here the same caution about separating the wheat from the chaff applies. Many of our dreams reflect personal or archetypal contents that may be useful in therapeutic analysis but have little apparent connection to the movements of the spirit in our lives. There are some, however, that clearly reflect an intelligence superior to our own and have about them a sort of teleological quality. They seem to be positively pulling us toward some future way of being that is, when we look at it, exactly what God would do if he were interested in furthering our growth toward him. These are incredibly valuable ways to listen to God, because in sleep our conscious defenses against the transcendent are so low. Small wonder that many great men and women throughout history have sought to understand their dreams and sometimes found powerful guidance in them. Paying attention to our dreams—the purest form of unconscious incursion—and learning their often baffling language can accelerate your own growth and attune you to God's leadings in your life in ways few other practices can.[9]

For both the physical events of our outer lives and the psychic events of our inner lives, many find that keeping a journal aids in their listening to God's messages. Journal writing forces us to objectify and write down our thoughts, and in that very process we tend to examine these events with much more thoughtfulness than we otherwise would. A journal also provides a permanent record of inner and outer events that might otherwise be forgotten (dreams are particularly elusive to memory) and provides a rich biography to use in reading your life backwards. You may just find the proof of God's caring existence hidden right in the pages of your own life story.

———◈———

There is a mystery inherent in our *Service* to others. Nothing has the capacity to strike us so close to our spiritual core or to nurture our growth toward wholeness quite like genuine acts of selfless service. One of the simplest but most powerful images recorded in all the gospels is that of Jesus, on the night before his crucifixion, on his hands and knees washing the feet of men too concerned about their place in the pecking order to wash each other's—or their own. I know people whose lives were changed forever by the sight of Mother Teresa simply holding a dying child. Service seems capable of doing on the outside what prayer and listening can do from the inside: connecting us intimately to the ground of being.

Perhaps this is because service, when done aright, has the power to *dis-illusion* us in ways that break down the normal barriers between ourselves and God, ourselves and others. It strips away our illusion of invulnerability to help feed a man whose strength is eaten away by bone cancer. It dis-illusions us of our immortality when we watch the rest-home resident we have been visiting fall further into the suffocating clutches of ALS. And we can lose our sense of superiority in listening to the story of a homeless woman and realizing that her circumstances were once no different from our own. Whether we like to think about it or not, most of us are simply a mutated gene or a blind-side accident away from death and a few paychecks or a stock market crash away from poverty.

To be with others in their diminishment, to spend our time with the "unproductive" among us, seems to have the power to confront us with who we truly are as persons. It gets us down beneath the level of pretenses and defenses to our essence. In that sense service can be a truly liberating and joyous experience, freeing us from our own self-images and our endless judgments, allowing us to just *be* ourselves with others. We experience not so much our prized separateness and uniqueness but our commonality and our commonness. And in the midst of all that we seem quite mysteriously to come closer to the heart of God.

Yes, service can be rendered from a sense of duty or to discharge of some obligation, and it may sometimes be difficult to tell the difference between that and the discipline of selfless service we are describing. But service rendered out of duty or obligation does not necessarily quicken our growth and development. Stage 4 Achievers can be some of the most duty-bound people on earth, their conversations liberally peppered with *should, ought,* and *gotta,* but this does not necessarily mean that they will progress beyond that level of development. Service rendered from this mind-set will generally produce either self-righteousness or resentment, depending on how one feels about the results achieved, the "strokes" received, and other such factors. True selfless service is not rendered with regard to whether some problem will be solved or one's reputation enhanced, or really for any other reason than that the *need* is there.

A number of years ago, two events happened within a single week that brought home to me the meaning of service—if in a rather negative way. The first was in watching my company give a large grant to a local minority college that was in something of a financial crisis. Dozens of people were involved in preparations for the gift—not in getting the money together, mind you, for that was as simple as stroking a check—but in planning publicity, securing the desired endorsements from community leaders, binding the college to ongoing advertisement of the award, and doing projections on the "payback" in increased business from the African American customer base. Community service, indeed.

The second event involved one of those big, downtown churches of which we spoke earlier. I went to them to request a small contribution to help pay the electric bill of a young single mother on welfare. Although she had had two children out of wedlock, Doreen was now working toward her high school equivalency, struggling to maintain the small apartment she rented for her family. The electric bill had busted her budget when she had tried, unwisely, to use the oven to help heat the cold apartment. After studying the situation, the staff person in charge of "outreach" startled me with this judgment about a young woman he had never met: "I just resent being asked to throw money at something that won't *solve* the problem. Someone like this will just be back next month for something new or else will just get pregnant again." He then proceeded to write me a check for the electric bill. Charity, indeed.

Service that most connects us to ourselves, to others, and to God is not given out of some grudging sense of obligation or some hope for reward. It eschews grandiosity both in the giving and in the expectation of results. It is small, hidden, and unseen, and is given (insofar as one is capable) only because the need is there. Here we would do well to remember the words of a man who, by all accounts, didn't do a lick of "productive" work for the last three years of his life and lived from town to town off the hospitality of others: "Take heed that you do not do your charitable deeds before men, to be seen by them. When you do a charitable deed, do not sound a trumpet before you as the hypocrites do in the synagogues and in the streets, that they may have praise from men. Assuredly, I say to you, they have their reward. But when you do a charitable deed, do not let your left hand know what your right hand is doing, that your deed may be in secret; and your Father who sees in secret will Himself reward you openly."[10]

Can you find a couple of hours a month to be with others in their diminishment, to subject yourself to the dis-illusionment that will follow? No, it is *not* sufficient for you to make a monetary contribution so that someone *else* can do this in your stead, or to be chair of some safely distant committee that is studying "the problem." *Be* of service directly to someone who is in need of that service and in need of your presence. You need that person perhaps more than you know.

For all that we have said about focusing our *attention* with the spiritual disciplines, it avails us little unless we focus our *intention* on Ultimate Reality. This is the all-important matter of our *Will* and the direction in which we point it. One person may study and gain such knowledge that he can write volumes on the intricacies of theology. Another may practice and gain such mental and physical agility that she can meditate for hours on end. But unless both have aimed their intention fully toward God and the things of God, their efforts have little to do with the spiritual life.

The great voices of the past speak of a kind of near obsession that comes from fully devoting oneself to this path. "Taste God, and only God will do," is Augustine's famous line. The Psalmist writes, "As the deer pants for the water brooks, so pants my soul for You, O God" (Psalm 42:1). "A naked intent toward God, the desire for him alone, is enough," says the unknown author of *The Cloud of Unknowing*.[11] The sheer longing with which we pursue this journey is the one thing both necessary and sufficient to sustain us.

The will is the arm of consciousness, determining where we will put our disposable energy and what will draw our intention. But the will can be either the friend or foe of our spirituality, depending on how it is aimed. I have never thought much of our traditional notions of sin in Western Christianity, but I am impressed by the fact that the word for sin in the biblical Greek was *amartia,* which means "to miss the mark." If sin means anything, it is to aim our will in a way that misses the mark in life, that aims at altogether the wrong circle of meaning.

A distinction made by my friend Gerald May in his book *Will and Spirit* has great value here. When we are will*ful* we seek by the use of our will to set ourselves apart from others and from life's essence in an attempt to control and manipulate our existence. But to be will*ing* "implies a surrendering of one's self-separateness, an entering-into, an immersion in the deepest processes of life itself."[12] It is less submission to something outside yourself than it is a yielding to the strongest and deepest yearnings within yourself, rather like flowing with the current of a river rather than forever swimming willfully against it.

To follow the spiritual path of opening, acknowledging, aligning, and cultivating is to be will*ing* to direct one's will in a way that serves one's highest self and the ultimate values in life. It adds the intention of our will to the attention of our spirit in planting the seeds of spiritual growth.

The Cultivation: Study, Guidance, Discipline, and Action

> For now, if you wish to keep growing you must nourish in
> your heart the lively longing for God. Though this loving
> desire is certainly God's gift, it is up to you to nourish it.
> THE CLOUD OF UNKNOWING

If you wish to keep a fire going, you should add wood and not water, paper and not stones. If you wish to tend your own spiritual blaze, give yourself fuel that will make you grow hotter still. And nothing does that more reliably than the reading and *Study* of great spiritual works. By these I mean not only the sacred texts of the great religions—the Bible, the Koran, the Upanishads, and the rest. Those are obvious starting places. But what seems most to stir people out of their spiritual slumber is to discover in someone else's journey just the right message or tone or feeling that makes us say, "Why, this person has experienced the same things as I have. I am not alone!" For C. S. Lewis it was the nineteenth-century Scottish poet George Macdonald; for T. S. Eliot it was an obscure seventeenth-century bishop named Lancelot Andrewes. Whoever it may be for you, it will be an experience like the one Walt Whitman recorded when he first read Emerson: "I was simmering, and he brought me to a boil."

Sometimes, when we have begun to turn our intention and attention toward God, the right book will just "appear." Do not distrust the power of synchronicity here. In 1985, not long after the experience of hearing the voice of my unconscious (recounted earlier in this chapter), I was sitting at my desk when one of my colleagues came in carrying something in her hand. Now, Trish was a good friend, but we were not prone to religious or philosophical discussions, much less to the sharing of books. "I don't know why," she said, "but something told me you would enjoy this book." After I gave my usual—and dishonest—assurance that I'd read it, she handed me a copy of M. Scott Peck's *The Road Less Traveled*. It made its way to my bedside table, but I didn't pick it up for weeks. When I did, I read the first few words—something about life being hard or such—and decided it probably wasn't for me. Over the next few months I picked it up a dozen or more times, read a bit, and put it back in its resting place. But when I got to the chapter on grace, something happened: I am at a loss to explain it, but it drew together all of my episodic and fragmented spiritual life as I had lived it to that point and provided fuel for some dramatic changes I was soon to make.

When I finished that book I didn't know quite where to turn next, but I remember being intrigued by one of Peck's footnotes that cited a work by psychologist Carl Jung. When I next went to the bookstore, I edged over toward the psychology section to see if they had anything by this guy whom I vaguely remembered from college Psych 101. Quite literally the first book I saw, with a cover that seemed veritably to spring off the shelf toward me, was Jung's *Modern Man in Search of a Soul.* I didn't stop until, some ten years later, I had read all of Jung's collected works.

If you're not so lucky as to have a friend like Trish or to have a book fly off the shelf at you (Shirley MacLaine, by the way, reports a similar experience), then you may want to graze around a bit and find what peculiarly suits you. Fortunately, there is an incredible wealth of material out there, covering centuries (millennia, even) of the spiritual journey. Particularly in more recent times spiritual fuel takes a wide variety of forms, from traditional prose to poetry to plays to music. Experiment with several different forms. "Feeling" types (in Myers-Briggs language) will be drawn to poetry and lyrical prose but might be better off grounded in more systematic approaches. "Thinkers" can be overly analytical and might be better off with works that explore—but leave unanswered—the mystery of God.

What follows, then, with my apologies for its inevitable incompleteness, are some wonderful places to start. In terms of the classics, I would begin with Augustine's *Confessions,* the story of his adult conversion that still strikes a modern tone. ("Save me, Oh Lord, but not yet.") Thomas à Kempis's *Imitation of Christ* and the anonymous *Cloud of Unknowing* have been read by countless millions over the centuries. I would also recommend the *Pensées* of Blaise Pascal, the *Journals* of either George Fox or John Woolman, and virtually anything by the mystic Meister Eckhart. Although William Law can be a bit puritanical in spots, *A Serious Call to a Devout and Holy Life* is a beautiful and compelling work. I find Kierkegaard difficult, but his *Purity of Heart* is an exquisite and delicate piece.

In more modern times, the starting place for me has always been C. S. Lewis, particularly *Mere Christianity, The Four Loves,* and *The Great Divorce.* There are also wonderful anthologies of selected passages of his works (one is called *The Joyful Christian*) which are perfect for short devotional readings. The father of modern Jewish mysticism is Abraham Joshua Heschel, and I have been profoundly influenced by his *Man Is Not Alone* and *God in Search of Man*. Others who have to be mentioned are the modern martyr Dietrich Bonhoeffer (*The Cost of Discipleship*), Evelyn Underhill (*Letters*), and Dorothy Sayers (the transcripts of her evocative radio plays of the 1940s, published as *The Man Born to Be King*). The plays and poetry of T. S. Eliot reach the depth and height of the spiritual life, as do many of the novels of Charles Williams. Many find the same sustenance in Tolstoy and Dostoyevsky.

Thomas Kelly's *Testament of Devotion* and Anthony Bloom's *Beginning to Pray* are invaluable aids from master pray-ers, and Tilden Edwards of the Shalem Institute gives a wonderful contemporary perspective on the ancient spiritual disciplines in his *Living Simply Through the Day* and *Living in the Presence*. But for me the greatest nourishment has come from two men who came from very different backgrounds but who shared both an intense love of God and a too-early death. Thomas Merton was a Trappist monk who lived most of his life in solitude until his writings (*No Man Is an Island, The Seven Story Mountain, Seeds of Contemplation,* and many more) earned him worldwide recognition. Tragically, he died while on a mission of understanding to a Buddhist monastery in 1968. Dag Hammarskjöld, in contrast, led a very public life as secretary-general of the United Nations until he was killed in route to a peacekeeping mission in the Congo in 1961. He left behind his journal, *Markings,* which is the most powerful statement of personal devotion I have ever read.

If you wish to come to the spiritual path from more of a psychological perspective, the seminal book for me is John Sanford's *The Kingdom Within.* Jung himself is just too dense for most people, and prone to mighty digressions. Better at first to stick to the Jungians such as Sanford, Morton Kelsey, and Robert Johnson.

A word of caution is in order. Some of the works I have suggested do not in all respects translate well into modern times (such as many of the things St. Paul had to say about women). But it's been said that reading the spiritual classics is like sitting down to a fish dinner: there is no requirement that you eat the fish bones and all. Better that you pull that which nourishes you off the bone and throw the rest away. Do not give in to our normal tendency to analyze the hell out of everything or to throw out a whole body of thought because you don't like one part of it. Let the author, through his or her experience, speak to you in the way only that person can. The experience of God was real for them—see how it matches your own reality.

So as you grow along the way, I want to suggest that you find those people who can be George Macdonald or Lancelot Andrewes to you. You may find yourself befriended and mentored by someone who time has taken away but whose thoughts and experiences are as timeless as Ultimate Reality itself. Give a part of your solitary time to this effort, and you will find that it becomes one of the most important times of your day or week. You can put part of your Sabbath time to particularly good use through the discipline of study. And, for goodness sake, the next time you go on vacation or an extended trip, leave the trashy pulp novel at home in favor of something that will inflame you, not merely entertain you—something that's wood, not water.

<hr />

The spiritual journey is largely an inward process, but that does not mean it should be undertaken alone. In fact, as we would for any sojourn into new territory, we need the company of experienced guides and the encouragement of friends. Without the discipline of *Guidance* we dramatically increase our chances of becoming lost along the way, detoured by our own fantasies, fallacies, and foibles.

The ideal situation is to find someone who is spiritually mature and steeped in his or her own faith who will be willing to act as a spiritual guide or friend to you. This tradition, known as spiritual direction or spiritual guidance, has deep roots in Hasidic Judaism as well as in Catholicism, but it was practically unknown in the Protestant church until recent years. The Reformist doctrine of the priesthood of the believer and the disdain for the moral hierarchy of the papacy gave many Protestants a natural skepticism about anyone who would purport to "guide" or "direct" others in their religious lives.

Properly understood, spiritual direction is not about submission to human authority but about shared attentiveness to God's movements in the life of the directee. The guide not so much directs as points toward those places where God's presence might be sensed or God's leadings felt. So understood, spiritual guidance is becoming increasingly popular, even among mainstream Protestants. The director may well be a member of the clergy, but then again may not—it is important only that he or she has experienced this particular calling. An inquiry to your minister, priest, or rabbi about the possibilities for spiritual direction in your community may open the door for you to the discipline of guidance. (You might also wish to explore one or more of the listings in the Resources section at the end of this book.)

Where a formal relationship with a spiritual director is not possible, a "spiritual friendship" may prove just as profitable. Find someone who is equally committed to his or her growth and development and agree to spend an hour or two a month providing this kind of guidance and support for one another. A good model for such meetings, I believe, is the one I employed with Bryce during the two years I was privileged to know him. We would meet in the sanctuary of a small church near where we both worked and spend the first ten minutes or so in silent prayer. We would ask during that time for the patience and insight to be attentive to God's movements in the life of the other, as well as in our own. Then, for the remainder of the time, we would let the spotlight rest on one of us and the inner and outer events that had taken place since our last meeting. The other person would try to maintain the kind of receptive openness we had in prayer, silently seeking to be a conduit for whatever encouragement, questions, insights, or suggestions God might wish to prompt from within. Because Bryce and I both maintained a journal of our dreams and other important inner events, our entries provided endless grist for our conversation.

My relationship with Bryce, cut all too short by his early death from cancer, was a wonderful example of what can happen if both parties make time for deep friendship in the belief that God can truly use the other for God's purposes. Remarkable wisdom, healing, and preparation—for life's beginnings *and* endings—can flow from these sacred conversations.

The same dynamic can be achieved in a small group, but I think it more difficult. It is hard to find the right mix of people and then to sustain it over time. There will often be one person who wants the floor more often than he should, and another whose voice is not heard nearly enough. It also seems to me that it would be an uncommon married couple who could provide guidance for one another, either as a pair or part of a group. Familiarity may not breed contempt, but it doesn't breed objectivity either.

Along the path of growth and development, there may well come a point where you are capable of being your own psychotherapist. That may, in fact, be one laudable goal of psychological and spiritual growth. But there will never come a point when you cannot benefit from the spiritual guidance of others. God still uses messengers, even clumsy ones such as ourselves, far more than we realize.

———

Emerson observed that "All men plume themselves on the improvement of society, and no man improves." Overly pessimistic, perhaps, but it is certainly true that we seem to spend boundless time and energy on plans and policies and programs designed to make our world (or nation or community or organization) a better place, while our own inner growth gets far too little attention. This is why the practices discussed here are so important. They are central to the process of growth and development. Indeed they are essential in one degree or another to experiential religion. But they are critical to the process of opening, acknowledging, aligning, and cultivating, which forms the basis of human spirituality.

For every *Discipline* there is a corresponding freedom. A track star has the freedom to run a four-minute mile because he has the discipline to run twenty-five miles a week. A musician has the freedom to play a certain piece flawlessly because she has the discipline to practice interminably. The discipline is only a means to an end. Likewise the practices here set forth need not be seen as having intrinsic value in and of themselves; they are important because of the relationships they help us build with our deepest selves, with others, and with God. And ultimately they are important because of the kind of people we are capable of becoming through them.

Discipline is a stern word. But I would encourage you not to see the cultivation of these practices in that way. Think of them rather as little vacations from the swirling, externally oriented world in which we usually dwell. Think of them as setting aside time to focus on inward reality, or to speak and listen to Ultimate Reality, or to be refreshed by the written words of someone who lived an inspired life, or to be in the presence of a friend of spirit. These provide the moorings from which we can set out on the active life.

———————

Which leads us to the last practice, without which all else can become just pious vainglory. Inner work must always be followed by outer *Action,* a making-real on the outside of what we have accomplished on the inside. After all, the fruits of a spiritual life, no less than those of a tree, must be used and consumed in order to be of any value in the world. Parker Palmer puts it this way in his book *The Active Life:* "[T]rue contemplation is never a mere retreat. Instead, it draws us deeper into right action by getting us more deeply in touch with the gifts that we have to give, with our need to give them, with the people and problems that need us."[13]

Spiritual growth is not measured in terms of chronology or linear progress or steps. Even our "stages of development" are just our attempts to conceptualize the process. Spiritual and psychological growth is measured by who you are to the next person you meet, in the next crisis you face, in the next decision you make, in the next action you take. Spirituality stands over against the exteriority that pervades most of our culture, yet it insists that only by going inside *out* can we truly live the spiritual life.

The Harvest: Living and Working from the Center

> *Change takes place slowly inside each of us and by choices*
> *we think through in quiet wakeful moments lying in bed*
> *just before dawn. Culture is changed not so much by*
> *carefully planned, dramatic, and visible events as by*
> *focusing on our own actions in the small, barely noticed,*
> *day-to-day activities of our work. . . . It is change from the*
> *inside out.*
> PETER BLOCK

The Congruent Life is living in our outer reality the truth we have learned from our journey into inward reality. It is about finding in our life and work those places where we can manifest and refine the fruits of our inner growth. The Congruent Life begins with our *opening* to Ultimate Reality, to a power beyond our finite selves, through solitude, silence, Sabbath time, and meditation. It continues along this inward journey by *acknowledging* that power as the central motivation and source of meaning in our life and, through the discipline of prayer, by responding boldly to this incredible invitation that has been issued to us to come into a real and living relationship with the ground of being. It is quickened through our desire to *align* ourselves with God's purposes in the world through watching and listening, the exertion of our will, and service to God's creation. And it is *cultivated,* deepened, and sustained through study, guidance, discipline, and action. It is a life devoted to the harmonious consonance of inner and outer, work and life, self and other, creature and creator.

We are only now starting to see what the search for congruence means for business and organizational life. As our explorations in this book have shown, personal, inner, spiritual growth is positively and definitely connected to identifiable traits and qualities that are not merely "leadership skills" but are ways of being and looking at the world that are critical to organizational success. They are also key to personal happiness and effectiveness.

What remains is for this realization to take root in business, and indeed in all of our organizations, in ways that honor and encourage that kind of growth. It needs to move from the realm of committed individuals to the realm of organizational discourse. We need to be able to openly acknowledge that the age-old process of which we speak has its place—not merely in churches or monasteries or feel-good nonprofits or New Age enclaves—but where *we* live and work and spend our time and energy. This is the next great task of business: the marriage of the "modern" with the "ancient and ever new."

Questions and Exercises for Further Reflection

1. Given that we schedule practically all of our waking time, it is very difficult for us to have an experience of solitude that allows us to become fully grounded in the present. If you find that you need some help breaking through the habits you have created for yourself, try the following. Pick an afternoon when the weather is very pleasant and choose a spot some distance from your home that you would enjoy visiting. Be sure you have nothing else

planned for the rest of the day that you absolutely "must" get back for. Now have someone take you to that spot and leave you. Have no set time for the person to come back and pick you up—intentionally keep that vague. When you find yourself with nothing to do and no way to do it (perhaps for the first time in a long while), you can slowly begin to let the present moment assumes its rightful place in your attention.

2. Tilden Edwards has suggested a way to listen to sounds in silence that can aid in our becoming still. He observes that within a fraction of a second after we hear a sound we tend to do one of two things: we either name the sound ("That is a mockingbird singing"), or we judge the sound by whether we like or dislike it. The next time you are in solitude, let one of the sounds that surround you come into your awareness as simply the vibration that it is, without naming or judging it. If you find your mind doing its normal thing, just continue to return to the sound itself, letting it wash through you. You may find upon later reflection that you experienced the sounds around you much more vibrantly and that they had an ability to center you in the present.

3. One profitable way to focus our attention in meditation is through reviewing the events and emotions of the day. Begin by simply relaxing for a few minutes, with eyes closed or focused on a particular object. Then open yourself up to thoughts of the last twenty-four hours of your life. What events, encounters, or emotions come up for you? Where have you been most authentically yourself, or failed to be? Where have you felt the greatest attachment to your ego-needs, and where have you been most able to let them go? Where have you sensed God's presence, and where have you felt most distant? For those moments in which you have felt most yourself, least invested in your ego, and most graced, simply smile and say "Thank you." For the others, gather them together in a sort of mental basket, say a short prayer for forgiveness, and simply let them go. Your act of recollecting them and seeking forgiveness is enough for them to change you over time.

4. Look at the flow of your life over its last significant phase. Where are the moments when something really fortuitous and

unforseen happened? When did just the right person appear, or situation occur, that made possible some significant breakthrough? Where did you find yourself frustrated or defeated? Did some "window" open up when that "door" was closed? If you were to assume for the moment that an intelligence greater than your own was using those events to move you toward something in your life, or away from something else, what would that something be?

5. One wonderful way to combine the discipline of study with meditation and prayer is through a version of the ancient practice of *lectio divina* (divine reading). First, assume a mental posture of openness to whatever God may have to say to you through your readings. Then begin reading the scripture or other inspiring text you are currently studying. Be aware if a particular phrase or sentence strikes you deeply within, and stop right there for the moment. Don't indulge your normal tendency to want to "finish" the passage just yet; instead, step back from the passage and reflect on the phrase or sentence that has affected you so. What is its particular meaning for your life and work? What may God be trying specifically to say to you through it and your reaction to it? This may serve as a good beginning place for prayer.

Conclusion

The Hundredth Seeker

To believe what has not occurred in history will not occur at all, is to argue disbelief in the dignity of man.
MOHANDAS K. GANDHI

Great ideas, Camus observed, come into the world as gently as doves. They don't come on sounding trumpet, or command the cover of *Newsweek,* or highlight the debate in anybody's congressional race. Truly great ideas claim one individual heart and mind at a time, convicting and convincing us in ways that make us want to live life differently, in accordance with *their* truth, and thus transform that small ambit which is ours to control.

But it doesn't end there. There is a peculiar economy in this place called The Future; things are calculated differently there. Jesus tried to tell us this when he talked of a future way of being that he called the Kingdom of Heaven. He said that the Kingdom of Heaven—a "great idea" if there ever was one—was like a tiny bit of leaven that a woman hid deep within a half-bushel of flour, only to find that when left alone in the unseen silence it came to leaven the entire loaf (Matthew 13:33). Or perhaps it was like a mustard seed, the tiniest of all seeds; which by giving itself to the earth became a huge tree where the birds of the air could build their nests (Matthew 13: 31–32).

In the calculations of our normal economy, of course, such things are not possible. Ideas "win" in the marketplace by making majorities; forming consensus; and translating into policies and programs, rules and laws. The small, insignificant, drop-in-a-bucket individual is important only when it's time for a head count. But as Jesus taught, the great ideas that will form the basis of our future do not operate on the principle of majority rule. There is no use keeping score or determining who's ahead at the half. The great ideas come and alight and flourish in ways that seem to obey their own laws, the economic laws of a place called The Future.

On Japan's Koshima Island, so the story goes, there lived a small troop of macaque monkeys who were being observed by a team of anthropologists. During 1952 the scientists began to dump sweet potatoes on the beach both to provide food for the monkeys and to increase the opportunities for observation. One day, a young female (named Imo by her observers) took her potato down to the sea and began to wash it in the gentle surf. Apparently, this helped remove sand and grit and gave the meal a more pleasant flavor. Imo soon taught her new trick to her mother and a few playmates, who would join her down by the shore for the daily dinner ritual. Over the next six years, the habit of washing the potatoes in the ocean gradually spread, one by one, to a number of other monkeys in the colony, who seemed to learn it from the younger members of the troop.

Then one day in 1958 something remarkable happened. As anthropologist Lyall Watson recounts,[1] in the autumn of that year, on a particular day, one more insignificant little monkey—Watson calls him the hundredth monkey—was converted in the usual way to washing his potato before eating. But by nightfall of that same day, every single remaining monkey on the island had adopted the habit and was busy dunking his or her dinner in the salty surf. Some sort of invisible threshold had been crossed, some critical mass achieved. It was as if, to the monkeys, it had always been done exactly that way.

Yet it didn't stop there. Before long there were reports that other troops of monkeys on other islands, completely separated from the colony at Koshima, had suddenly and inexplicably taken to washing their food in the surf before eating it. The yeast had leavened the entire loaf. The mustard seed was now a huge tree. One plus one had become incalculable.

The cultivation of a spiritual life and its fruits is a "great idea"—not because it is in this book but because it has *always* been a great idea. It has been an idea pursued over thousands of years by mil-

lions of seekers whose ideal it has been to live the central principles of their lives in all of life's outer manifestations. Those ideas
and ideals are not new, but the outer circumstances are. We stand
at a point in history that not only invites us to a more congruent
life but *demands* it of us. We simply cannot achieve the promise of
the new millennium and the goals of our own society without a sizable number of people reaching the kind of maturity that only psychospiritual growth can foster. They may constitute a minority of
us for now—what Carl Sandburg called the saving minority—but
we will need to see more and more of them in leadership positions
in our businesses and nonprofits, our churches and government
agencies, if our institutions are to transform themselves sufficiently
to meet the challenges they will surely face. Ancient ideas, but a
new, immediate, and critical need for them.

George Bernard Shaw once said that while the reasonable man
adapts to the world, the unreasonable one persists in trying to
make the world adapt to him. Thus, he concluded, all progress depends on the unreasonable man. By that standard, we should all
be wholly *unreasonable* men and women. We should not adapt ourselves to our inherited view of work, our culturally defined split between religion and the rest of life, or our assigned place in the
mechanism of a consumerist society. If we have deep values, if we
have vibrant beliefs dying to find life in what we do for a living, if
we yearn for the Congruent Life—then we should insist that the
world conform itself to us. If the potato just tastes better washed in
the ocean, then maybe we should insist on eating it like that. Who
knows? In the mysterious ways in which great ideas come into the
world—or into communities or organizations—you just may be the
hundredth monkey.

It was of this hope that Jung wrote shortly before his death: "I
am neither spurred on by excessive optimism nor in love with high
ideals, but am merely concerned with the fate of the individual
human being—that infinitesimal unit on whom a world depends,
and in whom, if we read the meaning of the Christian message
aright, even God seeks his goal."[2]

Seek, and be found.

Notes

Introduction
1. Harman, W., *Global Mind Change* (Boston: Sigo Press, 1991), p. 121.
2. One version is in Luke 15:11–32.
3. Schumacher, E. F., and Gillingham, P. N., *Good Work* (New York: HarperCollins, 1985), p. 120.
4. McKnight, R., "Spirituality in the Workplace," in J. D. Adams (ed.), *Transforming Work* (Alexandria, VA: Miles River Press, 1984), p. 145.
5. "Company Memo to Stressed-Out Employees: 'Deal With It,'" *Wall Street Journal,* Oct. 2, 1996, p. B-1.
6. "Leaders Learn to Heed the Voice Within," *Fortune,* Aug. 22, 1994, p. 92.
7. According to a poll conducted by ABC News (broadcast Mar. 31, 1997), 95 percent of those surveyed indicated a belief in God or some supreme being, and 82 percent considered themselves "religious." A similar poll conducted by Gallup ten years earlier (Gallup Report No. 259, Apr. 1987) found that 94 percent of the sample believed in God or a Universal Spirit.
8. Harman, W., and Hormann, J., *Creative Work* (Indianapolis: Knowledge Systems, 1990), p. 13.
9. Chenu, M.-D., *The Theology of Work: An Exploration* (Chicago: Regnery, 1966), p. 4.
10. The term *lost provinces* is borrowed from L. Ryken, *Redeeming the Time: A Christian Approach to Work and Leisure* (Grand Rapids, MI: Baker Books, 1995).
11. Block, P., *Stewardship: Choosing Service over Self-Interest* (San Francisco: Berrett-Koehler, 1993), p. 77.

Chapter One
1. *At Work,* July/Aug. 1994, p. 2.
2. Eliade, M., *The Sacred and the Profane* (New York: HarperCollins, 1966).
3. See, for example, Dale, E. S., *Bringing Heaven Down to Earth* (New York: Lang, 1991), pp. 37–44.

4. Brother Lawrence, "The Practice of the Presence of God," in *The Kitchen Saint* (Princeton, NJ: Princeton Theological Monograph Series, 1989).
5. Frey, D. E., "Economic Individualism in Puritan Thought," unpublished manuscript, 1993.
6. Williams, O. F., and Houck, J. W., *The Judeo-Christian Vision and the Modern Corporation* (Notre Dame, IN: University of Notre Dame Press, 1982), p. 10.
7. Bell, D., *Work and Its Discontents* (Boston: Beacon Street Press, 1956).
8. Smith, A., *The Theory of Moral Sentiments* (New York: Kelley, 1966), p. 297.
9. Williams and Houck, *The Judeo-Christian Vision and the Modern Corporation,* p. 15.
10. Sayers, D., *Creed or Chaos?* (Orlando: Harcourt Brace, 1949), p. 56.
11. Sayers, *Creed or Chaos?* p. 51.
12. Weber, M., *The Protestant Ethic and the Spirit of Capitalism* (London: Allen & Unwin, 1930), p. 182.
13. Maccoby, M., *Why Work: Motivating the New Workforce* (Alexandria, VA: Miles River Press, 1995).
14. Gini, A. R., and Sullivan, T. J. (eds.), *It Comes with the Territory: An Inquiry Concerning Work and the Person* (New York: Random House, 1989), pp. 66–67.
15. Bloom, A. D., *The Closing of the American Mind* (New York: Simon & Schuster, 1987), p. 194.

Chapter Two

1. Haughey, J. C., *Converting Nine to Five: A Spirituality of Daily Work* (New York: Crossroad, 1989), p. 19.
2. Gini, A. R., and Sullivan, T. J. (eds.), *It Comes with the Territory: An Inquiry Concerning Work and the Person* (New York: Random House, 1989), p. 23.
3. Schumacher, E. F., and Gillingham, P. N., *Good Work* (New York: HarperCollins, 1985), pp. 3–4.
4. Burns, J. M., *Leadership* (New York: HarperCollins, 1978), p. 384.
5. Maslow, A., *Eupsychian Management,* quoted in Gini and Sullivan (eds.), *It Comes with the Territory,* p. 237.
6. Fort, T. L., "Business as a Mediating Institution," *Business Ethics Quarterly,* 6(2), 1996, pp. 149–163.
7. Greenleaf, R. K., *Servant Leadership* (Mahwah, NJ: Paulist Press, 1977), p. 134.
8. Bellah, quoted in M. Naughton and G. R. Laczniak, "A Theological Context of Work from the Catholic Social Encyclical Tradition," *Journal of Business Ethics,* 12(12), 1993, p. 983.

9. Fox, M., *On Becoming a Musical Mystical Bear* (Mahwah, NJ: Paulist Press, 1972).

10. Buechner, F., *Wishful Thinking: A Theological ABC* (New York: Harper-Collins, 1973), p. 95.

11. Peck, M. S., *A World Waiting to be Born* (New York: Bantam Books, 1993), p. 71.

12. "Crosscurrents," *At Work*, May/June 1994, p. 16.

13. "More Employees Say They Are Working on Weekends," *Winston-Salem Journal*, May 19, 1997, p. D-1.

14. "Work vs. Play," *Wall Street Journal*, Sept. 29, 1995, p. A-1.

15. Kahn, R. L., *Work and Health* (New York: Wiley, 1981), p. 11.

16. Davidson, J. C., and Caddell, D. P., "Religion and the Meaning of Work," *Journal for the Scientific Study of Religion*, *33*(2), 1994, pp. 135–147.

17. Davidson and Caddell, "Religion and the Meaning of Work," p. 145.

Chapter Three

1. Bolman, L. G., and Deal, T. E., "What Makes a Team Work," *Organizational Dynamics*, *21*(2), Fall 1992, p. 44.

2. The term *participation mystique* was coined by Lucien Levy-Bruhl in describing subject-object relations in primitive peoples. Jungian psychology uses the term more in the way we are employing it here. See Jung, C. G., *Psychological Types* (Princeton, NJ: Princeton University Press, 1974), pp. 456–457.

3. Vaill, P. B., "Spirituality in the Age of the Leveraged Buyout," keynote address at the conference on Spirituality in Life and Work, Georgetown University, July 21, 1989, p. 26.

4. Owen, H., *Spirit: Transformation and Development in Organizations* (Potomac, MD: Abbott, 1987), p. vii.

5. Vaill, P. B., *Managing as a Performing Art: New Ideas for a World of Chaotic Change* (San Francisco: Jossey-Bass, 1991), p. 213.

6. Underhill, E., *The Spiritual Life*, quoted in R. P. Job and N. Shawchuck, *A Guide to Prayer* (Nashville, TN: Upper Room Books, 1983), p. 320.

7. Vaill, P. B., *Learning as a Way of Being* (San Francisco: Jossey-Bass, 1996), pp. 178–180.

8. Spretnak, C., *States of Grace: The Recovery of Meaning in the Postmodern Age* (San Francisco: Harper San Francisco, 1991), pp. 208–209.

9. Lao Tzu, Chapter Twenty-Three of the *Tao Te Ching*, quoted in *The Guiding Light of Lao Tzu*, trans. H. Wei (Wheaton, IL: Theosophical Publishing House, 1982), p. 158.

10. James, W., *The Varieties of Religious Experience: A Study in Human Nature* (New York: Longman, 1902), p. 506.

11. Underhill, E., *The Spiritual Life*, quoted in Job and Shawchuck, *A Guide to Prayer*, p. 315.

12. Conger, J. A., and Associates, *Spirit at Work: Discovering the Spirituality in Leadership* (San Francisco: Jossey-Bass, 1994), p. 17.

13. Allport, G. W., *The Person in Psychology* (Boston: Beacon Press, 1968), p. 242.

14. Allport, *Person in Psychology*, p. 243.

15. Kanungo, R. N., and Mendonca, M., "What Leaders Cannot Do Without: The Spiritual Dimensions of Leadership," in J. A. Conger and Associates, *Spirit at Work*, p. 175.

16. James, *Varieties of Religious Experience*, p. 410.

17. James, *Varieties of Religious Experience*, pp. 498–499.

18. James, *Varieties of Religious Experience*, p. 507.

19. Jung, C. G., *Two Essays on Analytical Psychology* (Princeton, NJ: Princeton University Press, 1966), pp. 173 and the following pages. For an excellent summary of Jung's theory of individuation, see Sanford, J. A., *The Man Who Wrestled with God* (Mahwah, NJ: Paulist Press, 1974), pp. 125–132.

20. Jung, *Two Essays*, p. 238.

21. Sanford, J. A. (ed.), *Fritz Kunkel: Selected Writings* (Mahwah, NJ: Paulist Press, 1984), pp. 140 and the following pages.

22. Jung, C. G., *The Archetypes and the Collective Unconscious* (Princeton, NJ: Princeton University Press, 1959), p. 121.

23. Jung, C. G., *Psychological Types* (Princeton, NJ: Princeton University Press, 1971), p. 448.

24. Sanford, *Man Who Wrestled with God*, p. 128.

25. Jung, C. G., *Psychology and Religion: West and East* (Princeton, NJ: Princeton University Press, 1958), p. 89.

26. Kanungo, R. N., and Mendonca, M., *Ethical Dimensions of Leadership* (Thousand Oaks, CA: Sage, 1996), p. 88.

27. Dehler, G. E., and Welsh, M. A., "Spirituality and Organizational Transformation: Implications for the New Management Paradigm," *Journal of Managerial Psychology*, 9(6), 1994, p. 21.

28. McCormick, D. W., "Spirituality and Management," *Journal of Managerial Psychology*, 9(6), 1994, p. 5.

Chapter Four

1. Peters, T., "Spirituality Has No Place in the Secular Corporation," *Star Tribune*, Apr. 6, 1993.

2. Peters, "Spirituality Has No Place."

3. Peters, "Spirituality Has No Place."

4. Lee, C., and Zemke, R., "The Search for Spirit in the Workplace," *Training*, 30(6), June 1993, p. 26.

5. Owen, H., *Spirit: Transformation and Development in Organizations* (Potomac, MD: Abbott, 1987), p. 29.

6. Autry, J. A., *Life and Work: A Manager's Search for Meaning* (New York: Morrow, 1994), p. 100.

7. Ibrahim, N. A., Rue, L. W., and Green, G. R., "Characteristics and Practices of Christian-Based Companies," *Journal of Business Ethics, 10*(2), 1991, pp. 123–132.

8. Hawley, J., *Reawakening the Spirit in Work: The Power of Dharmic Management* (San Francisco: Berrett-Koehler, 1993), p. 93.

9. Jung, C. G., *The Undiscovered Self* (New York: Little, Brown, 1957), pp. 22–23.

10. "EEOC May Pit Church vs. State at Work," *Wall Street Journal,* June 8, 1994, p. B-8.

11. "EEOC May Pit Church vs. State at Work."

12. *Rosen v. Baker,* 1995 WL 264169 (EDNY).

13. The only exception to this statement, curiously, is the federal government itself. On August 14, 1997, President Clinton signed Policy Guidance #2, "Religious Exercise and Religious Expression in the Workplace," which is applicable only to civilian federal employees. It permits certain specified forms of personal religious expression in federal workplaces, including limited attempts to "persuade fellow employees."

14. Lee and Zemke, "The Search for Spirit," p. 27.

15. Csikszentmihalyi, M., *Flow: The Psychology of Optimal Experience* (New York: HarperCollins, 1990).

16. Csikszentmihalyi, M., *Beyond Boredom and Anxiety: The Experience of Play in Work and Games* (San Francisco: Jossey-Bass, 1975), p. 36.

17. Dehler, G. E., and Welsh, M. A., "Spirituality and Organizational Transformation: Implications for the New Management Paradigm," *Journal of Managerial Psychology, 9*(6), 1994, pp. 17–26.

18. See Fassel, D., *Working Ourselves to Death* (San Francisco: Harper San Francisco, 1990).

19. See Leviticus 16:8–10.

20. For an excellent exposition of the psychological dynamics of scapegoating, see Coleman, A. D., *Up from Scapegoating: Awakening Consciousness in Groups* (Wilmette, IL: Chiron, 1996).

21. Niebuhr, R., *Moral Man and Immoral Society: A Study in Ethics and Politics* (New York: Scribner, 1960).

22. Sayers, D., *Creed or Chaos?* (Orlando: Harcourt Brace, 1949), p. 59.

23. Peck, M. S., *People of the Lie: The Hope for Healing Human Evil* (New York: Simon & Schuster, 1983).

24. Nichols, M., "Does New Age Business Have a Message for Managers?" *Harvard Business Review, 72*(2), Mar. 1994, pp. 52–60.

25. Nichols, "Does New Age Business Have a Message for Managers?" p. 53.
26. Nichols, "Does New Age Business Have a Message for Managers?" p. 55.
27. Nichols, "Does New Age Business Have a Message for Managers?" p. 56.

Chapter Five

1. "America, Land of the Shaken," *Business Week*, Mar. 11, 1996, pp. 64–65.
2. "America, Land of the Shaken."
3. http://www.depression.com.
4. DeFrank, R. S., and Ivancevich, J. M., "Stress on the Job: An Executive Update," *Academy of Management Executive*, 12(3), 1998, p. 55.
5. Vaill, P. B., "The Rediscovery of Anguish," keynote address at the annual meeting of the Association for Creative Change, Cincinnati, OH, June 1989.
6. Behrman, J. N., *Essays on Ethics in Business and the Professions* (Englewood Cliffs, NJ: Prentice Hall, 1988).
7. Toffler, A., *The Third Wave* (New York: Morrow, 1980), p. 401.
8. Toffler, *The Third Wave*.
9. Yankelovich, D., "The New Psychological Contracts at Work," *Psychology Today*, May 1978, reprinted in A. R. Gini and T. J. Sullivan (eds.), *It Comes with the Territory* (New York: Random House, 1989), p. 85.
10. Earley, J., "Questions of Spirit: An Interview with Steve Boehlke," *Spectrum*, Apr. 1996, p. 5.
11. Flynn, G., "Why Employees Are So Angry," *Workforce*, Sept. 1998, p. 27.
12. Kelly, M., "Unpaid Overtime," *Business Ethics* 12(4), July/Aug. 1998, pp. 12–14. At this writing a class action lawsuit is pending against the largest bank in the United States for just such practices.
13. "Companies Hit the Road Less Travelled," *Business Week*, June 5, 1995, p. 82.
14. Dorsey, D., "The New Spirit of Work," *Fast Company*, Aug. 1998, p. 134.
15. Schifrin, M., "The Unkindest Cuts," *Forbes*, May 4, 1998, p. 44–45.
16. "Who Is the Real 'Chainsaw Al'?" *Business Week*, Dec. 2, 1996, p. 40–41.
17. Sloan, A., "Chainsaw Massacre," *Newsweek*, June 29, 1998, p. 62.
18. Peck, M. S., *A World Waiting to Be Born: Civility Rediscovered* (New York: Bantam Books, 1993), p. 353.

19. Autry, J. A., *Love and Profit: The Art of Caring Leadership* (New York: Morrow, 1991), p. 13.
20. Kallen, B., "Praying for Guidance," *Forbes,* Dec. 1, 1986.
21. Conger, J. A., and Associates, *Spirit at Work: Discovering the Spirituality in Leadership* (San Francisco: Jossey-Bass, 1994), p. 203.
22. Vaill, "Rediscovery of Anguish."

Chapter Six
1. Levinson, D. J., "A Theory of Life Structure Development in Adulthood," in C. N. Alexander and E. J. Langer (eds.), *Higher Stages of Human Development: Perspectives on Adult Growth* (New York: Oxford University Press, 1990), p. 35.
2. Cook-Greuter, S. R., "Maps for Living: Ego-Development Stages from Symbiosis to Conscious Universal Embeddedness," in M. L. Commons and others (eds.), *Adult Development,* vol. 2 (New York: Praeger, 1990), p. 89.
3. Cook-Greuter, "Maps for Living," p. 91.
4. Fowler, J. W., *Stages of Faith: The Psychology of Human Development and the Quest for Meaning* (San Francisco: HarperCollins, 1981), pp. 200–201.
5. Fraedrich, J., Thorne, D. M., and Ferrell, O. C., "Assessing the Application of Cognitive Moral Development Theory to Business Ethics," *Journal of Business Ethics, 13,* 1994, pp. 829–838.
6. See Torbert, W. R., *Managing the Corporate Dream* (Homewood, IL: Dow Jones-Irwin, 1987); and Fisher, D., and Torbert, W. R., *Personal and Organizational Transformations* (London: McGraw-Hill, 1995).
7. Vogelsang, J. D., "Personality, Faith, Development, and Work Attitudes," *Journal of Religion and Health, 22*(2), Summer 1983, p. 133. I am indebted to Dr. Vogelsang for his insights on the work attitudes associated with the developmental stages.
8. Fisher and Torbert, *Personal and Organizational Transformations,* pp. 77–78.
9. Burns, J. M., *Leadership* (New York: HarperCollins, 1978), p. 78–79.
10. Merron, K., Fisher, D., and Torbert, W. R., "Meaning Making and Management Action," *Group and Organizational Studies, 12*(3), Sept. 1987, pp. 274–286.
11. Torbert, *Managing the Corporate Dream,* p. 121.
12. See Graham, J. W., "Leadership, Moral Development, and Citizenship Behavior," *Business Ethics Quarterly, 5*(1), Jan. 1995, pp. 43–54; and Organ, D. W., *Organizational Citizenship Behavior: The "Good Soldier" Syndrome* (San Francisco: New Lexington Press, 1988).
13. Loevinger, J., *Ego Development: Conception and Theories* (San Francisco: Jossey-Bass, 1976).

14. Merron, Fisher, and Torbert, "Meaning Making," p. 275.
15. Bartunek, J., Gordon, J., and Weathersby, R. P., "Developing Complicated Understanding in Administrators," *Academy of Management Review, 8,* 1982, pp. 273–284.
16. Cook-Greuter, "Maps for Living," pp. 96–97.
17. Hood, R. W., Jr., "Religious Orientation and the Experience of Transcendence," *Journal for the Scientific Study of Religion, 12,* 1973, pp. 441–448; and Clouse, B., "Religious Experience, Religious Belief and Moral Development of Students at a State University," *Journal of Psychology and Christianity, 10*(4), 1991, pp. 337–349.
18. Schumacher, E. F., and Gillingham, P. N., *Good Work* (New York: HarperCollins, 1985), p. 115.
19. de Foucauld, C., *Meditations of a Hermit,* quoted in R. P. Job and N. Shawchuck, *A Guide to Prayer for All God's People* (Nashville, TN: Upper Room Books, 1990), p. 111.
20. Bergin, A. E., "Values and Religious Issues in Psychotherapy and Mental Health," *American Psychologist, 46*(4), Apr. 1991, pp. 394–403.
21. Bergin, "Values and Religious Issues," p. 400.
22. Kohlberg, L., and Ryncarz, R. A., "Beyond Justice Reasoning: Moral Development and Consideration of a Seventh Stage," in C. N. Alexander and E. J. Langer (eds.), *Higher Stages of Human Development.*
23. See, for example, Alexander, C. N., and others,"Growth of Higher Stages of Consciousness: Maharishi's Vedic Psychology of Human Development," in C. N. Alexander and E. J. Langer (eds.), *Higher Stages of Human Development.*
24. Wilber, K., Engler, J., and Brown, D. P., *Transformations of Consciousness: Conventional and Contemplative Perspectives on Development* (Boston: Shambhala, 1986), pp. 3–5.
25. Wilber, Engler, and Brown, *Transformations of Consciousness,* pp. 65–105.

Chapter Seven

1. Kanungo, R. N., and Mendonca, M., *Ethical Dimensions of Leadership* (Thousand Oaks, CA: Sage, 1996), p. 14.
2. Fisher, D., and Torbert, W. R., *Personal and Organizational Transformations* (London: McGraw-Hill, 1995), pp. 178–196.
3. Bartunek, J., Gordon, J., and Weathersby, R. P., "Developing Complicated Understanding in Administrators," *Academy of Management Review, 8,* 1982, pp. 272–284.
4. Bergin, A. E., "Values and Religious Issues in Psychotherapy and Mental Health," *American Psychologist, 46*(4), Apr. 1991, pp. 394–403;

and Baker, M., and Gorsuch, R., "Trait Anxiety and Intrinsic-Extrinsic Religiousness," *Journal for the Scientific Study of Religion, 21*(2), 1982, pp. 119–122.

5. Kramer, D. A., "Post-Formal Operations? A Need for Further Conceptualization," *Human Development, 26,* 1983, pp. 91–105.

6. Merron, K., Fisher, D., and Torbert, W. R., "Meaning Making and Management Action," *Group and Organizational Studies, 12*(3), Sept. 1987, pp. 274–286.

7. Senge, P. M., "The Leader's New Work: Building Learning Organizations," in Renesch, J. (ed.), *New Traditions in Business: Spirit and Leadership in the Twenty-First Century* (San Francisco: Berrett-Koehler, 1992), p. 89.

8. Basseches, M. A., "Dialectical Thinking as a Metasystematic Form of Cognitive Organization," in M. L. Commons, F. A. Richards, and C. Armon (eds.), *Beyond Formal Operations: Late Adolescent and Adult Cognitive Development* (New York: Praeger, 1984), pp. 216–238.

9. Cleveland, H., *The Future Executive,* quoted in R. W. Terry, *Authentic Leadership: Courage in Action* (San Francisco: Jossey-Bass, 1993), pp. xv–xvi.

10. Kramer, D. A., "Development of an Awareness of Contradictions Across the Lifespan and the Question of Postformal Operations," *Adult Development, 1,* 1989, pp. 133–159.

11. Souvaine, E., Lahev, L. L., and Kegan, R., "Life After Formal Operations: Implications for a Psychology of the Self," in C. N. Alexander and E. J. Langer (eds.), *Higher Stages of Human Development: Perspectives on Adult Growth* (New York: Oxford University Press, 1990), p. 236.

12. Cook-Greuter, S. R., "Maps for Living: Ego-Development Stages from Symbiosis to Conscious Universal Embeddedness," in M. L. Commons and others (eds.), *Adult Development,* vol. 2 (New York: Praeger, 1990), p. 88.

13. Jung, C. G., *Civilization in Transition* (Princeton, NJ: Princeton University Press, 1964), p. 154.

14. Erikson, E. H., *Gandhi's Truth on the Origins of Militant Nonviolence* (New York: Norton, 1969).

15. Quoted in R. P. Job and N. Shawchuck, *A Guide to Prayer for All God's People* (Nashville, TN: Upper Room Books, 1990), p. 259.

16. Quoted in E. Easwaran, *God Make the Rivers to Flow* (Tomales, CA: Nilgiri Press, 1994), p. 76.

17. Niebuhr, R., *The Irony of American History* (New York: Scribner, 1952), p. 63.

18. Cook-Greuter, "Maps for Living," p. 86.

19. Kelsey, M. T., *Companions on the Inner Way* (New York: Crossroad, 1984), p. 23.

20. Bennis, W., and Nanus, B., *Leaders: The Strategies for Taking Charge* (New York: HarperCollins, 1985), pp. 57–58.

21. Lao Tzu, *Tao Te Ching*, verse 36, in *The Way of Life*, trans. W. Bynner (New York: John Day, 1944).

22. Palmer, P., *The Active Life: A Spirituality of Work, Creativity, and Caring* (San Francisco: Harper San Francisco, 1990), p. 51.

23. Greenleaf, R. K., *Servant Leadership* (Mahwah, NJ: Paulist Press, 1977), p. 327.

24. "Leaders Learn to Heed the Voice Within," *Fortune*, Aug. 22, 1994, p. 92.

25. Quoted in M. L. Ray, "The Emerging New Paradigm in Business," in Renesch, J. (ed.), *New Traditions in Business: Spirit and Leadership in the Twenty-First Century* (San Francisco: Berrett-Koehler, 1992), p. 36.

26. Schaefer, C., and Darling, J., "Spirit Matters: Using Contemplative Disciplines in Work and Organizational Life," unpublished manuscript, Nov. 1996.

27. Murchland, B., "Creativity and the Social Order," in J. W. Houck and O. F. Williams (eds.), *Co-Creation and Capitalism: John Paul II's Laborem Exercens* (Lanham, MD: University Press of America, 1983).

28. Murchland, "Creativity and the Social Order," p. 87.

29. Maslow, A., *Eupsychian Management*, quoted in A. R. Gini and T. J. Sullivan (eds.), *It Comes with the Territory: An Inquiry Concerning Work and the Person* (New York: Random House, 1989), p. 239.

30. De Pree, M., *Leadership Jazz* (New York: Dell, 1993).

31. Easwaran, E., "Working in Freedom," *Yoga International*, May/June, 1995, p. 24.

32. James, W., *The Varieties of Religious Experience: A Study in Human Nature* (New York: Longman, 1902), p. 475.

33. Fox, E., *Your Heart's Desire*, quoted in R. F. Job and N. Shawchuck, *A Guide to Prayer* (Nashville, TN: Upper Room Books, 1983), pp. 44–45.

Chapter Eight

1. Covey, S. R., *The Seven Habits of Highly Effective People* (New York: Simon & Schuster, 1989), p. 185.

2. McCall, M. W., and Lombardo, M. M., *Off the Track: Why and How Successful Executives Get Derailed* (Greensboro, NC: Center for Creative Leadership, 1983).

3. Merron, K., Fisher, D., and Torbert, W. R., "Meaning Making and

Management Action," *Group and Organization Studies, 12*(3), Sept. 1987, pp. 274–286.

4. Merron, Fisher, and Torbert, "Meaning Making," p. 276.

5. Bunker, K. A., "The Power of Vulnerability in Contemporary Leadership," *Consulting Psychology Journal: Practice and Research, 49*(2), Spring 1997, pp. 122–136.

6. Bunker, "The Power of Vulnerability," p. 134.

7. Moore, T., *Meditations on the Monk Who Dwells in Daily Life* (New York: HarperCollins, 1994), p. 12.

8. Cook-Greuter, S. R., "Maps for Living: Ego-Development Stages from Symbiosis to Conscious Universal Embeddedness," in M. L. Commons and others (eds.), *Adult Development,* vol. 2 (New York: Praeger, 1990), pp. 92–93.

9. See Eyler, J., "Citizenship Education for Conflict: An Empirical Assessment of the Relationship between Principled Thinking and Tolerance for Conflict and Diversity," *Theory and Research in Social Education, 8*(2), Summer 1980, pp. 11–26.

10. Torbert, W. R., *Managing the Corporate Dream* (Homewood, IL: Dow Jones–Irwin, 1987).

11. Bergin, A. E., "Values and Religious Issues in Psychotherapy and Mental Health," *American Psychologist, 46*(4), Apr. 1991, pp. 394–403. The tolerance scale on the CPI identifies those with "permissive, accepting and nonjudgmental social beliefs and attitudes."

12. Drath, W. H., *Why Managers Have Trouble Empowering: A Theoretical Perspective Based on Concepts of Adult Development* (Greensboro, NC: Center for Creative Leadership, 1983). Another version of this work appears as "Managerial Strengths and Weaknesses as Functions of the Development of Personal Meaning," *Journal of Applied Behavioral Sciences, 26*(4), 1990, pp. 483–499.

13. Drath, *Why Managers Have Trouble Empowering,* p. 28.

14. Merron, Fisher, and Torbert, "Meaning Making."

15. Peck, M. S., *A World Waiting To Be Born* (New York: Bantam Books, 1993), p. 266.

16. Fowler, J. W., *Stages of Faith: The Psychology of Human Development and the Quest for Meaning* (San Francisco: HarperCollins, 1981), p. 199.

17. Smith, S., "Ego Development and the Problems of Power and Agreement in Organizations," unpublished doctoral dissertation, School of Business and Public Administration, George Washington University.

18. Autry, J. A., *Love and Profit: The Art of Caring Leadership* (New York: Morrow, 1991), p. 13.

19. Lewis, C. S., *The Four Loves* (Orlando: Harcourt Brace, 1958).

20. Lewis, *The Four Loves*, p. 175.
21. Lewis, *The Four Loves*, p. 11.
22. Thurman, H., *The Inward Journey* (New York: HarperCollins, 1961), p. 129.
23. Kanungo, R. N., and Mendonca, M., *Ethical Dimensions of Leadership* (Thousand Oaks, CA: Sage, 1996).
24. De Pree, M., *Leadership Is an Art* (New York: Dell, 1989), p. 11.
25. Fisher, D., and Torbert, W. R., *Personal and Organizational Transformations* (London: McGraw-Hill, 1995), p. 62.
26. Moore, *Meditations*, p. 29.

Chapter Nine

1. Harmon, W., *Global Mind Change* (Boston: Sigo Press, 1991), p. 8.
2. For many of these insights I am indebted to Dr. Clifford Christians of the University of Illinois, Urbana, and his unpublished manuscript "Business Ethics in a Post Enlightenment Age" (1993).
3. Toffler, A., *The Third Wave* (New York: Morrow, 1980).
4. See Cohn, N., *The Pursuit of the Millennium* (New York: Oxford University Press, 1970).
5. Adams, J. D. (ed.), *Transforming Work: A Collection of Organizational Transformation Readings* (Alexandria, VA: Miles River Press, 1984), p. vii.
6. Bennis, W. G., and Nanus, B., *Leaders: The Strategies for Taking Charge* (New York: HarperCollins, 1985), p. 39.
7. Nanus, B., *Visionary Leadership: Creating a Compelling Sense of Direction for Your Organization* (San Francisco: Jossey-Bass, 1992).
8. Denison, D. R., and Mishra, A. K., "Toward a Theory of Organizational Culture and Effectiveness," *Organization Science, 6*(2), 1995.
9. Kohn, A., *Punished by Rewards: The Trouble with Gold Stars, A's, Praise and Other Bribes* (Boston: Houghton Mifflin, 1993).
10. Vaill, P. B., "The Rediscovery of Anguish," keynote address at the annual meeting of the Association for Creative Change, Cincinnati, OH, June 1989.
11. Dehler, G. E., and Welsh, M. A., "Spirituality and Organizational Transformation: Implications for a New Management Paradigm," *Journal of Managerial Psychology, 9*(6), 1994, pp. 17–26.
12. Bennis and Nanus, *Leaders*, p. 92.
13. Tichy, N. M., and Devanna, M. A., *The Transformational Leader* (New York: Wiley, 1986), pp. 271–280.
14. Tichy and Devanna, *The Transformational Leader*, p. 278.
15. Greenleaf, R. K., *Servant Leadership* (Mahwah, NJ: Paulist Press, 1977), pp. 15, 23.

16. Greenleaf, *Servant Leadership,* pp. 17, 20.

17. Greenleaf, *Servant Leadership,* p. 25.

18. Greenleaf, *Servant Leadership,* p. 32.

19. Greenleaf, *Servant Leadership,* p. 327.

20. Greenleaf, *Servant Leadership,* p. 10.

21. Pascale, R., "The Agenda," *Fast Company,* Apr./May 1998, p. 114.

22. Kanungo, R. N., and Mendonca, M., *Ethical Dimensions of Leadership* (Thousand Oaks, CA: Sage, 1996).

23. Walton, M., *The Deming Management Method* (New York: Perigee Books, 1986).

24. Crosby, P. B., *Quality Without Tears: The Art of Hassle-Free Management* (New York: McGraw-Hill, 1984), p. 83.

25. Giroux, H., and Landry, S., "Schools of Thought in and Against Total Quality," *Journal of Management Issues,* X(2), 1998, p. 185.

26. Sayers, D., *Creed or Chaos?* (Orlando: Harcourt Brace, 1949), pp. 57–58.

27. Autry, J. A., *Life and Work: A Manager's Search for Meaning* (New York: Morrow, 1994), p. 102.

28. Giroux and Landry, "Schools of Thought," p. 183.

29. Giroux and Landry, "Schools of Thought," p. 193.

30. Giroux and Landry, "Schools of Thought."

31. Fisher, D., and Torbert, W. R., *Personal and Organizational Transformations* (London: McGraw-Hill, 1995), p. 128.

32. For further reflections on these themes, see Fox, M., *The Reinvention of Work: A New Vision of Livelihood for Our Time* (San Francisco: HarperCollins, 1994), pp. 70–74.

33. Hargrove, R., *Mastering the Art of Creative Collaboration* (New York: McGraw-Hill, 1998).

34. Vaill, P. B., *Learning as a Way of Being* (San Francisco: Jossey-Bass, 1996), p. 126.

35. Burns, J. M., *Leadership* (New York: HarperCollins, 1978), p. 117.

36. "Chaos Theory Seeps Into Ecology Debate, Stirring Up a Tempest." *Wall Street Journal,* July 11, 1994, p. A-1.

37. *Wall Street Journal,* July 11, 1994, p. A-8.

38. I am indebted to Dr. Peter B. Vaill for this example.

39. Maynard, H. B., and Mehrtens, S. E., *The Fourth Wave: Business in the Twenty-First Century* (San Francisco: Berrett-Koehler, 1993).

Chapter Ten

1. See, for example, Matthew 4:1–2, 14:13, 17:1–9; Luke 6:12; Mark 1:35, 6:31, 14:32.

2. In Job, R. P., and Shawchuck, N., *A Guide to Prayer for All God's People* (Nashville, TN: Upper Room Books, 1990), p. 25.

3. Schaefer, C., and Darling, J., "Spirit Matters: Using Contemplative Disciplines in Work and Organizational Life," unpublished manuscript, Nov. 1996.

4. Peck, M. S., *A World Waiting to Be Born* (New York: Bantam Books, 1993), pp. 81–92.

5. Bloom, A., *Beginning to Pray* (Mahwah, NJ: Paulist Press, 1970), p. 49.

6. Hart, T. N., *The Art of Christian Listening* (Mahwah, NJ: Paulist Press, 1980), p. 57.

7. Foster, R. J., *Celebration of Discipline* (New York: HarperCollins, 1978), p. 30.

8. Bloom, *Beginning to Pray*, p. 49.

9. There are a number of highly readable books on dreams and their interpretation from a religious perspective. I particularly recommend Robert A. Johnson's *Inner Work* (Harper San Francisco, 1989) and any of the books on the subject by John A. Sanford or Morton T. Kelsey.

10. Matthew 6:1–4, slightly adapted from the NKJV.

11. Johnston, W. (ed.), *The Cloud of Unknowing and the Book of Privy Counseling* (Garden City, NY: Image Books, 1973), p. 56.

12. May, G. G., *Will and Spirit: A Contemplative Psychology* (San Francisco: HarperCollins, 1982), p. 6.

13. Palmer, P. J., *The Active Life: A Spirituality of Work, Creativity, and Caring* (San Francisco: Harper San Francisco, 1990), p. 122.

Conclusion

1. Watson, L., *Lifetide* (New York: Simon & Schuster, 1979).

2. Jung, C. G., *The Undiscovered Self* (New York: Little, Brown, 1957), p. 113.

Further Readings

The Meaning and Purpose of Human Work

Gini, A. R., and Sullivan, T. J. (eds.), *It Comes with the Territory: An Inquiry Concerning Work and the Person* (New York: Random House, 1989).

Harmon, W. W., *Creative Work: The Constructive Role of Business in a Transforming Society* (Indianapolis: Knowledge Systems, 1990).

Ryken, L., *Redeeming the Time: A Christian Approach to Work and Leisure* (Grand Rapids, MI: Baker Books, 1995).

Schumacher, E. F., and Gillingham, P. N., *Good Work* (New York: Harper-Collins, 1985).

Williams, O. F., and Houck, J. W. (eds.), *The Judeo-Christian Vision and the Modern Corporation* (Notre Dame, IN: University of Notre Dame Press, 1982).

The Theology of Work

Dale, E. S., *Bringing Heaven Down to Earth: A Practical Spirituality of Work* (New York: Lang, 1991).

Fox, M., *The Reinvention of Work: A New Vision of Livelihood for Our Time* (San Francisco: Harper San Francisco, 1995).

Gillett, R. W., *The Human Enterprise: A Christian Perspective on Work* (Kansas City: Sheed and Ward, 1985).

Haughey, J. C., *Converting Nine to Five: A Spirituality of Daily Work* (New York: Crossroad, 1989).

Novak, M., and Cooper, J. W. (eds.), *Corporation: A Theological Inquiry* (Washington, DC: American Enterprise Institute for Public Policy Research, 1991).

Pierce, G. F. (ed.), *Of Human Hands: A Reader in the Spirituality of Work* (Chicago: ACTA Publications, 1991).

Volf, M., *Work in the Spirit: Toward a Theology of Work* (New York: Oxford University Press, 1991).

Spirituality/Religion and Business

Autry, J. A., *Love and Profit: The Art of Caring Leadership* (New York: Morrow, 1991).

Autry, J. A., *Life and Work: A Manager's Search for Meaning* (New York: Morrow, 1994).

Briskin, A., *The Stirring of Soul in the Workplace* (San Francisco: Jossey-Bass, 1996).

Cowan, J., *Small Decencies: Reflections and Meditations on Being Human at Work* (New York: Harper Business, 1993).

Cowan, J., *Common Table* (New York: Harper Business, 1994).

Marcic, D., *Managing with the Wisdom of Love: Uncovering Virtue in People and Organizations* (San Francisco: Jossey-Bass, 1997).

Neuhaus, R. J., *Doing Well and Doing Good: The Challenge to the Christian Capitalist* (New York: Doubleday, 1995).

Orsborn, C., *Inner Excellence: Spiritual Principles of Life-Driven Business* (San Rafael, CA: New World Library, 1993).

Palmer, P. J., *The Active Life: A Spirituality of Work, Creativity, and Caring* (San Francisco: Harper San Francisco, 1990).

Richards, D., *Artful Work: Awakening Joy, Meaning, and Commitment in the Workplace* (San Francisco: Berrett-Koehler, 1995).

Schaefer, C., and Voors, T., *Vision in Action: Working with Soul and Spirit in Small Organizations* (Hudson, NY: Lindisfarne Press, 1996).

Spirituality and Leadership

Autry, J. A., and Mitchell, S., *Real Power: Business Lessons of the Tao Te Ching* (New York: Riverhead, 1998).

Block, P., *Stewardship: Choosing Service over Self-Interest* (San Francisco: Berrett-Koehler, 1993).

Conger, J. A., and Associates, *Spirit at Work: Discovering the Spirituality in Leadership* (San Francisco: Jossey-Bass, 1994).

De Pree, M., *Leadership Is an Art* (New York: Dell, 1990).

De Pree, M., *Leadership Jazz* (New York: Dell, 1993).

Deal, T. E., and Bolman, L. G., *Leading with Soul: An Uncommon Journey of Spirit* (San Francisco: Jossey-Bass, 1995).

Fairholm, G., *Capturing the Heart of Leadership: Spirituality and Community in the New American Workplace* (New York: Praeger, 1997).

Greenleaf, R. K., *Servant Leadership: A Journey into the Nature of Legitimate Power and Greatness* (Mahwah, NJ: Paulist Press, 1977).

Greenleaf, R. K., *On Becoming a Servant Leader: The Private Writings of Robert K. Greenleaf* (San Francisco: Jossey-Bass, 1997).

Hawley, J., *Reawakening the Spirit in Work: The Power of Dharmic Management* (San Francisco: Berrett-Koehler, 1993).

Moxley, R. S., Jr., *Leadership and Spirit: Breathing New Vitality and Energy into Individuals and Organizations* (San Francisco: Jossey-Bass, 1999).

Palmer, P. J., *The Courage to Teach: Exploring the Inner Landscape of a Teacher's Life* (San Francisco: Jossey-Bass, 1998).

Renesch, J. (ed.), *New Traditions in Business: Spirit and Leadership in the Twenty-First Century* (San Francisco: Berrett-Koehler, 1992).

Spears, L. C. (ed.), *Insights on Leadership: Service, Stewardship, Spirit, and Servant Leadership* (Indianapolis: Greenleaf Center, 1998).

Vaill, P. B., *Managing as a Performing Art: New Ideas for a World of Chaotic Change* (San Francisco: Jossey-Bass, 1989).

Vaill, P. B., *Spirited Leading and Learning: Process Wisdom for a New Age* (San Francisco: Jossey-Bass, 1998).

Vocation and Business Management

Boldt, L. G., *How to Find the Work You Love* (New York: Arkana/Penguin, 1996).

Hillman, J., *The Soul's Code: In Search of Character and Calling* (New York: Random House, 1996).

Krishnamurti, J., *On Right Livelihood* (San Francisco: Harper San Francisco, 1992).

Leider, R. J., and Shapiro, D. A., *Repacking Your Bags: Lighten Your Load for the Rest of Your Life* (San Francisco: Berrett-Koehler, 1995).

Novak, M., *Business as a Calling: Work and the Examined Life* (New York: Free Press, 1996).

Paradigm Shift and the Role of Business

Drucker, P. F., *The New Realities* (New York: Harper Business, 1994).

Harmon, W., *Global Mind Change: The Promise of the Last Years of the Twentieth Century* (Boston: Sigo Press, 1991).

Land, G., and Jarman, B., *Breakpoint and Beyond: Mastering the Future—Today* (New York: Harper Business, 1993).

Maynard, H. B., and Mehrtens, S. E., *The Fourth Wave: Business in the Twenty-First Century* (San Francisco: Berrett-Koehler, 1993).

Peck, M. S., *A World Waiting to Be Born: Rediscovering Civility* (New York: Bantam, 1994).

Rinsler, A., and Ray, M. (eds.), *The New Paradigm in Business: Emerging Strategies for Leadership and Organizational Change* (New York: Putnam, 1994).

Toffler, A., *The Third Wave* (New York: Bantam, 1984).

Spiritual Direction and Spiritual Growth

Barry, W. A., and Connolly, W. J., *The Practice of Spiritual Direction* (San Francisco: HarperCollins, 1982).

Byrne, L. (ed.), *Traditions of Spiritual Guidance* (Collegeville, MN: Liturgical Press, 1990).

Dyckman, K. M., and Carroll, L. P., *Inviting the Mystic, Supporting the*

Prophet: An Introduction to Spiritual Direction (Mahwah, NJ: Paulist Press, 1981).

Edwards, T., *Spiritual Friend* (Mahwah, NJ: Paulist Press, 1980).

Guenther, M., *Holy Listening: The Art of Spiritual Direction* (Cambridge, MA: Cowley, 1992).

Hart, T. N., *The Art of Christian Listening* (Mahwah, NJ: Paulist Press, 1980).

Jones, A., *Exploring Spiritual Direction: An Essay on Christian Friendship* (San Francisco: HarperCollins, 1982).

Leech, K., *Soul Friend* (San Francisco: HarperCollins, 1977).

May, G. G., *Will and Spirit: A Contemplative Psychology* (San Francisco: HarperCollins, 1982).

May, G. G., *Care of Mind/Care of Spirit* (San Francisco: HarperCollins, 1982).

Studzinski, R., *Spiritual Direction and Midlife Development* (Chicago: Loyola University Press, 1985).

Resources

C. Michael Thompson works with individuals and organizations throughout the United States on issues related to the Congruent Life. An experienced speaker and workshop leader, Thompson can also assess an organization's climate for leadership development and personal growth and design customized programs that foster greater organizational purpose and employee commitment. He also works with individual managers and executives to develop their leadership potential and more fully integrate their personal, professional, and spiritual lives.

C. Michael Thompson
792 Arbor Road
Winston-Salem, NC 27104
Telephone: (336) 727-0149
E-mail: cmtwsnc@aol.com.

Readers wishing more information on the Soul of the Executive program (discussed in Chapter Five) may contact the Shalem Institute for more information. The institute sponsors a number of other programs in the contemplative disciplines and the spiritual life.

The Shalem Institute for Spiritual Formation
5430 Grosvenor Lane
Bethesda, MD 20814
Telephone: (301) 897-7334
Website: http://www.shalem.org.

Those wishing to pursue the discipline of spiritual guidance (discussed in Chapter Ten) may wish to contact Spiritual Directors

International (SDI). SDI is a voluntary association of spiritual directors, with more than twenty-eight hundred members in thirty-six countries. Although SDI does not recommend individual directors, the organization can refer you to a regional contact nearest to your location who may be able to assist you.

Spiritual Directors International
1329 Seventh Avenue
San Francisco, CA 94122-2507
Telephone: (415) 566-1560.
Website: http://www.sdiworld.org.

If you prefer the model of spiritual friendship discussed in Chapter Ten to a formal direction relationship, begin your preparation for this relationship by reading several of the books recommended in the section "Spiritual Direction and Spiritual Growth" in Further Readings, particularly those by Tilden Edwards, Thomas Hart, and Alan Jones.

About the Author

C. Michael Thompson's life and career draw together the threads that form the fabric of this book. For the past three decades he has been deeply involved in the world of business as an attorney, consultant, and management professor. At the same time, his search for deeper meaning and purpose in his own work has led him to an intentional spiritual path that included two years of study with the Shalem Institute, a nonsectarian organization that teaches the art of spiritual guidance. He has also nurtured a lifelong interest in psychology through an intensive study of the works of C. G. Jung. He brings his experience in business, spiritual guidance, and psychology to his work with business executives as well as to his writing.

Thompson's consulting practice focuses on organizational and individual assessment, leadership development, and executive coaching. In addition to his private practice, he is an adjunct and feedback coach with the prestigious Center for Creative Leadership in Greensboro, North Carolina. Before devoting himself primarily to his consulting and writing projects, Thompson served as assistant dean and professor of the Calloway School of Business of Wake Forest University, one of the top twenty-five undergraduate business schools in the United States, and was vice president and counsel of a Fortune 500 company. He still maintains an active legal practice for selected business clients and teaches business law as a member of the adjunct faculty of Salem College in Winston-Salem, North Carolina.

Thompson received his B.A. and J.D. degrees from the University of North Carolina at Chapel Hill, where he was a John Motley Morehead Scholar. He lives with his wife of twenty-six years and two daughters in Winston-Salem and Sunset Beach, North Carolina.

Index

A

Abdulla al-Ansari, 153–154

Achievers, 128–129, 151, 183, 189, 254

Action, for spiritual growth, 263

The Active Life (Palmer), 263

Adult development: applied to work behaviors, 123–132; balance and, 150; Conventional level of, 120–121, 125–129, 185; faith and, 154–155; humor and, 166; inner life's role in, 136–140; Kohlberg's theory of, 118–123, 138; leadership as promoting, 132–135; Postconventional level of, 121–122, 129–132, 183; Preconventional level of, 120, 124–125; thinking and, 146–149

Alienation, of workers, 21

Allen, S., 166

Allport, G., 59, 137

American Electric and Power (AEP), 96–97

Ames, W., 19

Andrewes, L., 257

Anguish, 93

Archetypes, 191

AT&T, 104, 107

Attenborough, R., 200

Augustine, Saint, 161, 232, 258

Autry, J., 27, 38, 110, 193; on business and values, 15, 74, 76; on excellence in work, 224; on management, 46–47, 197

B

Baby boomers, values shift due to, 98–102

Balance: adult development and, 150; between individual and community, 218–221

Barrett, R., 104

Basseches, M. A., 147

Beginning to Pray (Bloom), 259

Behrman, J., 96

Believeurism, 75–76

Bell, D., 21

Bellah, R., 40

Benedict, Saint, 16

Bennis, W., 10, 140, 159, 217

Berdyaev, N., 228–229

Bergin, A., 137–138, 187

Bernadone, F., 180

Bible: Corinthians, 196; Deuteronomy, 42; Galatians, 78–79, 142; Isaiah, 56; Job, 51; John, 56; Leviticus, 42; Matthew, 38, 42, 82, 117, 220, 238, 267; Psalms, 161, 241, 256

Big-picture thinking, 146–148, 171, 229–230

Bill of Rights, 76, 78

Block, P., 9, 27, 38, 193, 220, 263

Bloom, A., 26, 247, 259

Bloom, M., 244

Boehlke, S., 100

Boeing, 104

Bonhoeffer, D., 259

Buechner, F., 40–41, 45